NEW YORK REVIEW BOOKS
CLASSICS

POEM STRIP

DINO BUZZATI (1906–1972) came from a distinguished family that had long been resident in the northern Italian region of the Veneto. His mother was a veterinarian; his father, a professor of international law. Buzzati studied law at the University of Milan and, at the age of twenty-two, went to work for *Corriere della Sera*, where he remained for the rest of his life. He served in World War II as a journalist connected to the Italian navy and on his return published the book for which he is most famous, *The Tartar Steppes*. A gifted artist as well as writer, Buzzati was the author of five novels and numerous short stories, as well as books for children, including *The Bears' Famous Invasion of Sicily* (published in The New York Review Children's Collection).

MARINA HARSS is a translator and dance writer living in New York City. Her recent translations include Mariolina Venezia's *Been Here a Thousand Years*, Alberto Moravia's *Conjugal Love*, and Pier Paolo Pasolini's *Stories from the City of God*.

POEM STRIP

DINO BUZZATI

Translated from the Italian by

MARINA HARSS

NEW YORK REVIEW BOOKS

New York

THIS IS A NEW YORK REVIEW BOOK
PUBLISHED BY THE NEW YORK REVIEW OF BOOKS
435 Hudson Street, New York, NY 10014
www.nyrb.com

Published in Italy as *Poema a Fumetti* by Arnoldo Mondadori Editore, Milan
Hand lettering by Rich Tommaso

Library of Congress Cataloging-in-Publication Data
Buzzati, Dino, 1906-1972.
 [Poema a fumetti. English]
 Poem strip / by Dino Buzzati ; translated from the Italian by Marina Harss.
    p. cm.
 ISBN 978-1-59017-323-7 (alk. paper)
 1. Graphic novels. I. Harss, Marina. II. Title.
 PN6767.B89.P64 2009
 741.5'945—dc22

                    2009021713

ISBN 978-1-59017-323-7

Printed in the United States of America on acid-free paper.
10 9 8 7 6 5 4 3 2 1

POEM STRIP

I would like to thank my friend Antonio Recalcati, the painter, who posed for the character of the protagonist; my colleague Franco Gremignani, the green man of via Saterna; Runa Pfeiffer, who lent her face to the character of Trudy, the guide to Avernus. I would also like to thank the following for their valuable input: Waldemar Weimann and Otto Prokop (p. 8); Alberico Belgioioso, Enrico Peressutti, and Ernesto Rogers (p. 23); Salvador Dali (p. 29); Mademoiselle Féline (p. 87); Caspar David Friedrich (p. 108); Arthur Rackham (p. 116); Otto Greiner (p. 117); Irving Klaw (p. 119); F. W. Murnau (p. 128); Achille Beltrame (p. 148); Wilhelm Busch (p. 154); Hans Bellmer (p. 161); and Federico Fellini (pp. 190–193).

d.b.

THE SECRET OF VIA SATERNA

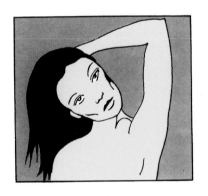

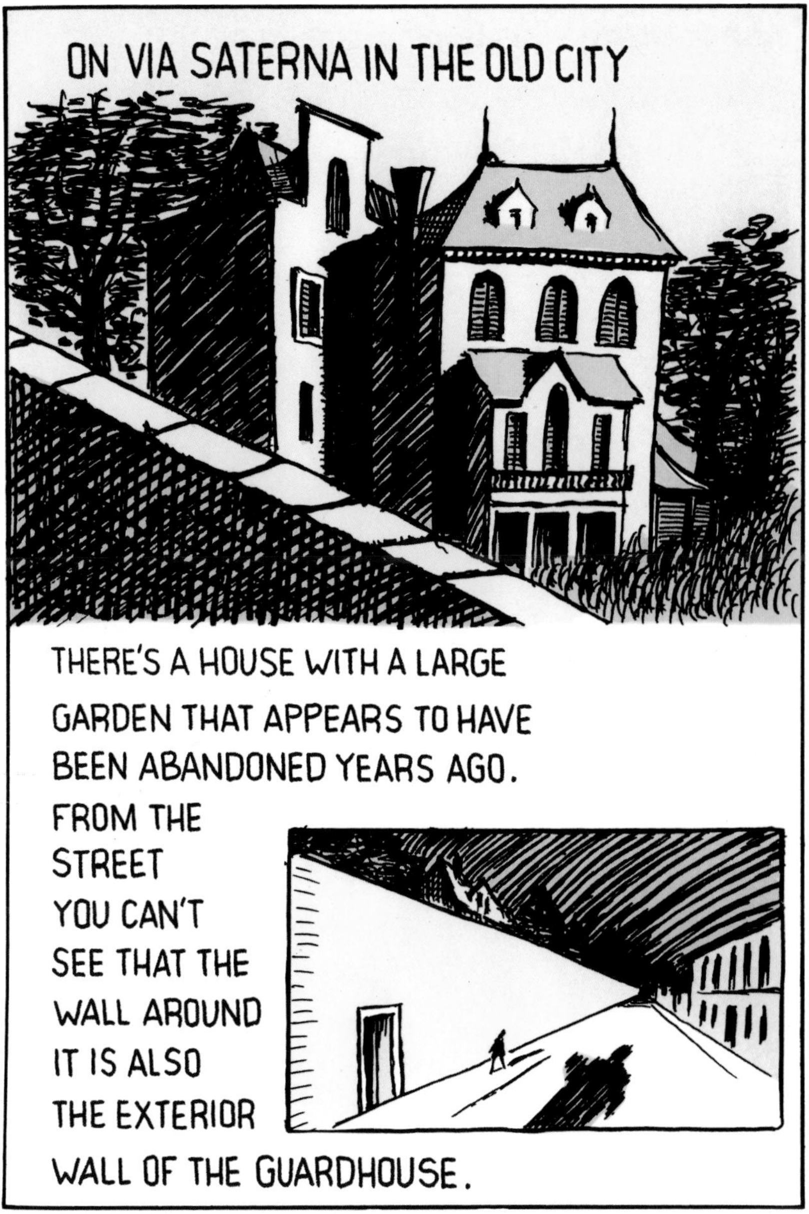
ON VIA SATERNA IN THE OLD CITY
THERE'S A HOUSE WITH A LARGE GARDEN THAT APPEARS TO HAVE BEEN ABANDONED YEARS AGO.
FROM THE STREET YOU CAN'T SEE THAT THE WALL AROUND IT IS ALSO THE EXTERIOR WALL OF THE GUARDHOUSE.

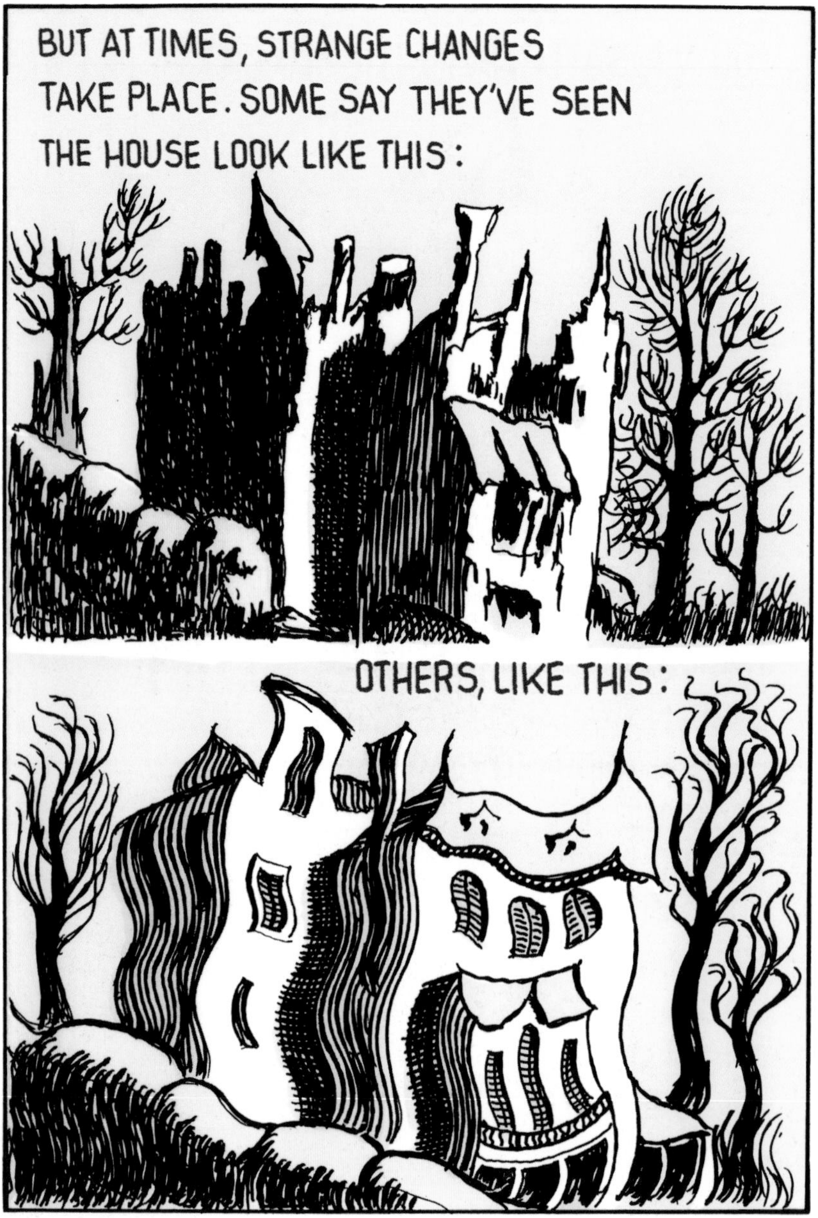
BUT AT TIMES, STRANGE CHANGES TAKE PLACE. SOME SAY THEY'VE SEEN THE HOUSE LOOK LIKE THIS:
OTHERS, LIKE THIS:

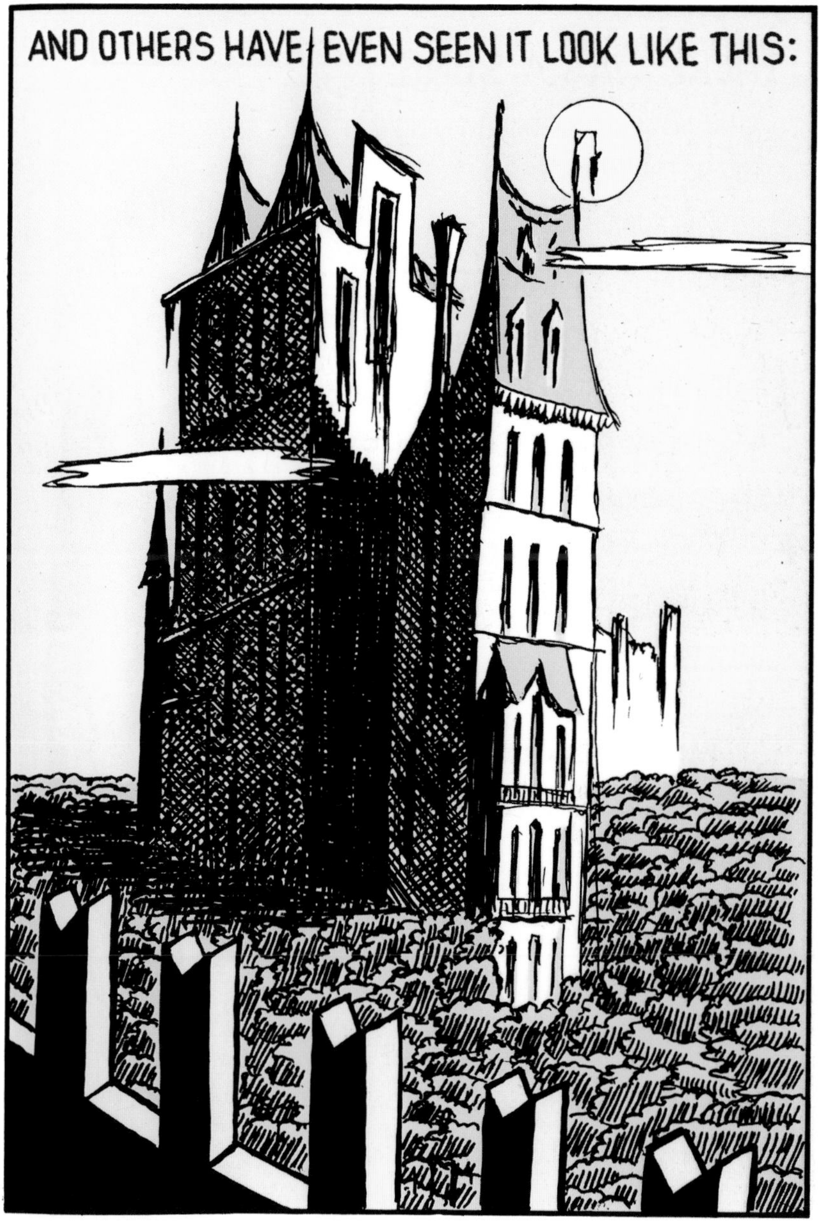
AND OTHERS HAVE EVEN SEEN IT LOOK LIKE THIS:

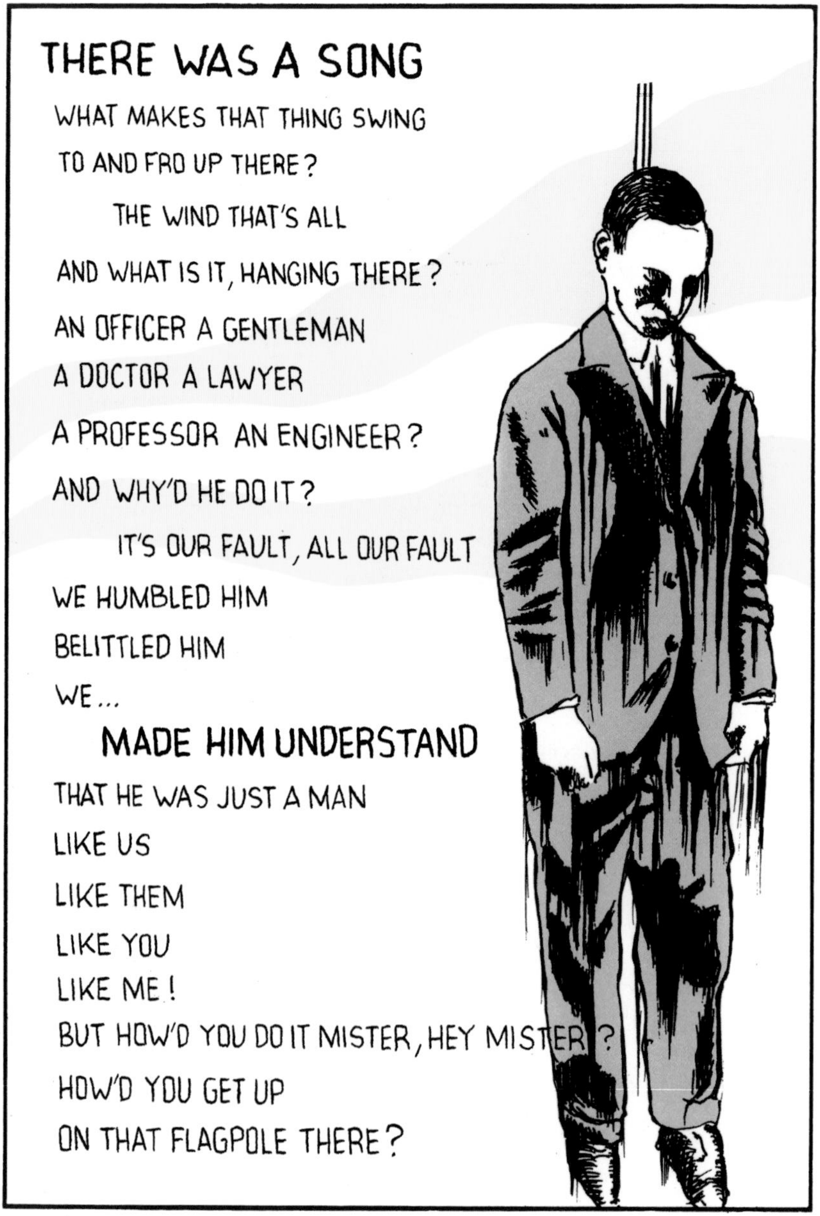
THERE WAS A SONG
WHAT MAKES THAT THING SWING
TO AND FRO UP THERE?
THE WIND THAT'S ALL
AND WHAT IS IT, HANGING THERE?
AN OFFICER A GENTLEMAN
A DOCTOR A LAWYER
A PROFESSOR AN ENGINEER?
AND WHY'D HE DO IT?
IT'S OUR FAULT, ALL OUR FAULT
WE HUMBLED HIM
BELITTLED HIM
WE...
MADE HIM UNDERSTAND
THAT HE WAS JUST A MAN
LIKE US
LIKE THEM
LIKE YOU
LIKE ME!
BUT HOW'D YOU DO IT MISTER, HEY MISTER?
HOW'D YOU GET UP
ON THAT FLAGPOLE THERE?

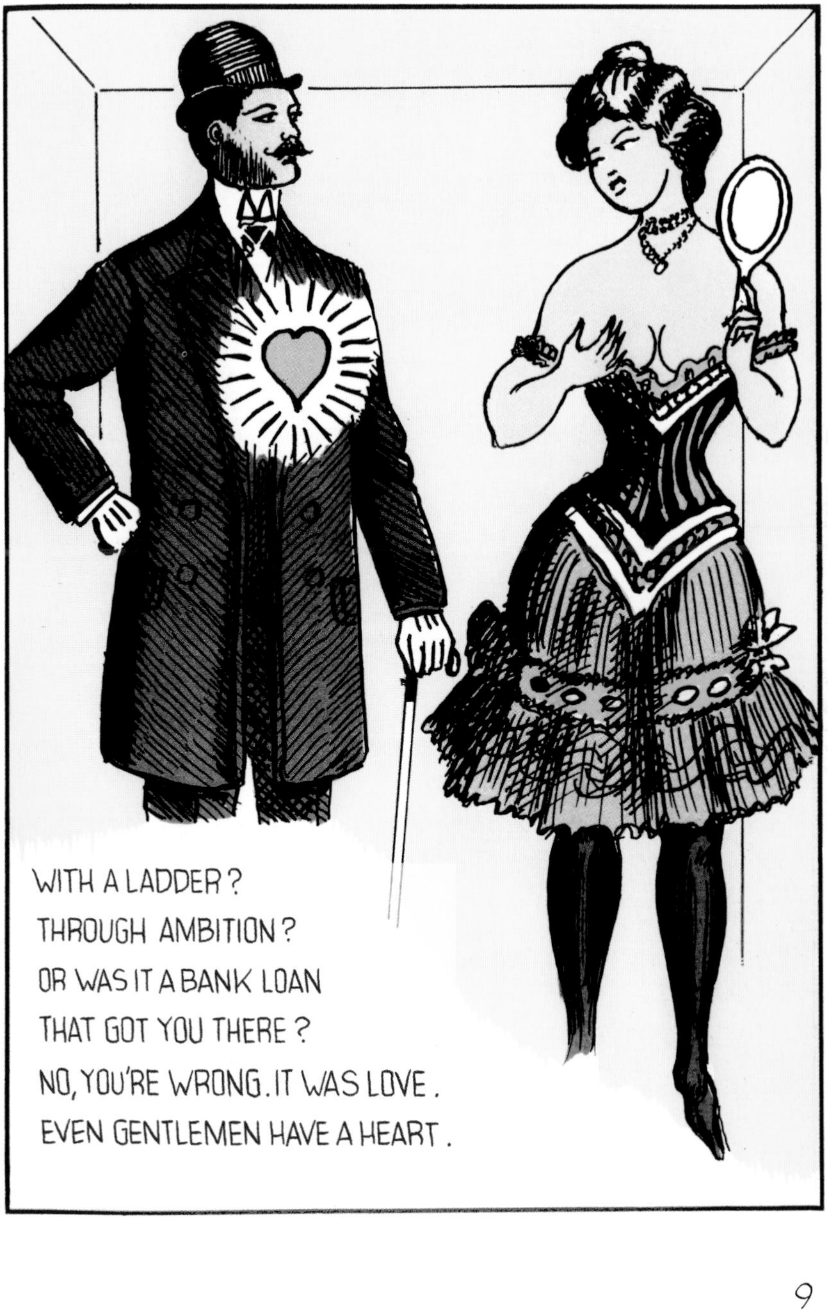
WITH A LADDER?
THROUGH AMBITION?
OR WAS IT A BANK LOAN
THAT GOT YOU THERE?
NO, YOU'RE WRONG. IT WAS LOVE.
EVEN GENTLEMEN HAVE A HEART.

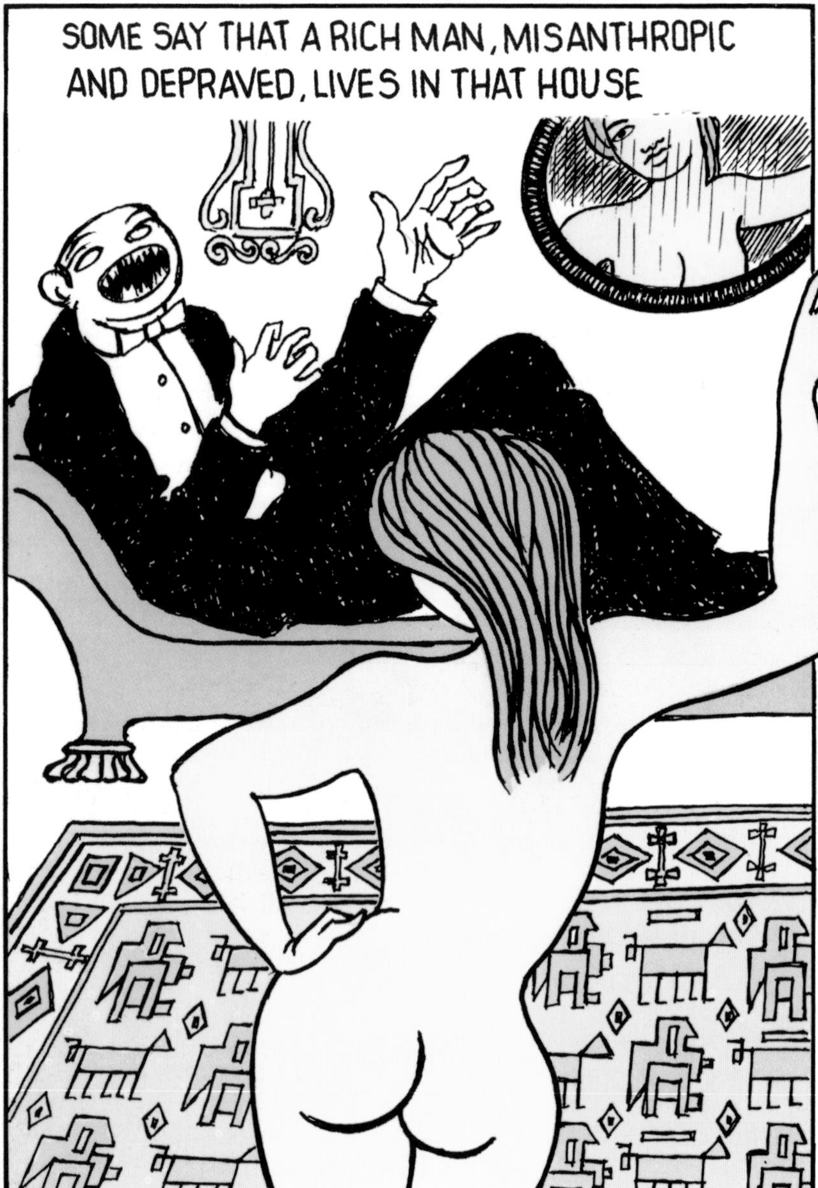
SOME SAY THAT A RICH MAN, MISANTHROPIC AND DEPRAVED, LIVES IN THAT HOUSE

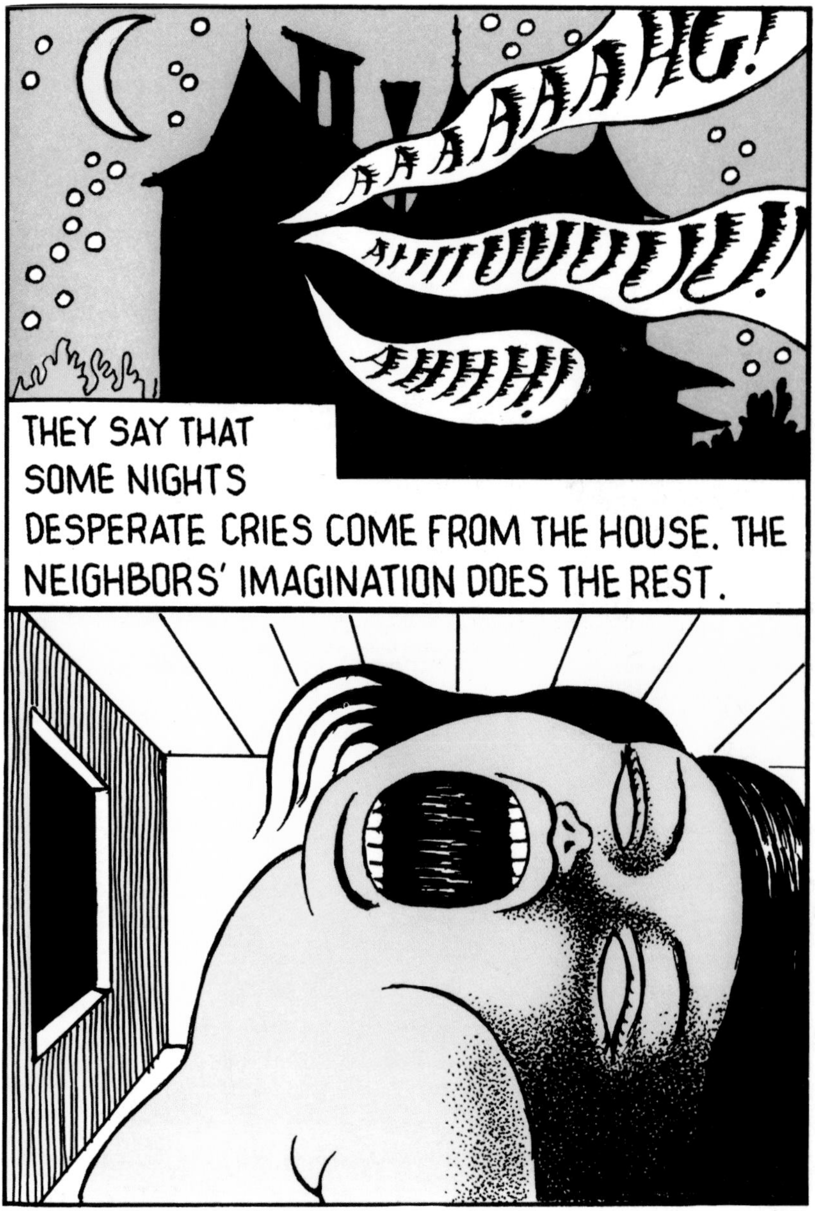
AAAAAAHG!
AHHHUUUEEL!
AHHHH!
THEY SAY THAT
SOME NIGHTS
DESPERATE CRIES COME FROM THE HOUSE. THE
NEIGHBORS' IMAGINATION DOES THE REST.

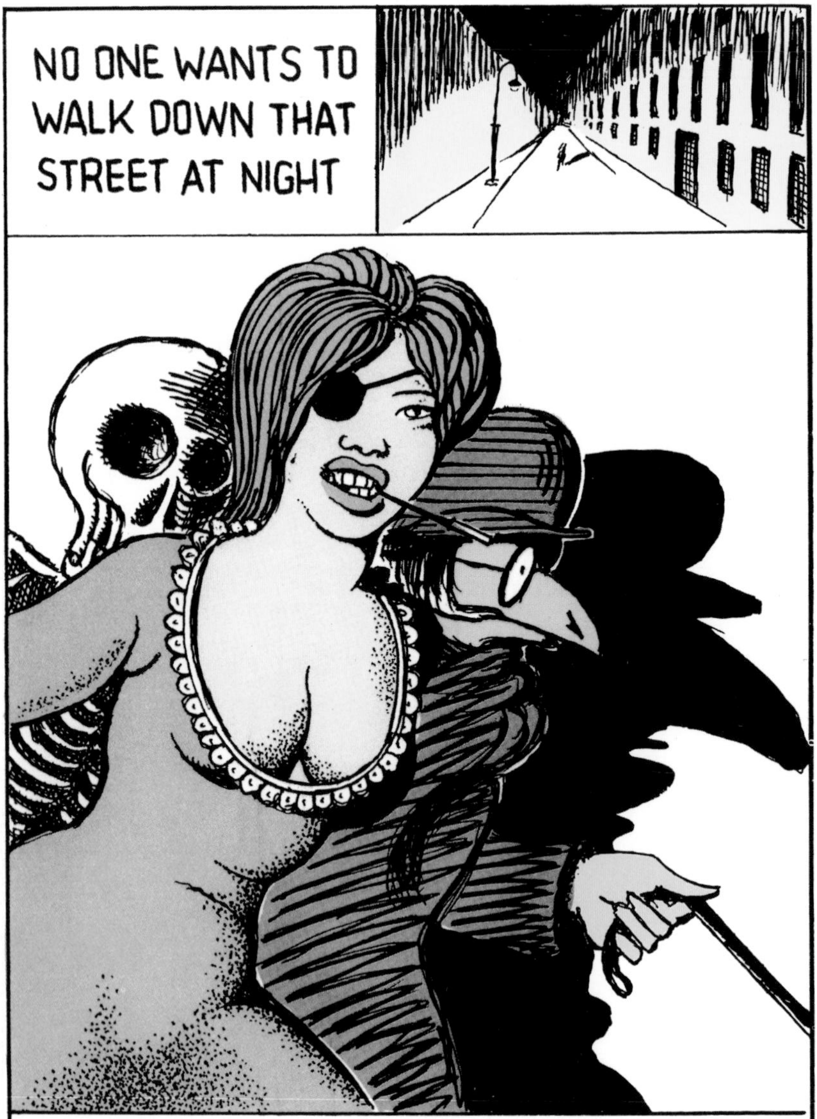
NO ONE WANTS TO WALK DOWN THAT STREET AT NIGHT
THEY SAY YOU CAN MEET SOME STRANGE TYPES!

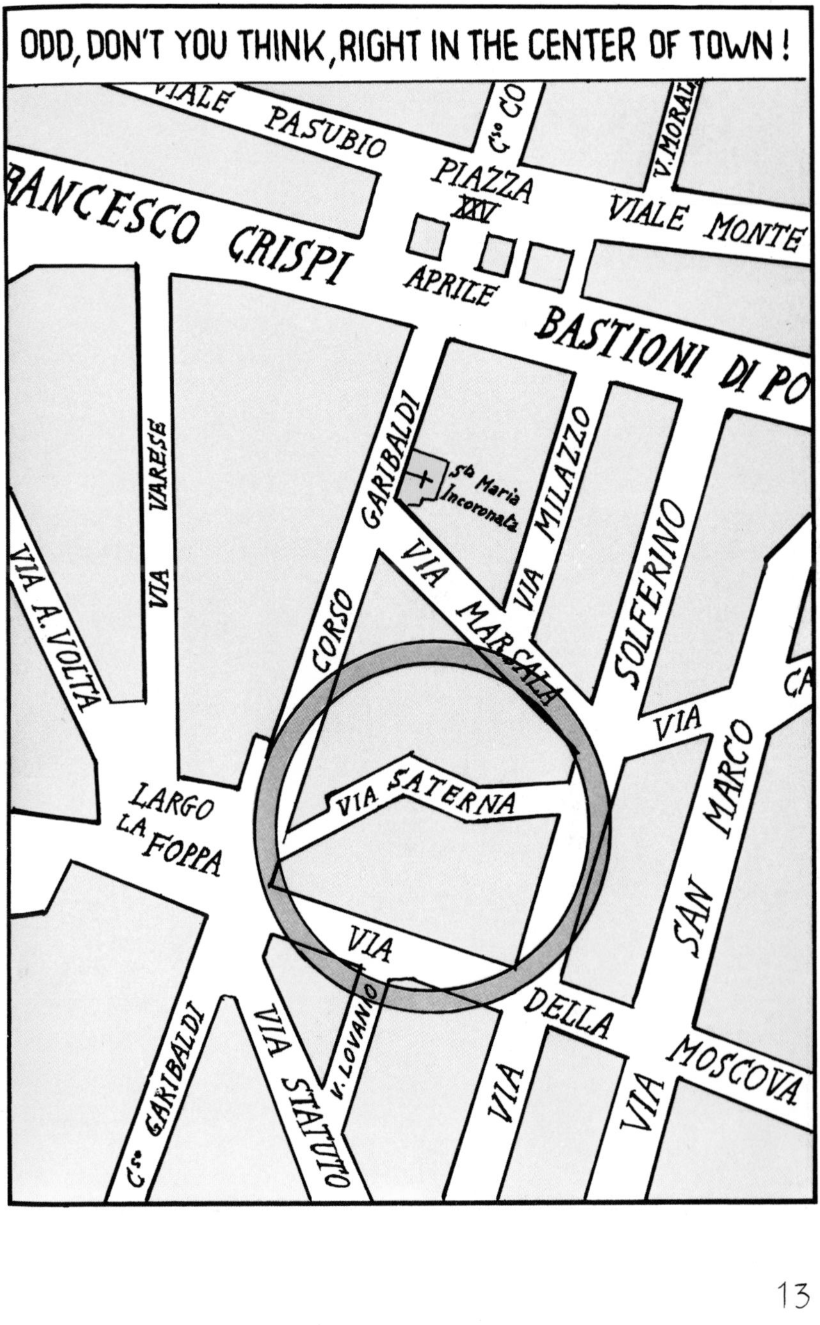
ODD, DON'T YOU THINK, RIGHT IN THE CENTER OF TOWN!
VIALE PASUBIO
C.so CO
V. MORAL
PIAZZA XXV APRILE
ANCESCO CRISPI
VIALE MONTE
BASTIONI DI PO
CORSO GARIBALDI
Sta Maria Incoronata
VIA MILAZZO
VIA VARESE
VIA A. VOLTA
VIA MARSALA
SOLFERINO
VIA SAN MARCO
CA
VIA SATERNA
LARGO LA FOPPA
VIA DELLA MOSCOVA
V. LOVANIO
VIA STATUTO
C.so GARIBALDI
VIA
VIA

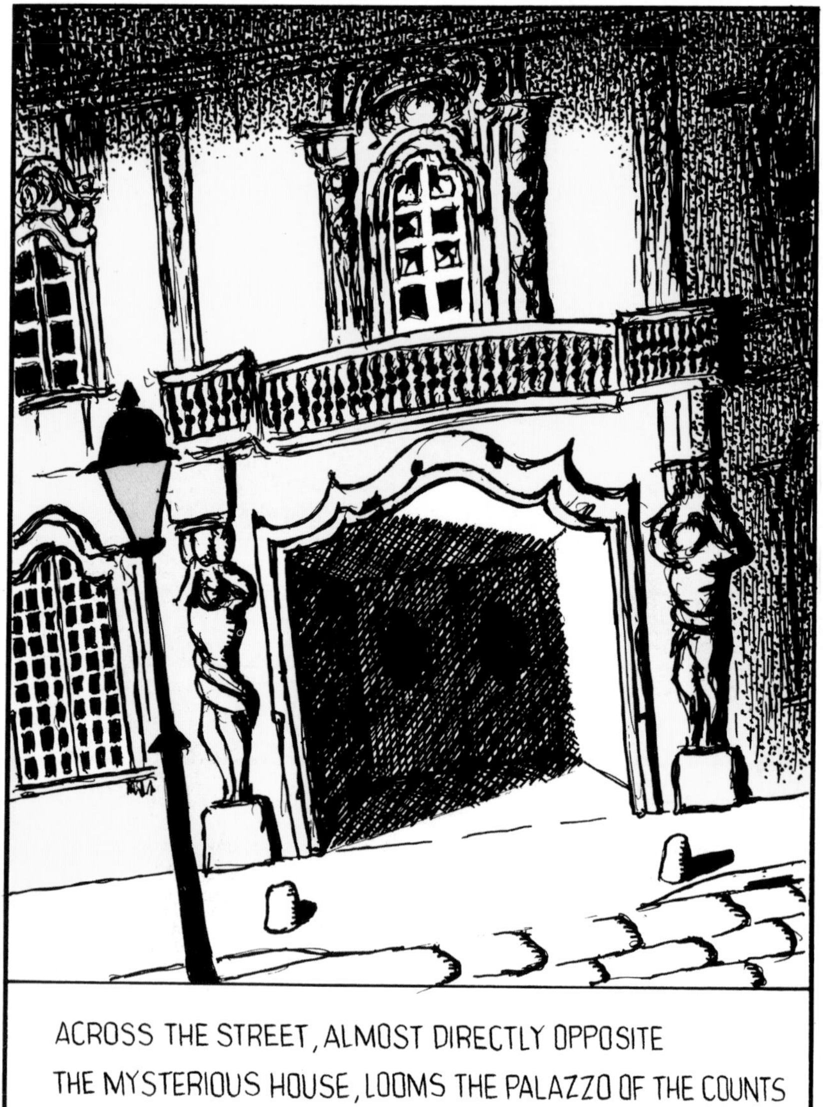
ACROSS THE STREET, ALMOST DIRECTLY OPPOSITE THE MYSTERIOUS HOUSE, LOOMS THE PALAZZO OF THE COUNTS OF BALTAZANO—THESE DAYS A FAMILY MORE NOBLE THAN RICH.

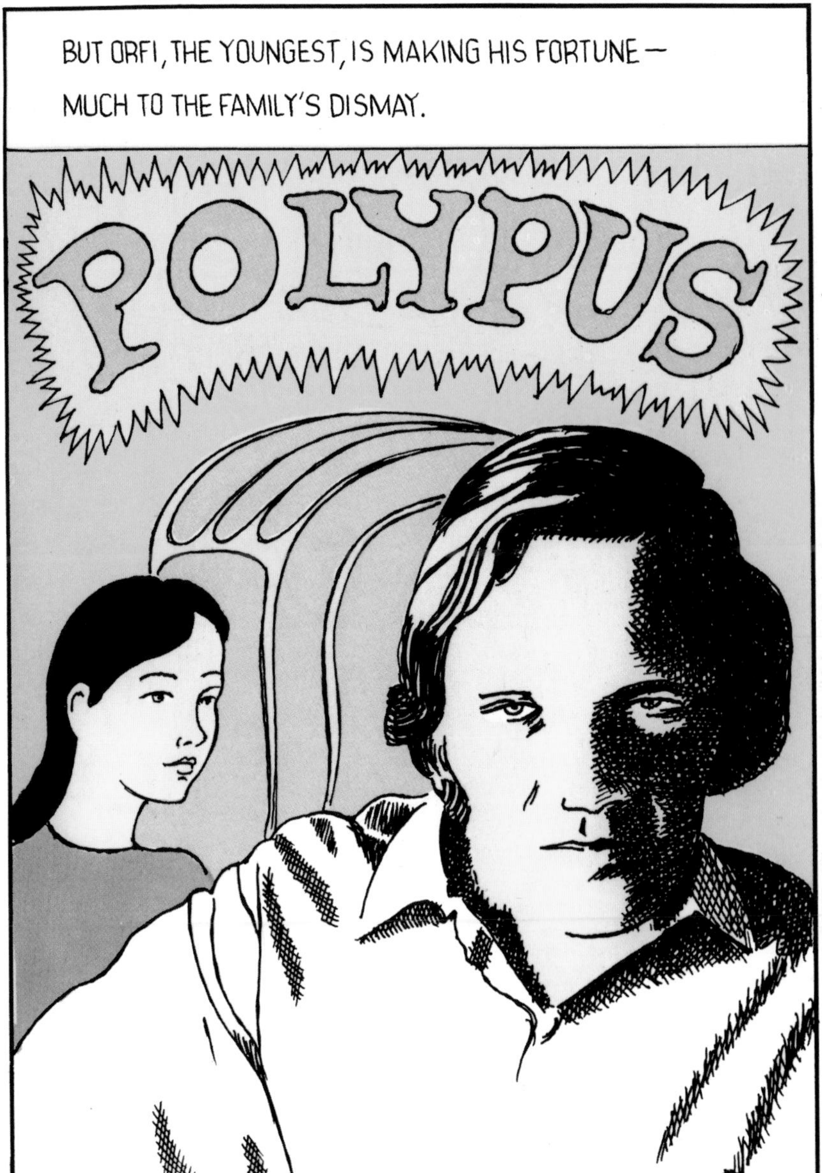
BUT ORFI, THE YOUNGEST, IS MAKING HIS FORTUNE — MUCH TO THE FAMILY'S DISMAY.
POLYPUS

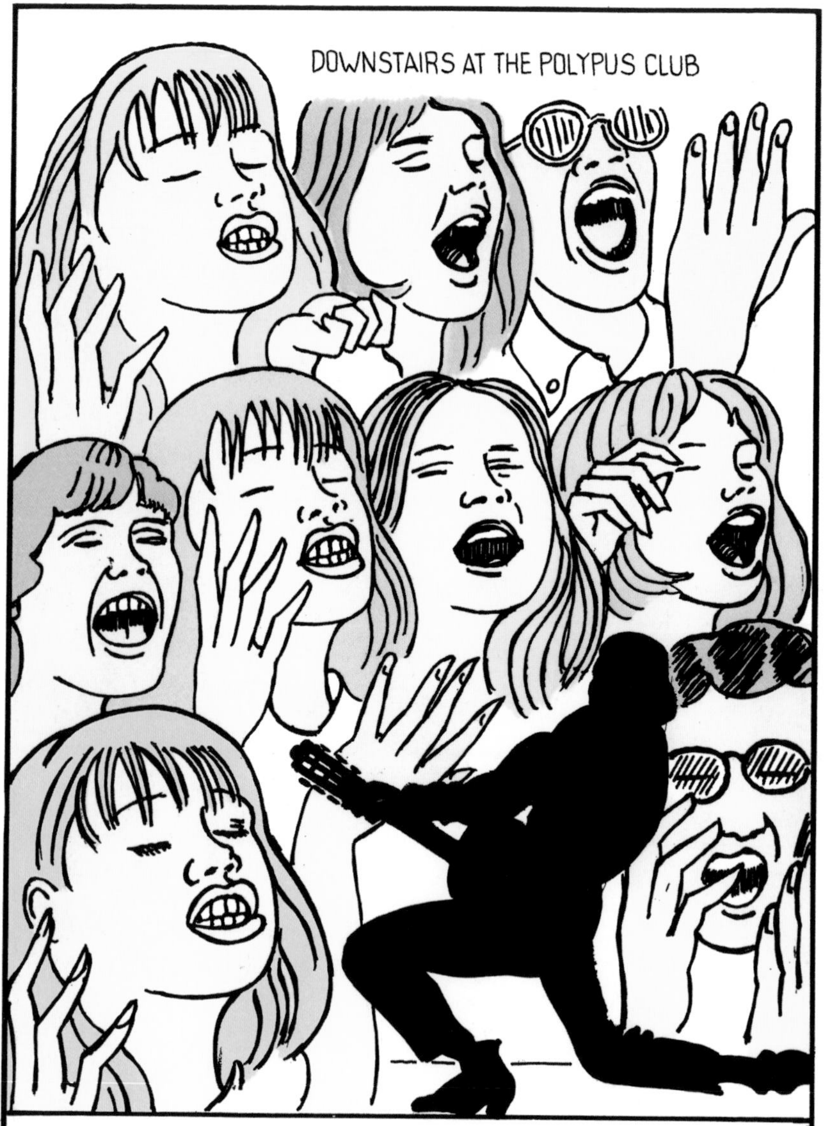
DOWNSTAIRS AT THE POLYPUS CLUB
EVERY NIGHT THE KIDS GO WILD

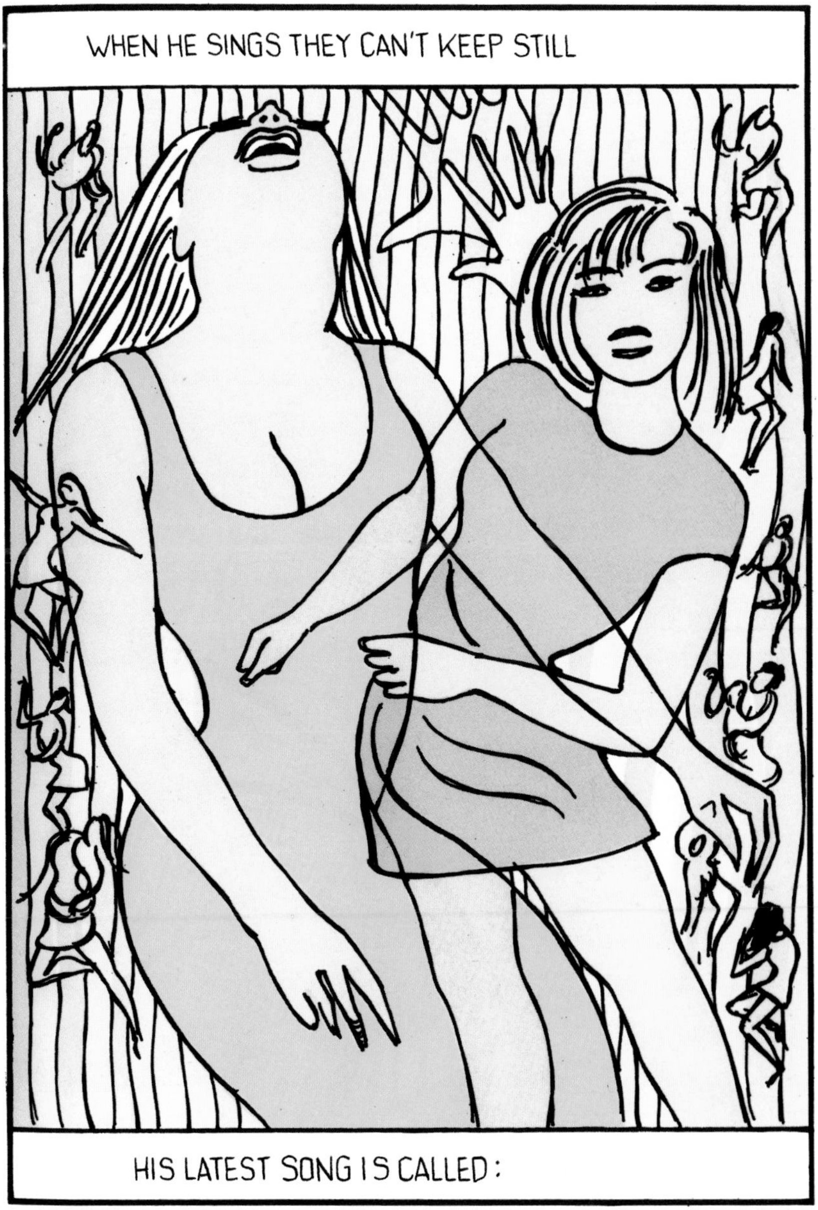
WHEN HE SINGS THEY CAN'T KEEP STILL
HIS LATEST SONG IS CALLED:

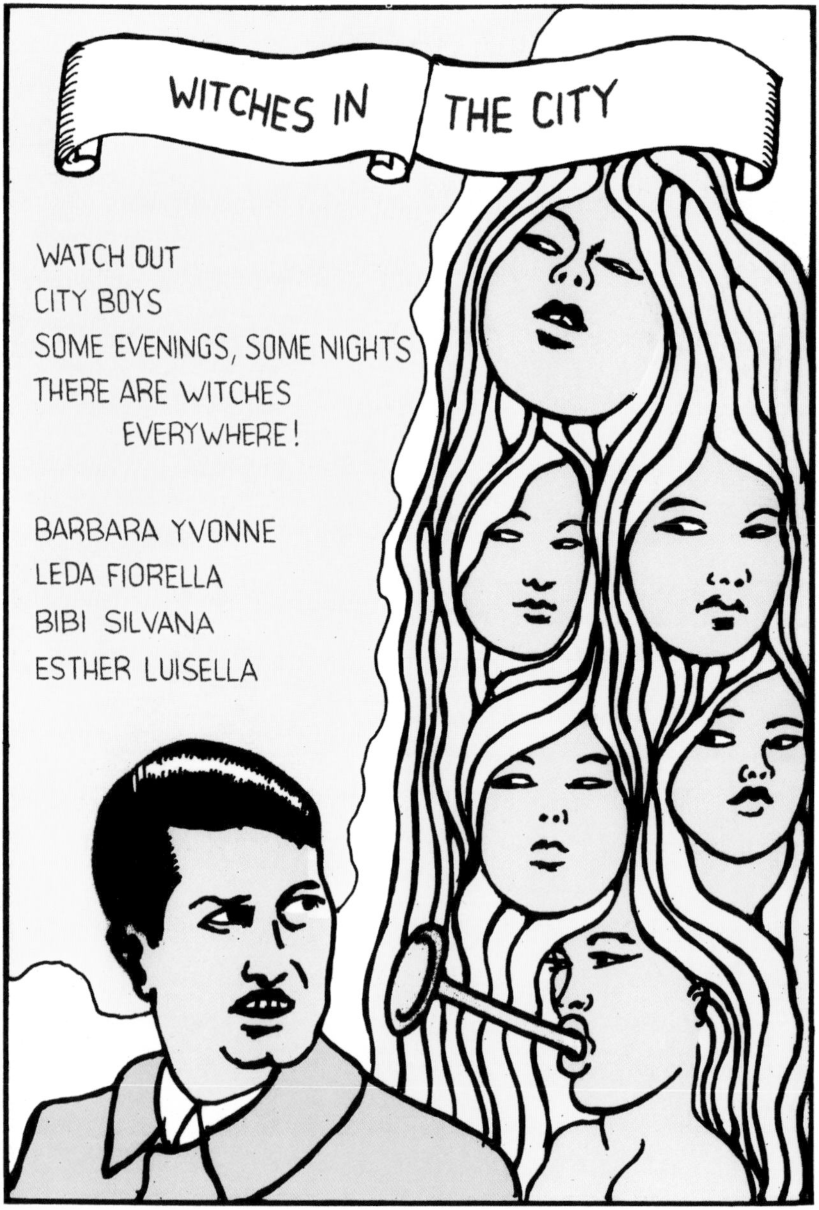
WITCHES IN THE CITY
WATCH OUT
CITY BOYS
SOME EVENINGS, SOME NIGHTS
THERE ARE WITCHES
EVERYWHERE!
BARBARA YVONNE
LEDA FIORELLA
BIBI SILVANA
ESTHER LUISELLA

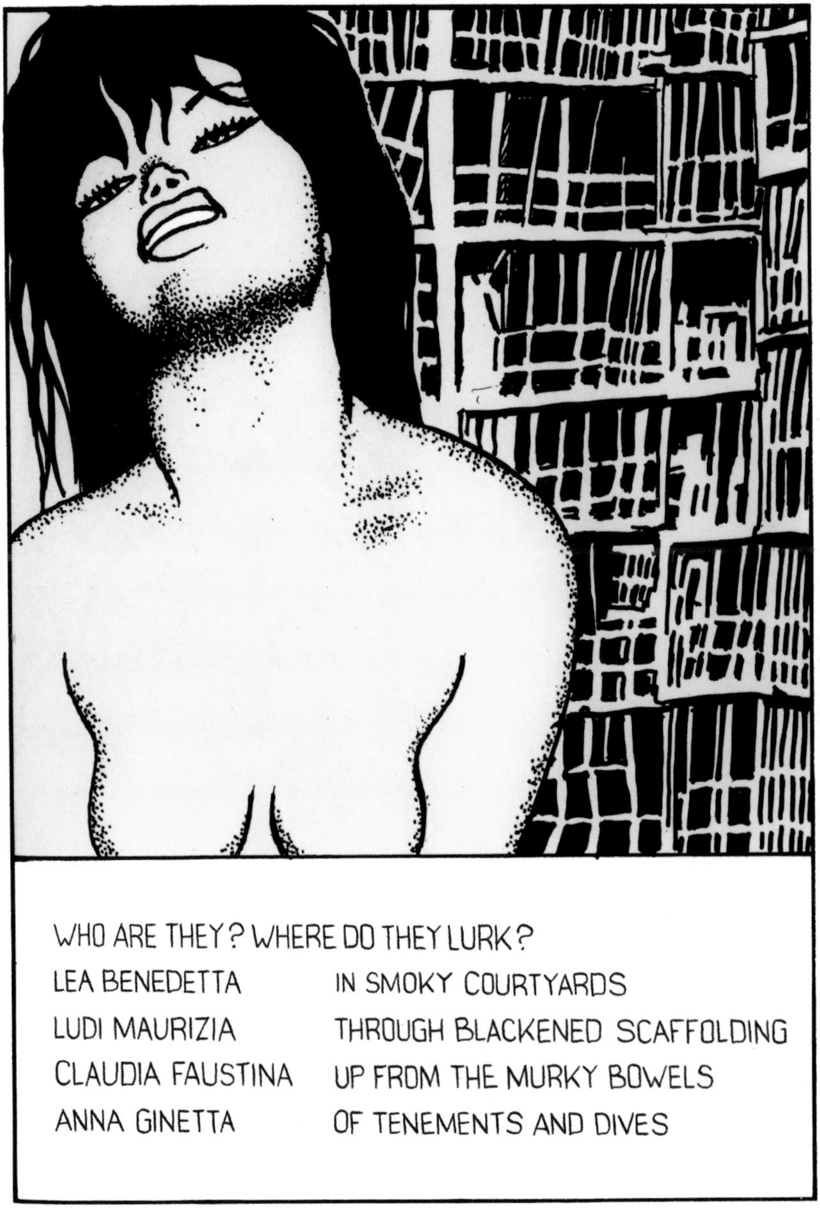
WHO ARE THEY? WHERE DO THEY LURK?
LEA BENEDETTA IN SMOKY COURTYARDS
LUDI MAURIZIA THROUGH BLACKENED SCAFFOLDING
CLAUDIA FAUSTINA UP FROM THE MURKY BOWELS
ANNA GINETTA OF TENEMENTS AND DIVES

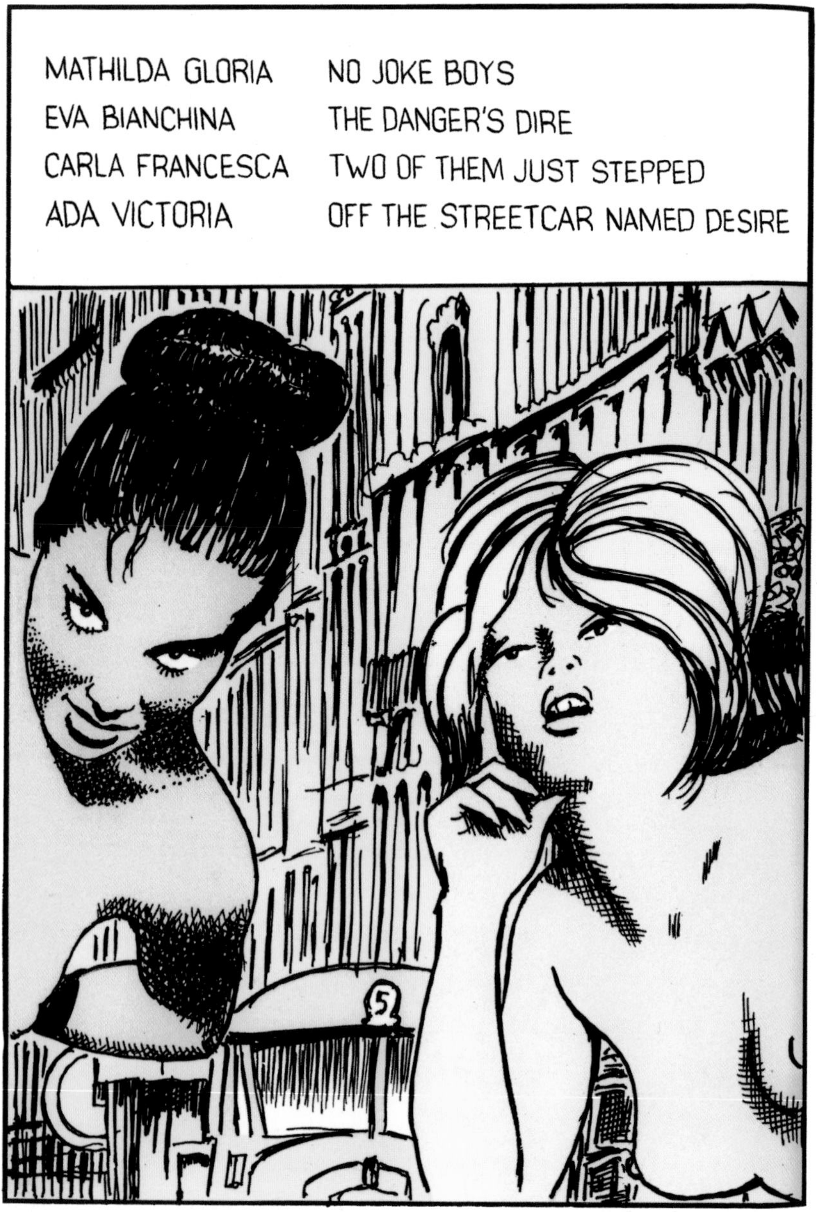
MATHILDA GLORIA NO JOKE BOYS
EVA BIANCHINA THE DANGER'S DIRE
CARLA FRANCESCA TWO OF THEM JUST STEPPED
ADA VICTORIA OFF THE STREETCAR NAMED DESIRE

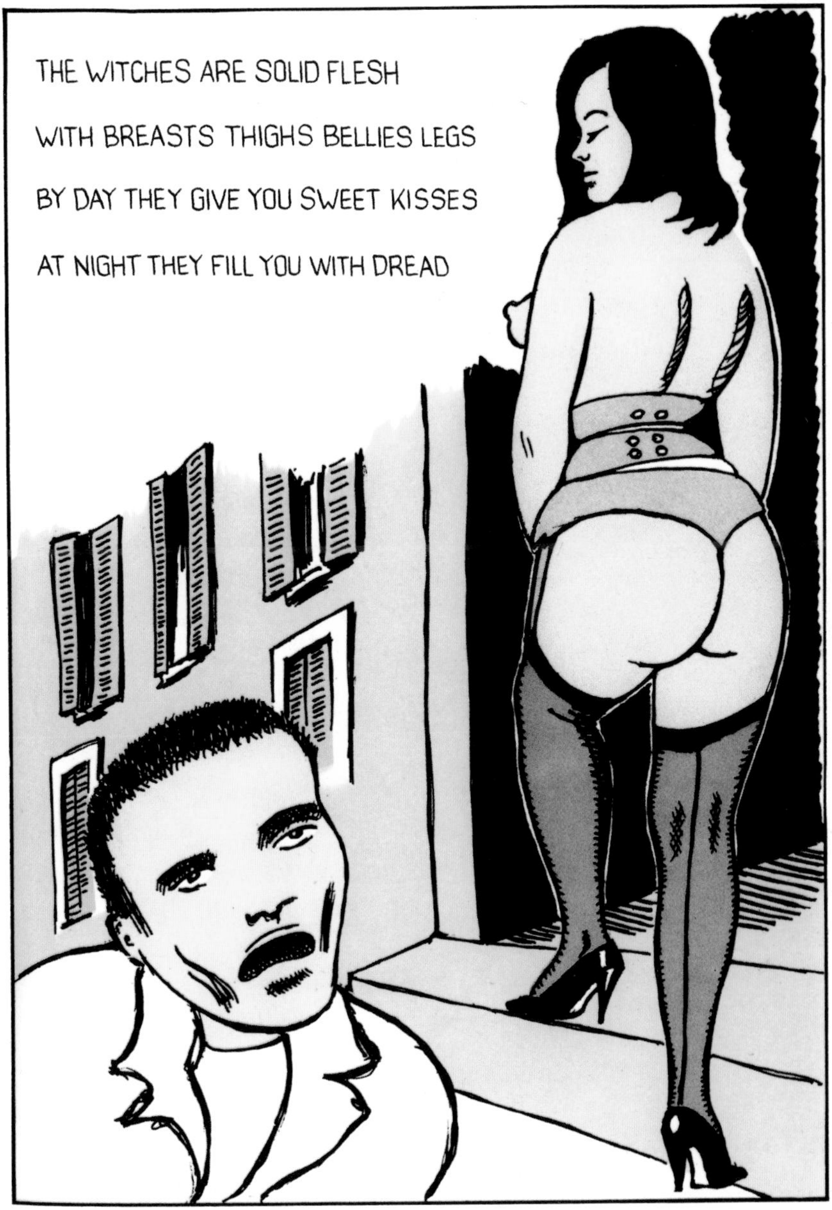
THE WITCHES ARE SOLID FLESH
WITH BREASTS THIGHS BELLIES LEGS
BY DAY THEY GIVE YOU SWEET KISSES
AT NIGHT THEY FILL YOU WITH DREAD

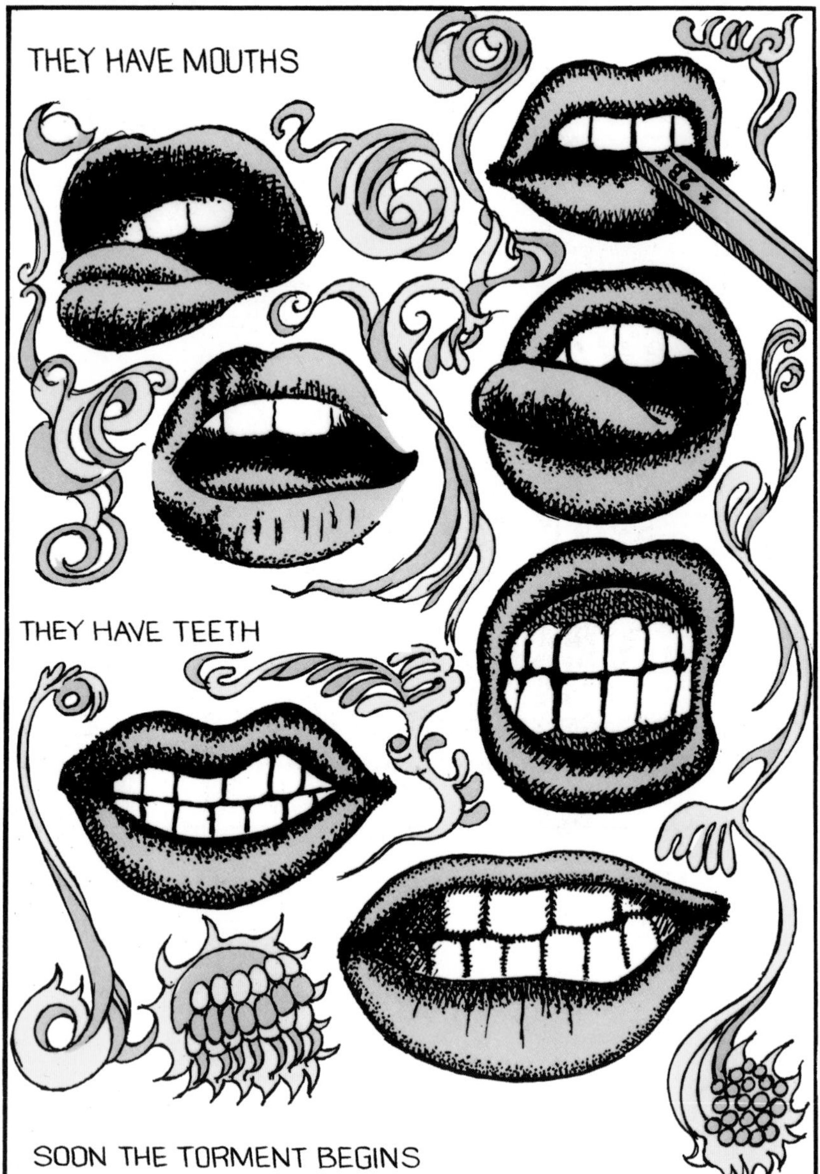
THEY HAVE MOUTHS
2B
THEY HAVE TEETH
SOON THE TORMENT BEGINS

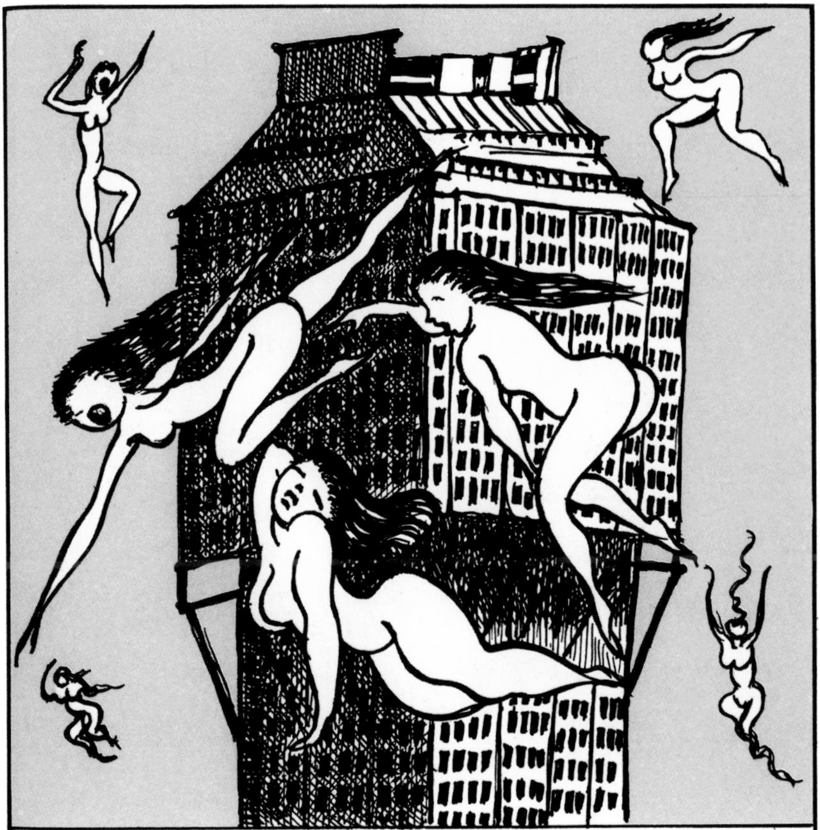

THERE'S NO POINT HIDING
IN THE CELLAR BELOW
THERE'S NO POINT BOLTING
THE GATE OR THE FRONT DOOR
THERE'S NO KEEPING THEM OUT
LOVELY LITTLE WITCHES

TERESA DANIELA MARIA
KATYA NADIA MIRELLA
LYDIA LALLA LUCIA
BIANCA SUZY GRAZIELLA

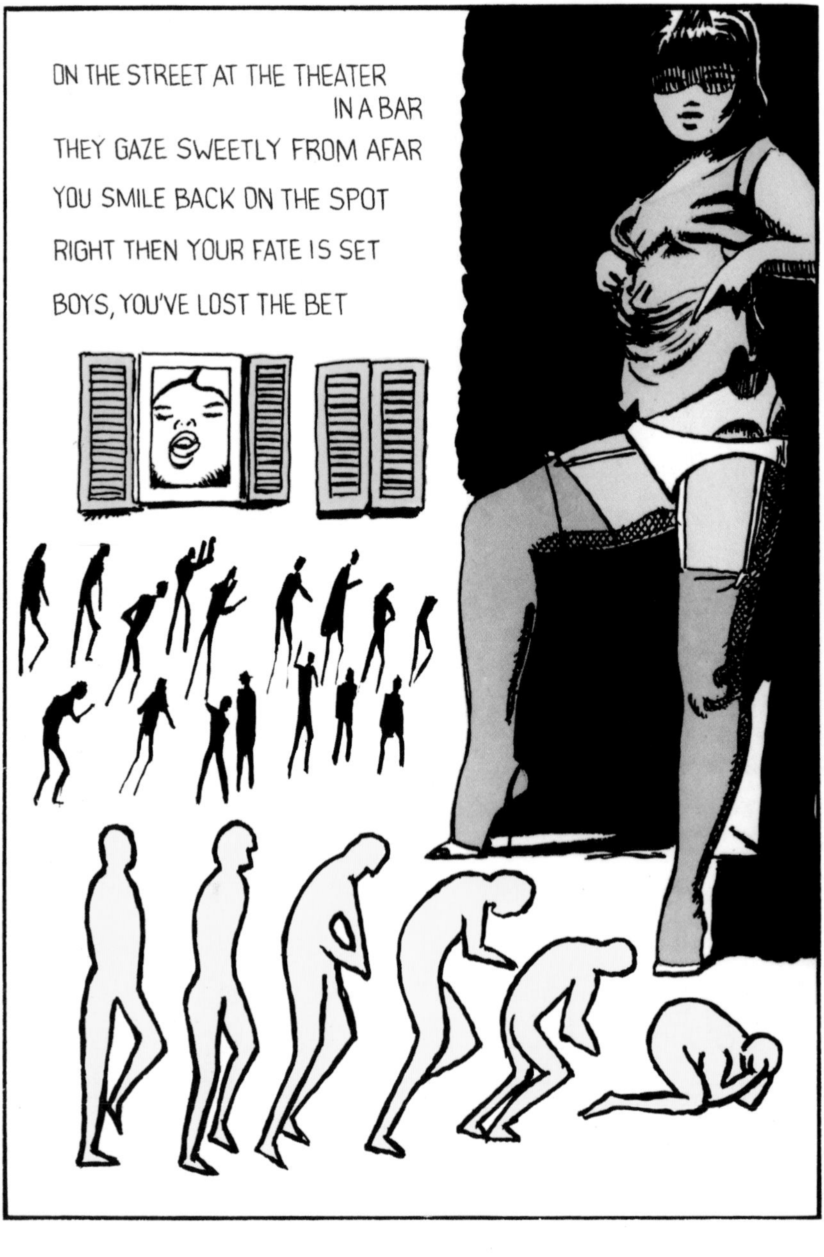
ON THE STREET AT THE THEATER
IN A BAR
THEY GAZE SWEETLY FROM AFAR
YOU SMILE BACK ON THE SPOT
RIGHT THEN YOUR FATE IS SET
BOYS, YOU'VE LOST THE BET

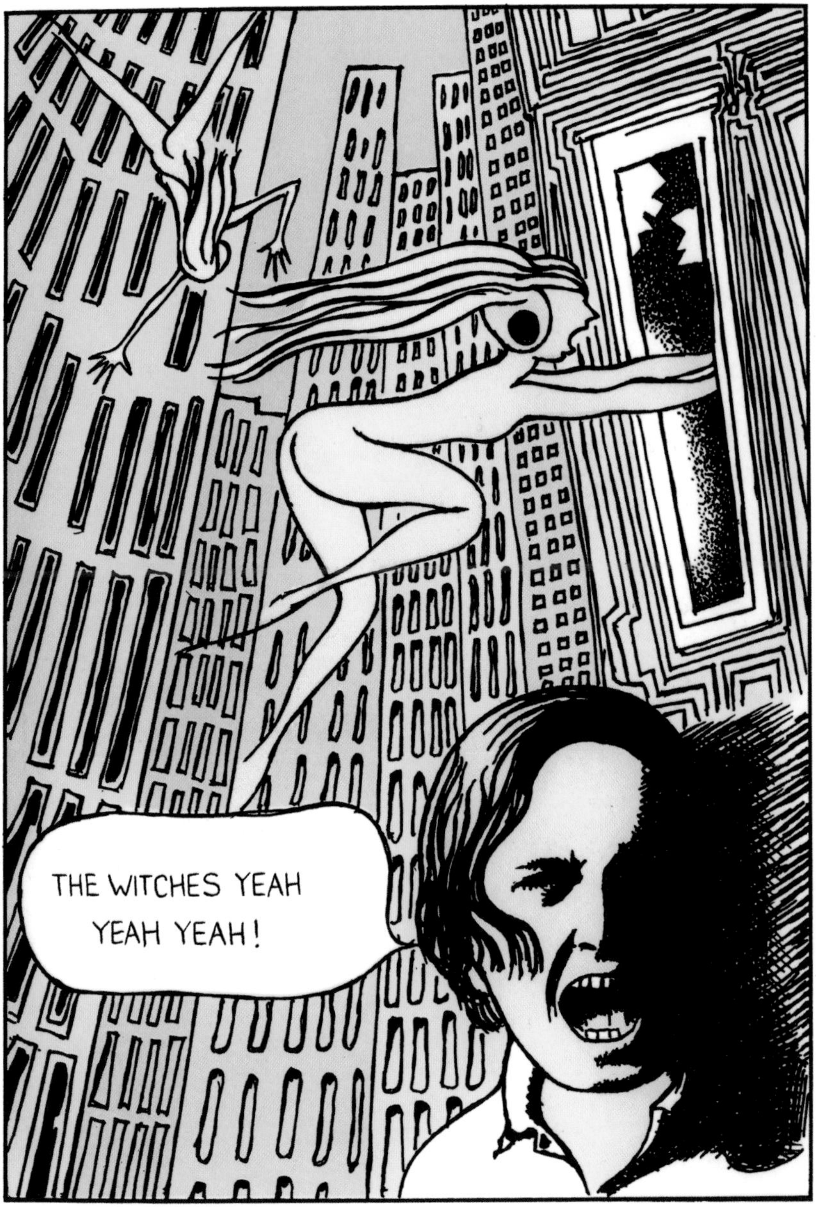
THE WITCHES YEAH YEAH YEAH!

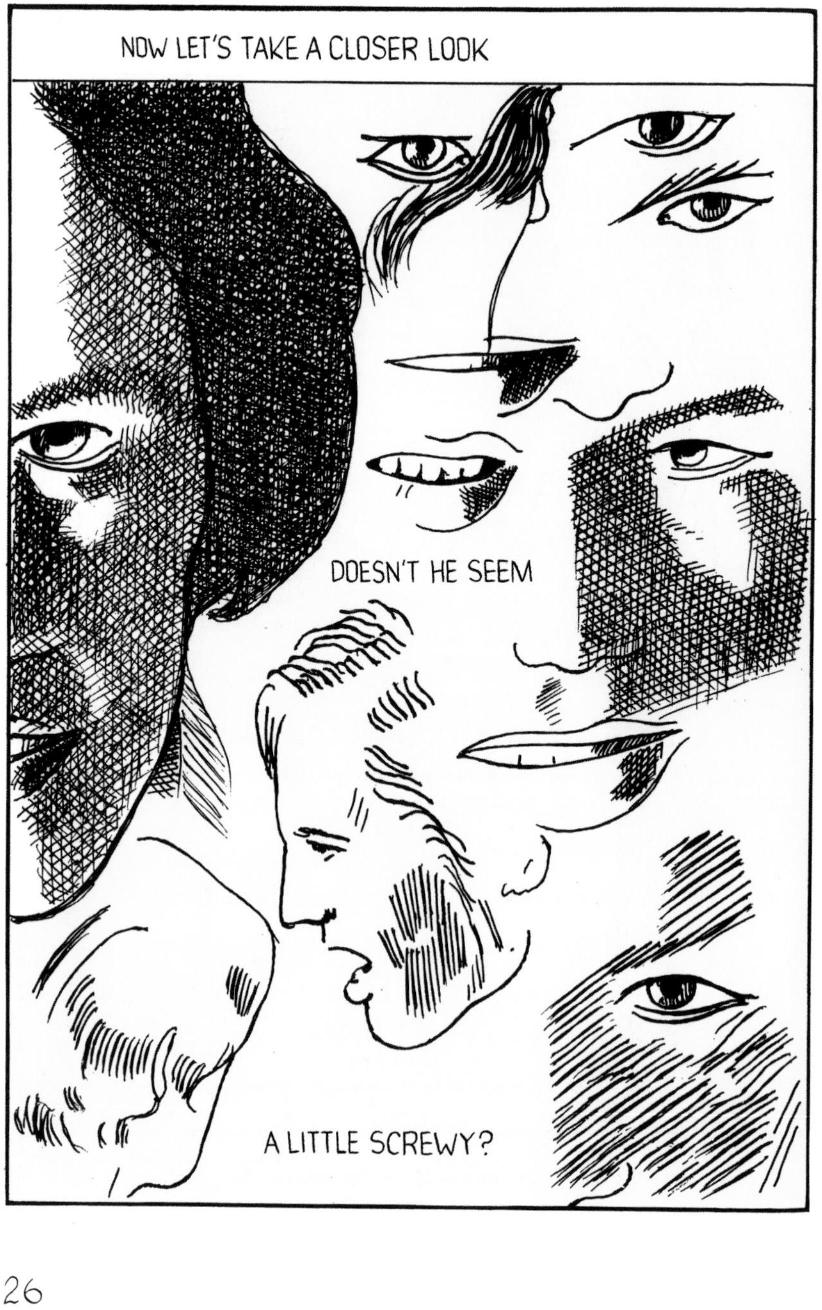
NOW LET'S TAKE A CLOSER LOOK
DOESN'T HE SEEM
A LITTLE SCREWY?

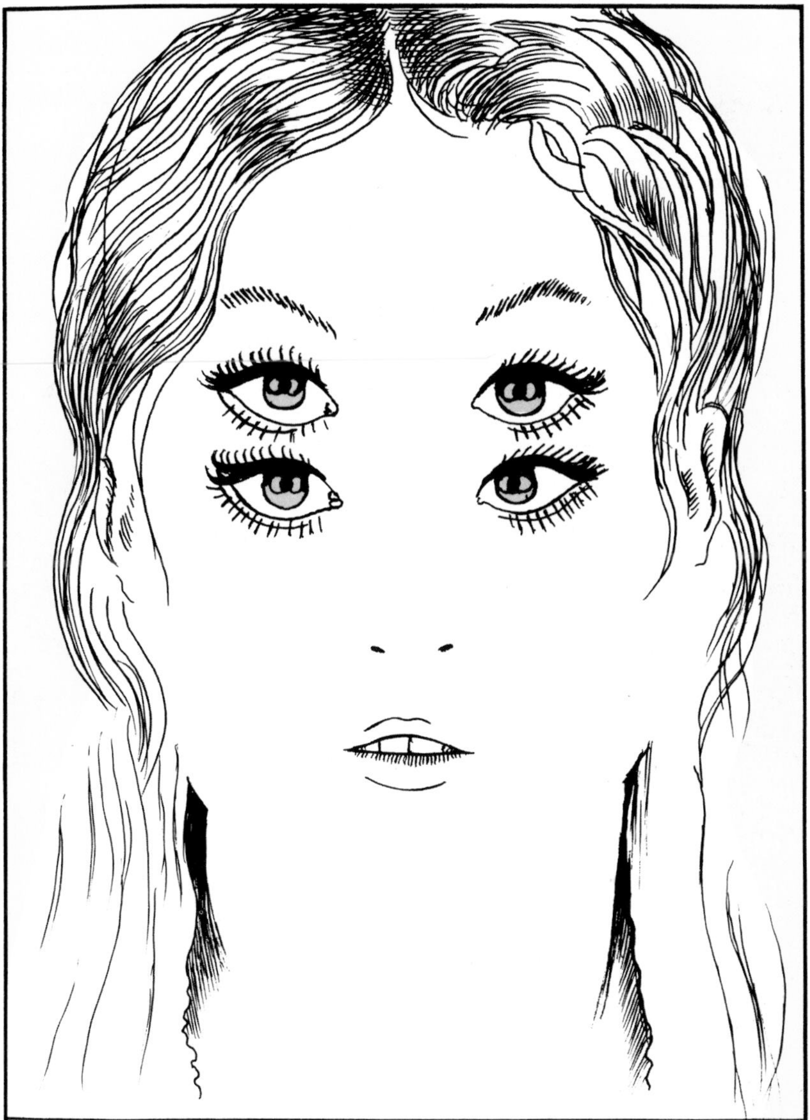

HIS BELOVED'S NAME IS EURA

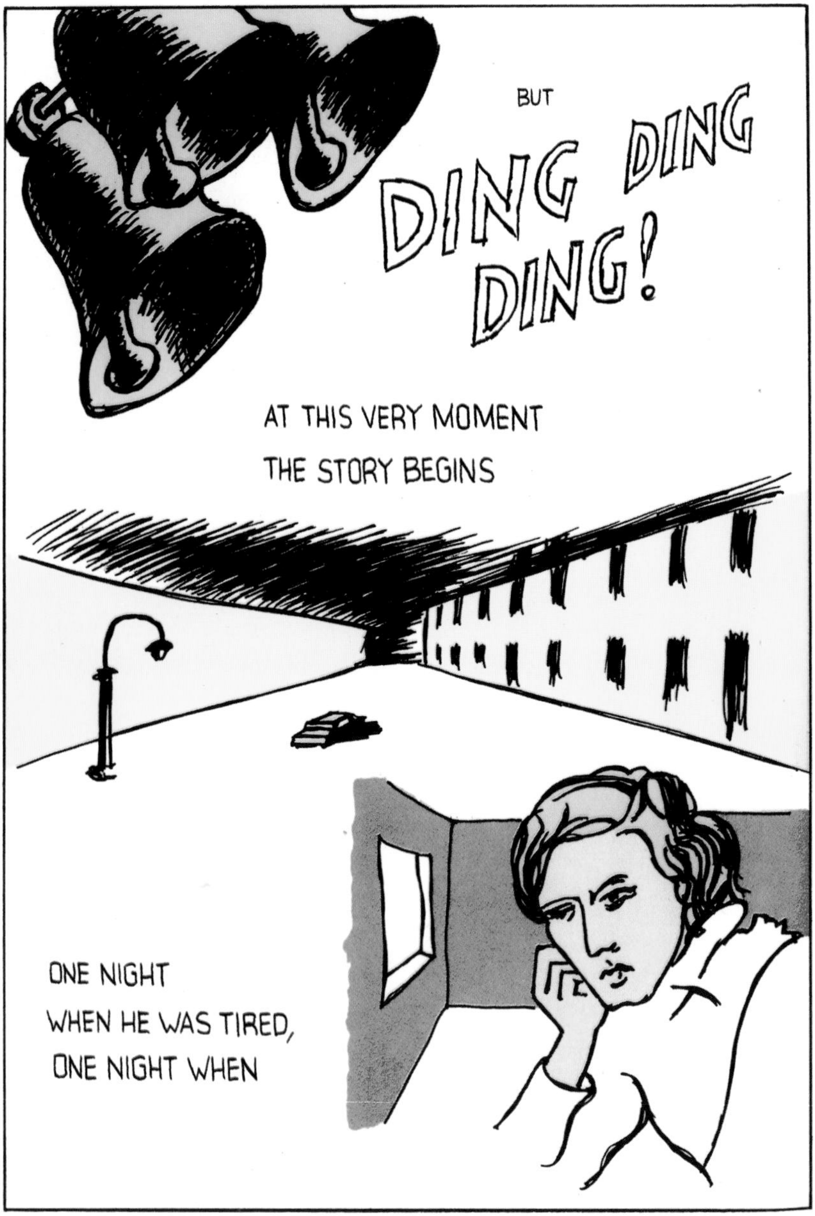
BUT
DING DING DING!
AT THIS VERY MOMENT
THE STORY BEGINS
ONE NIGHT
WHEN HE WAS TIRED,
ONE NIGHT WHEN

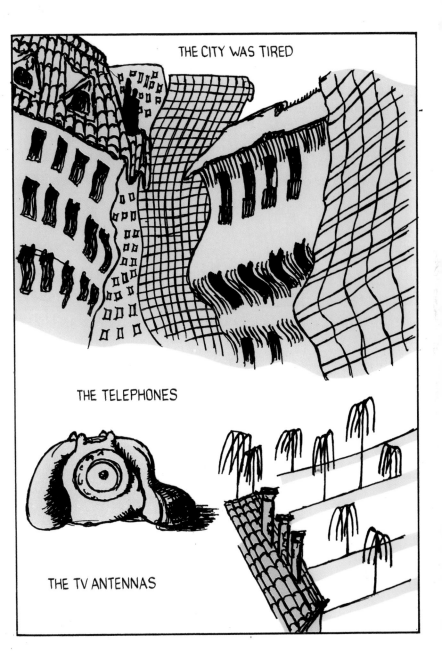

THE CITY WAS TIRED

THE TELEPHONES

THE TV ANTENNAS

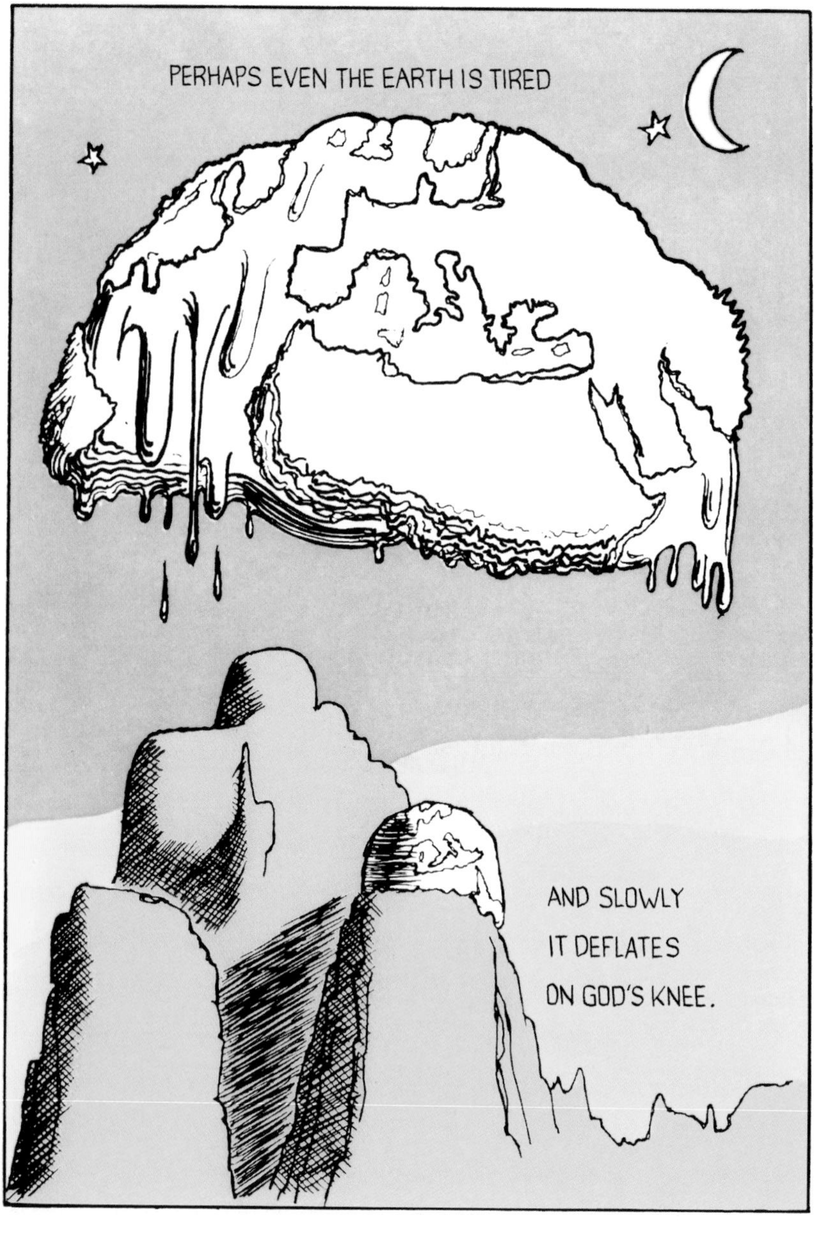
PERHAPS EVEN THE EARTH IS TIRED
AND SLOWLY
IT DEFLATES
ON GOD'S KNEE.

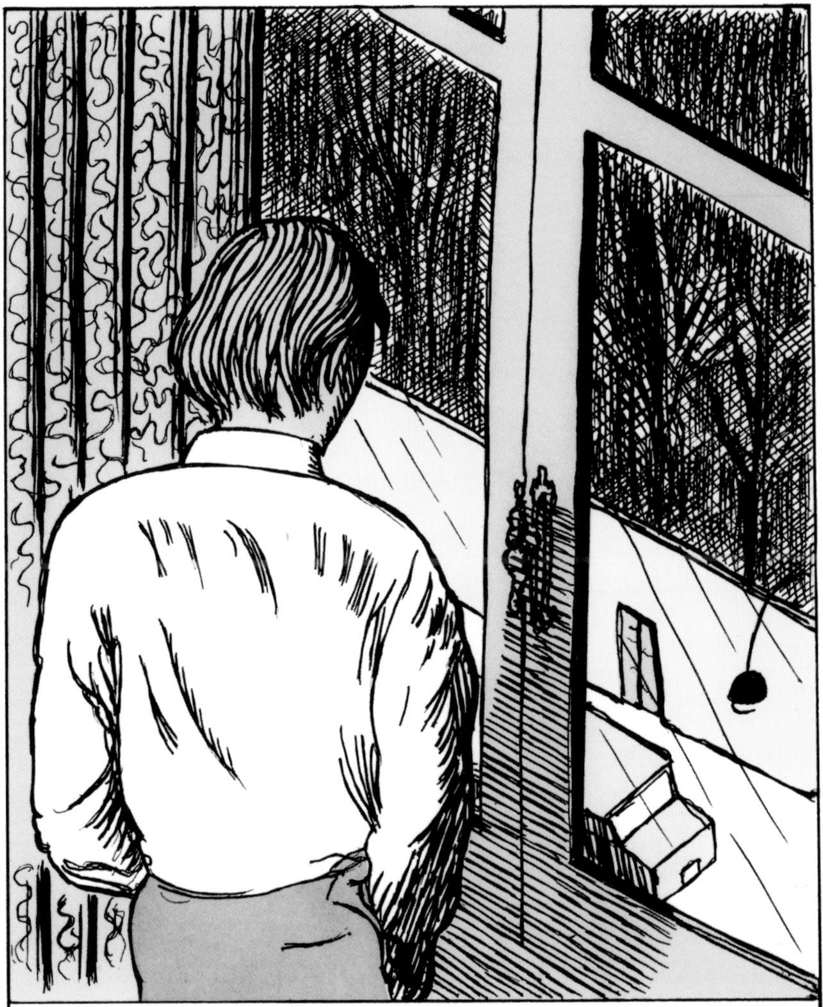

AS HE HAPPENED TO LOOK DOWN AT THE STREET
ON A COLD NIGHT IN MARCH, HE SAW
A TAXI PULL UP IN FRONT OF A LITTLE DOOR
IN THE MYSTERIOUS WALL.

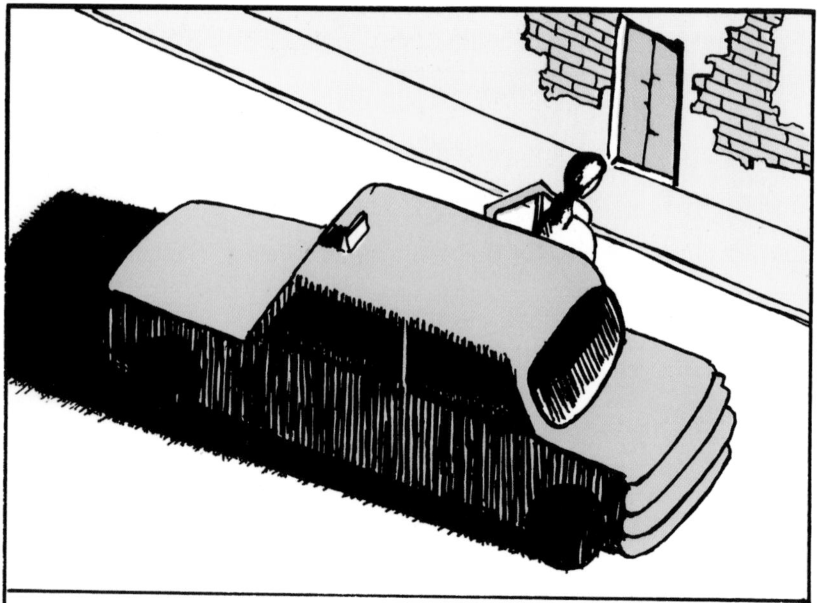

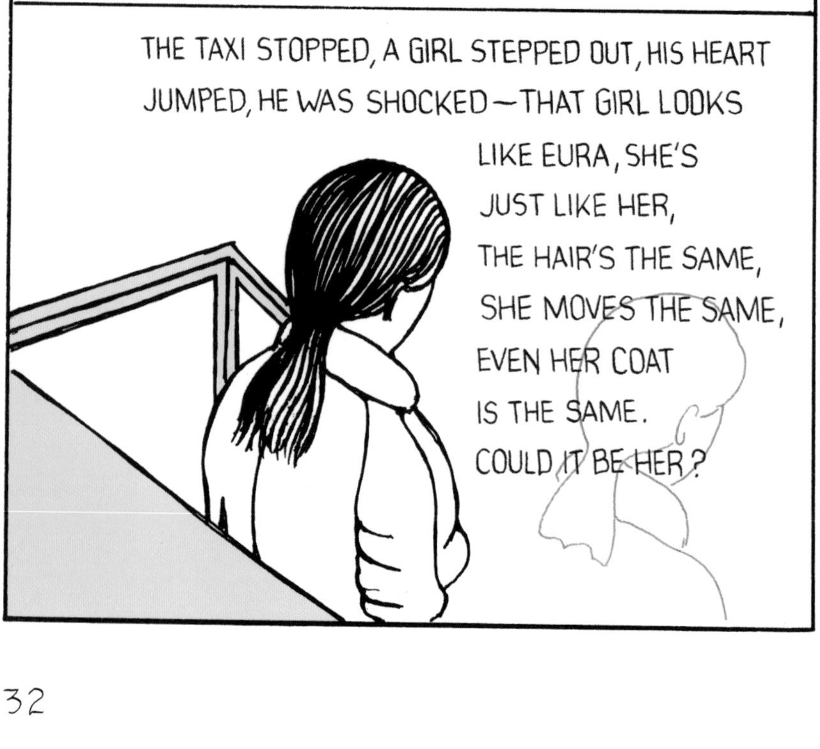
THE TAXI STOPPED, A GIRL STEPPED OUT, HIS HEART JUMPED, HE WAS SHOCKED—THAT GIRL LOOKS LIKE EURA, SHE'S JUST LIKE HER, THE HAIR'S THE SAME, SHE MOVES THE SAME, EVEN HER COAT IS THE SAME. COULD IT BE HER?

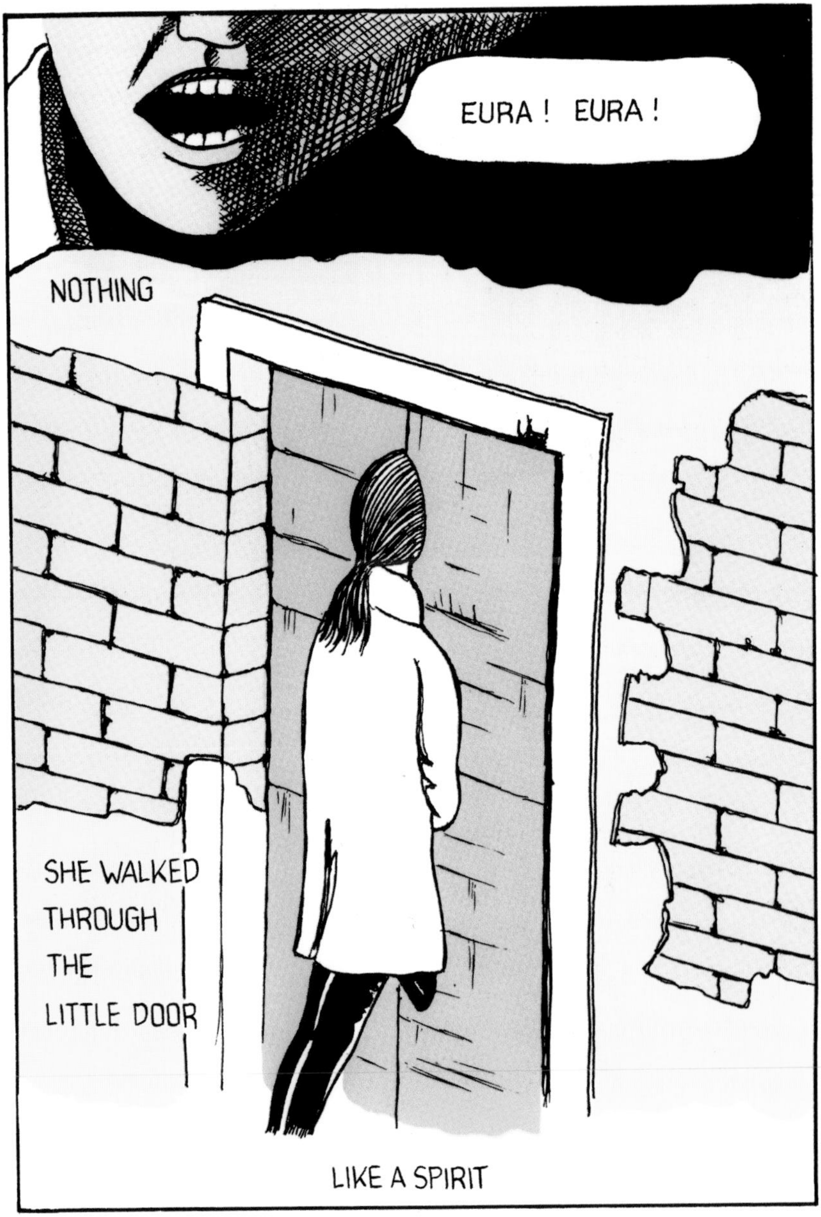
EURA! EURA!
NOTHING
SHE WALKED
THROUGH
THE
LITTLE DOOR
LIKE A SPIRIT

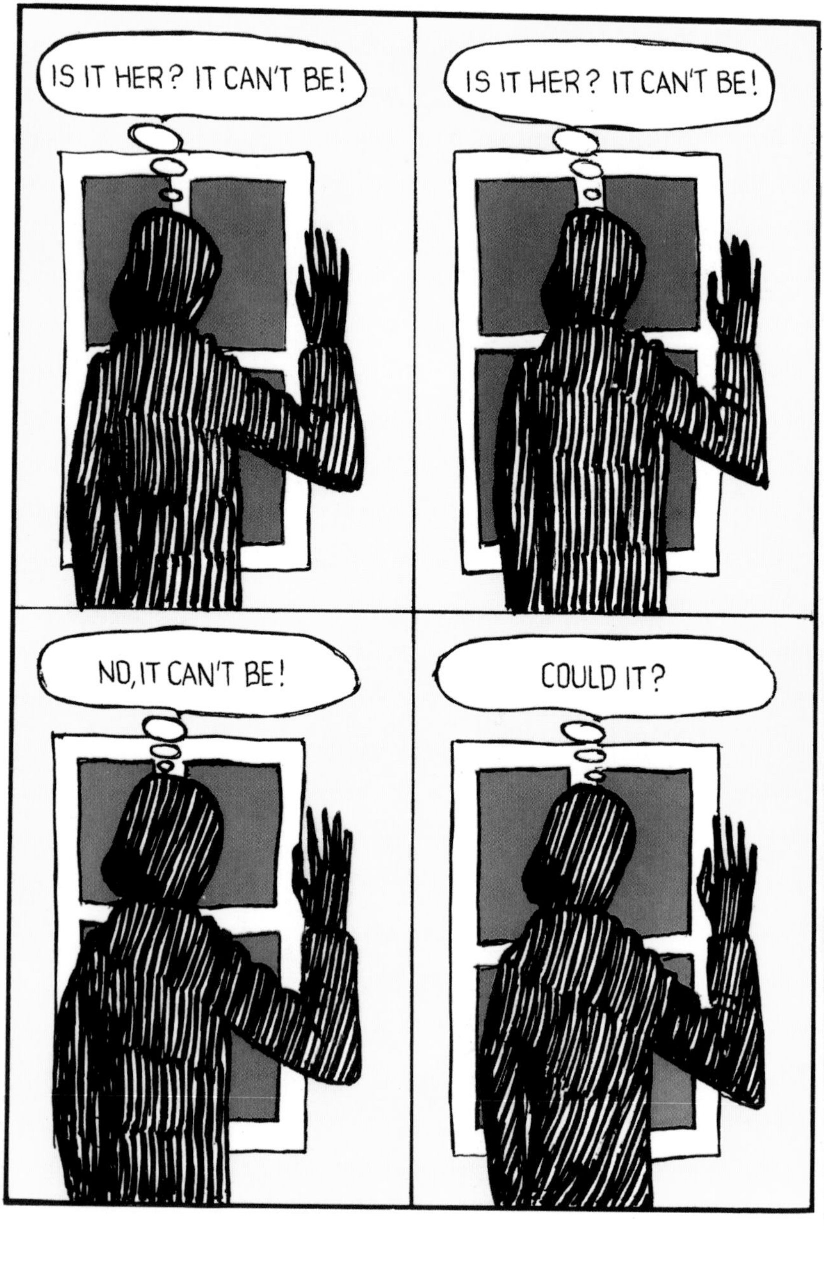
IS IT HER? IT CAN'T BE!
IS IT HER? IT CAN'T BE!
NO, IT CAN'T BE!
COULD IT?

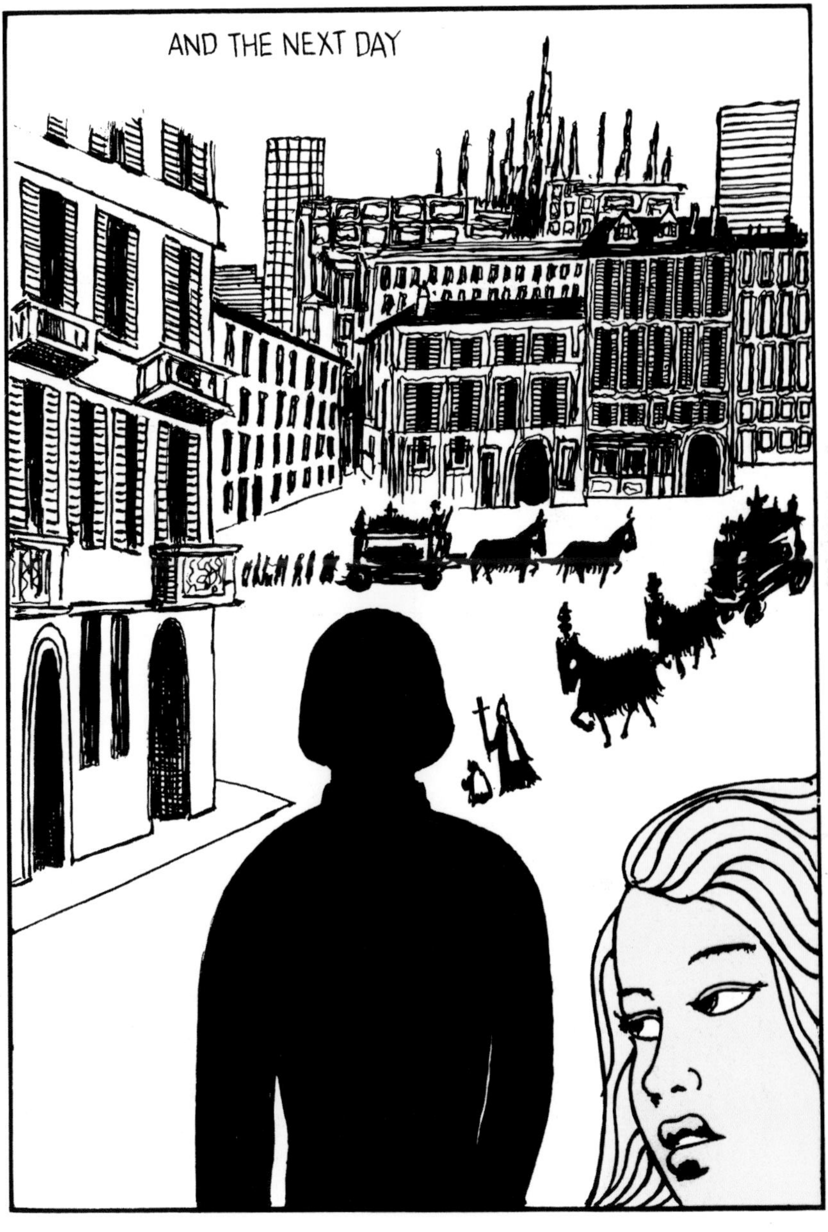
AND THE NEXT DAY

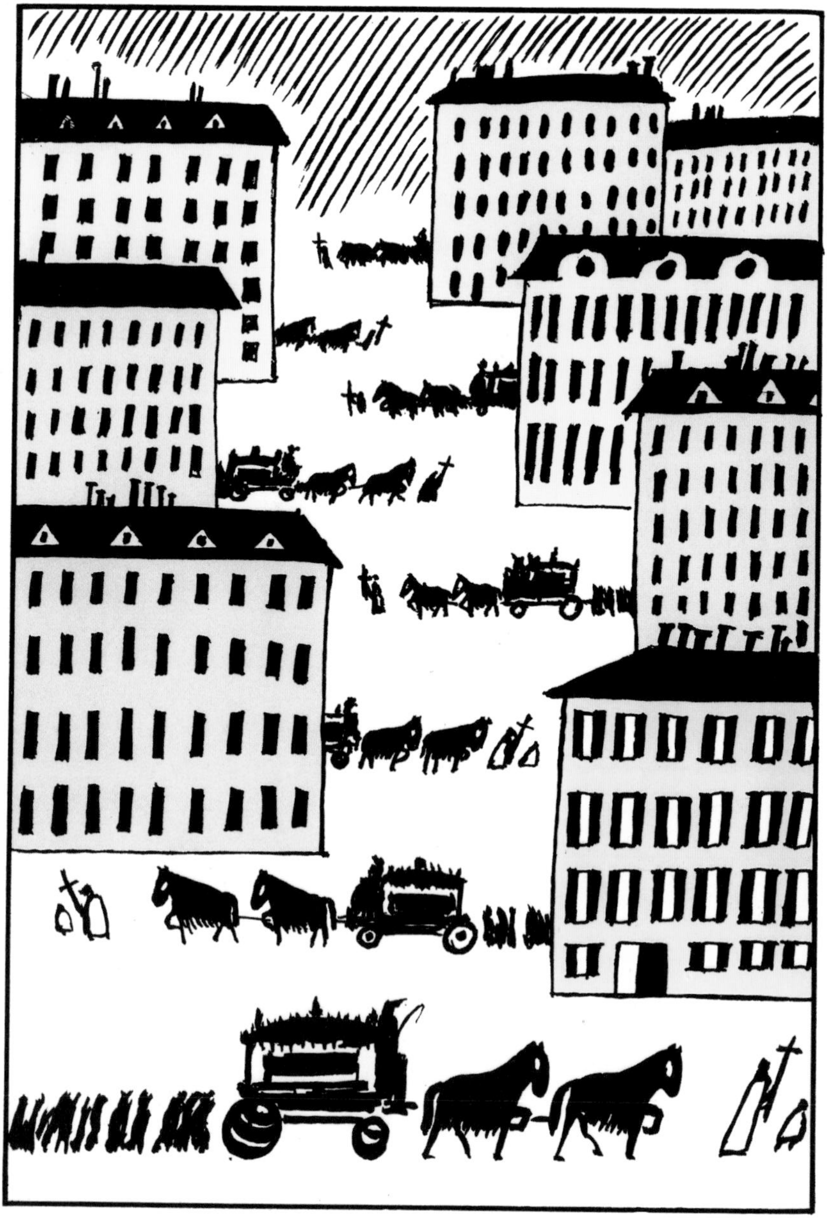

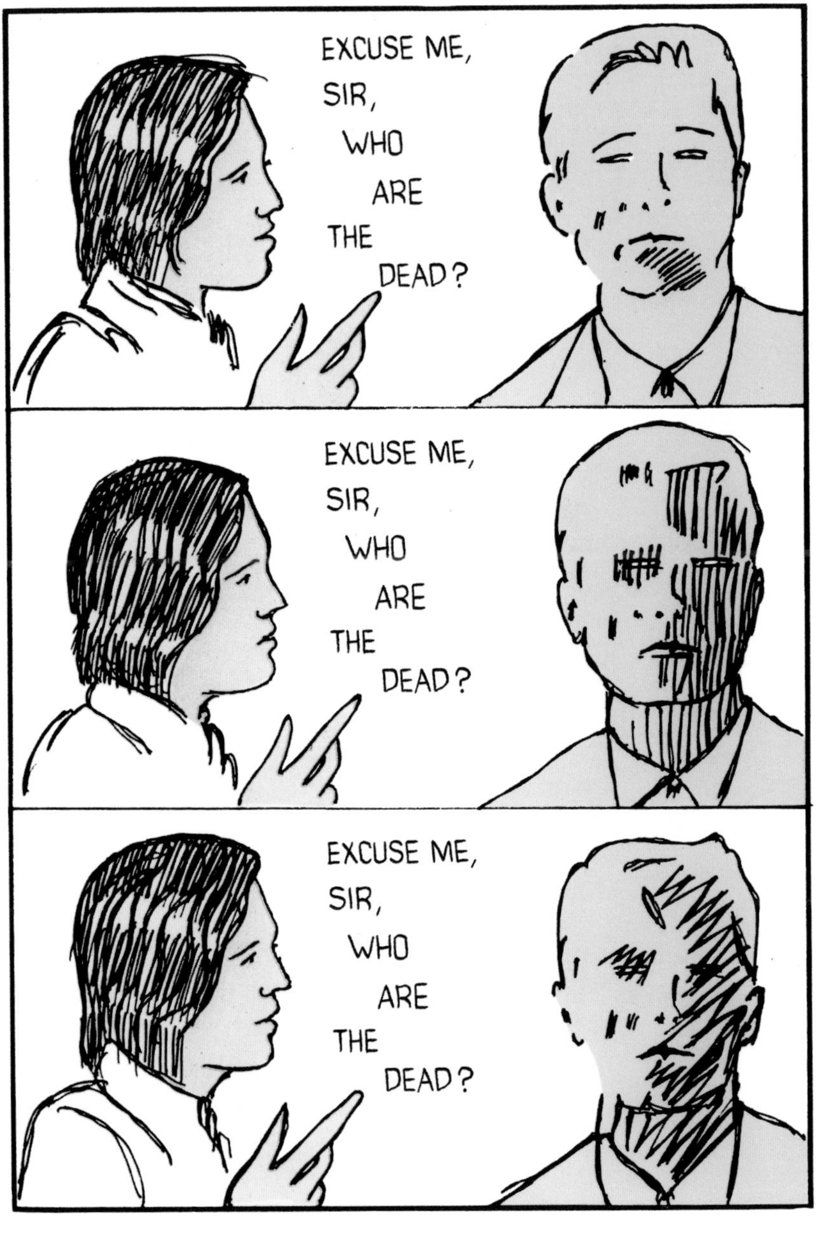
EXCUSE ME, SIR, WHO ARE THE DEAD?
EXCUSE ME, SIR, WHO ARE THE DEAD?
EXCUSE ME, SIR, WHO ARE THE DEAD?

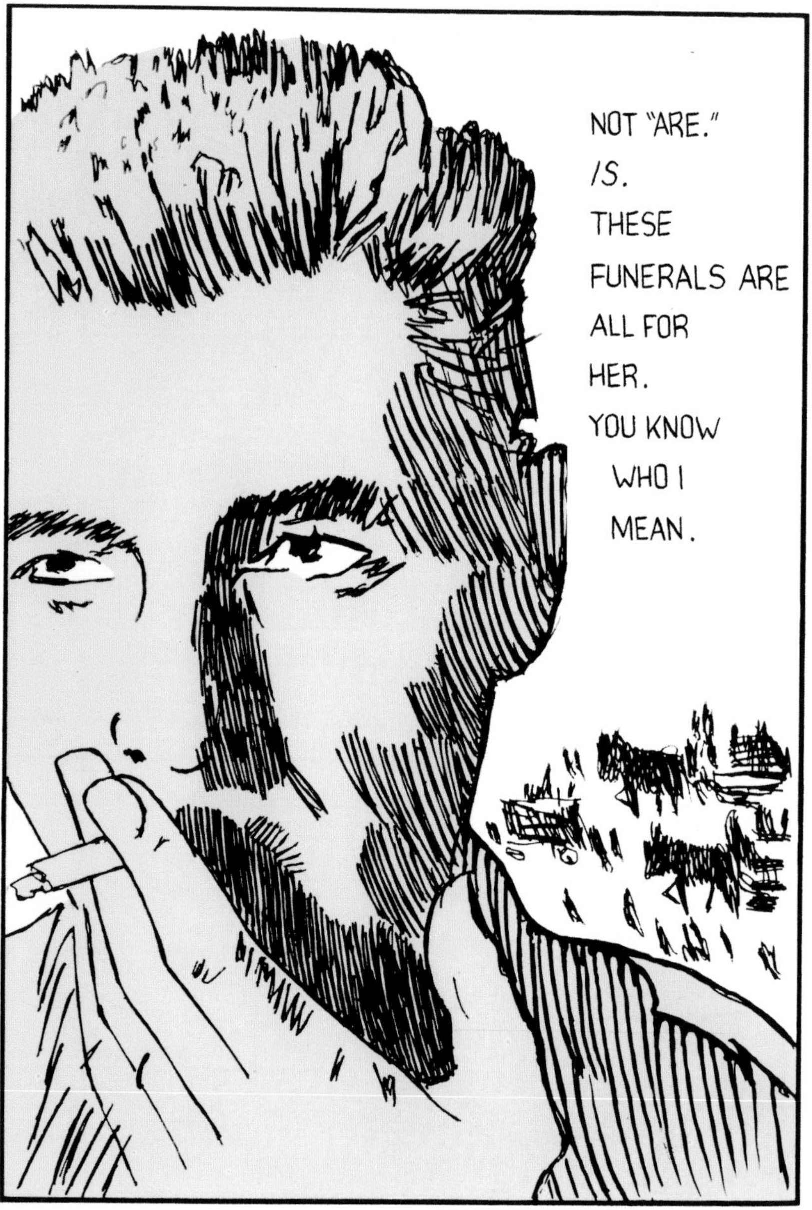
NOT "ARE."
IS.
THESE
FUNERALS ARE
ALL FOR
HER.
YOU KNOW
WHO I
MEAN.

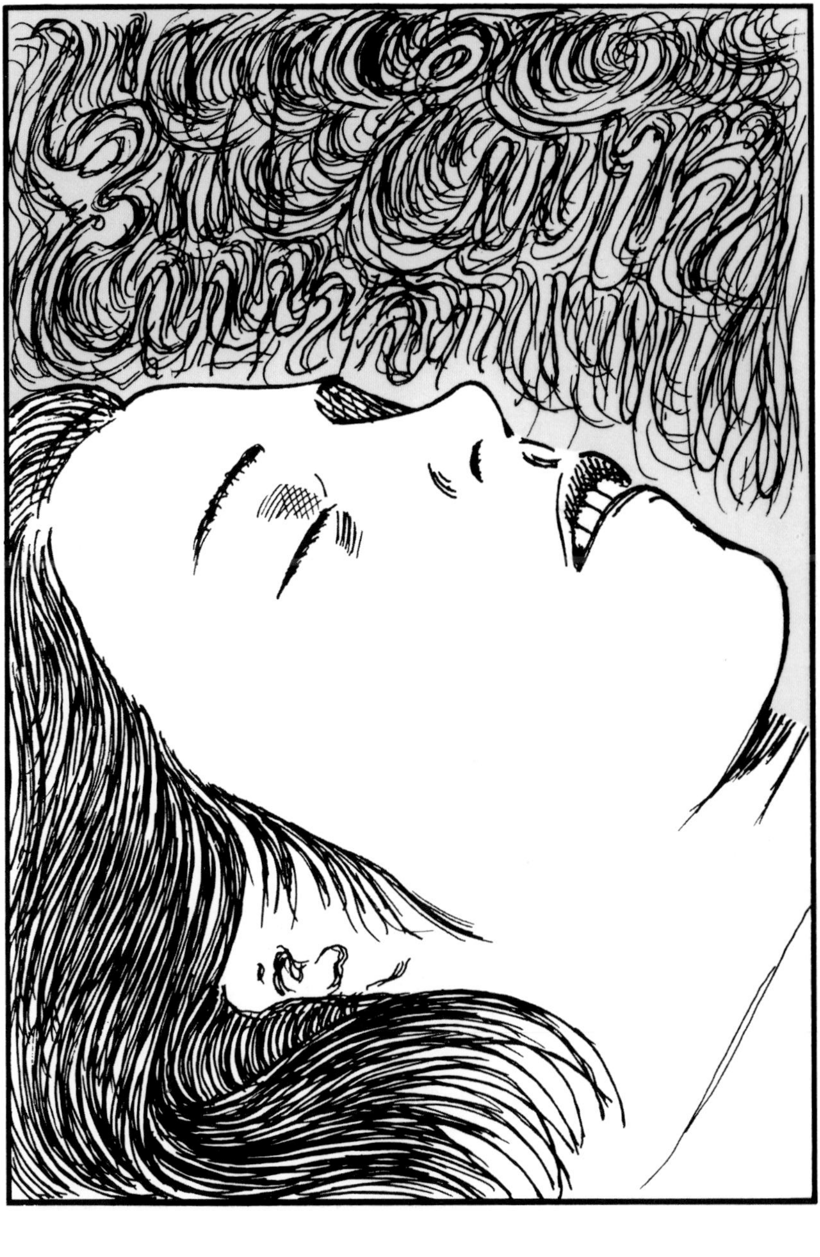

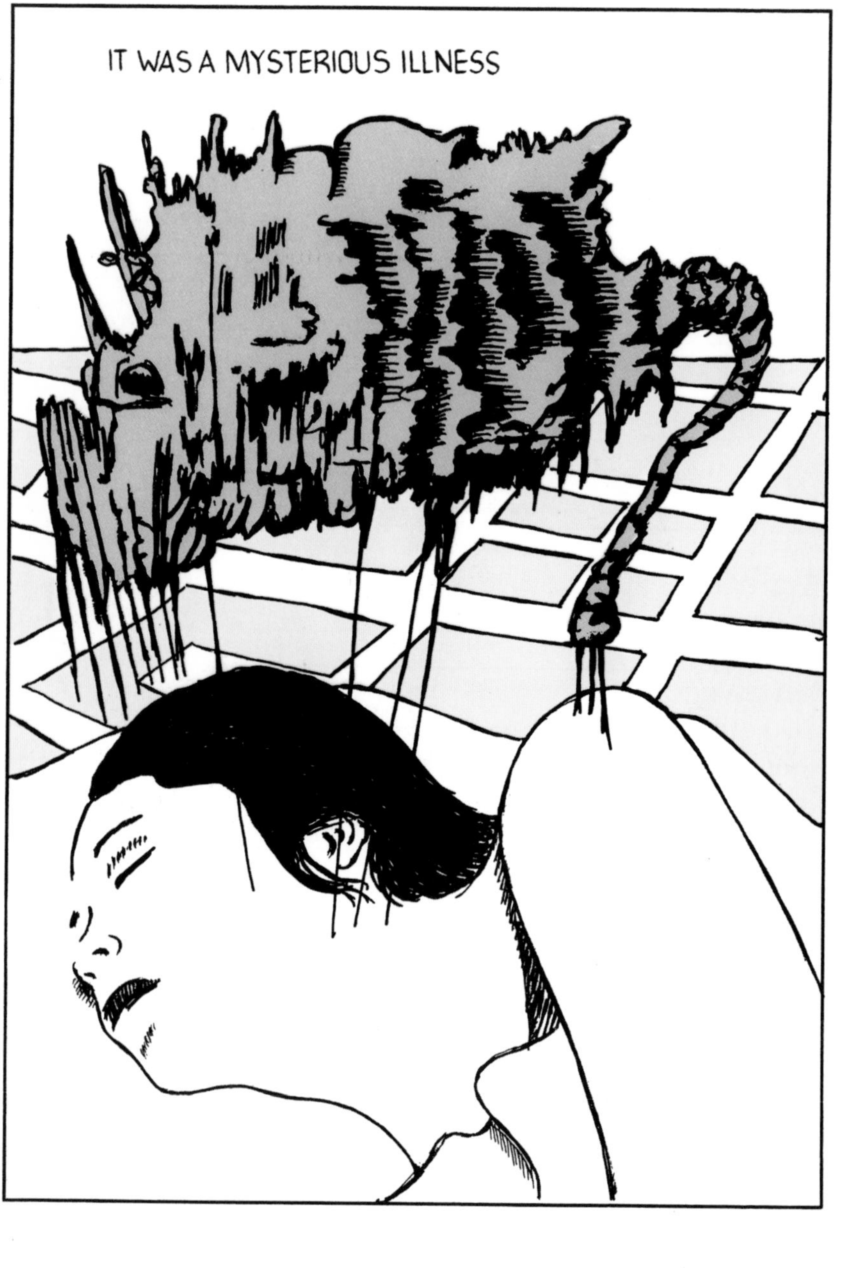
IT WAS A MYSTERIOUS ILLNESS

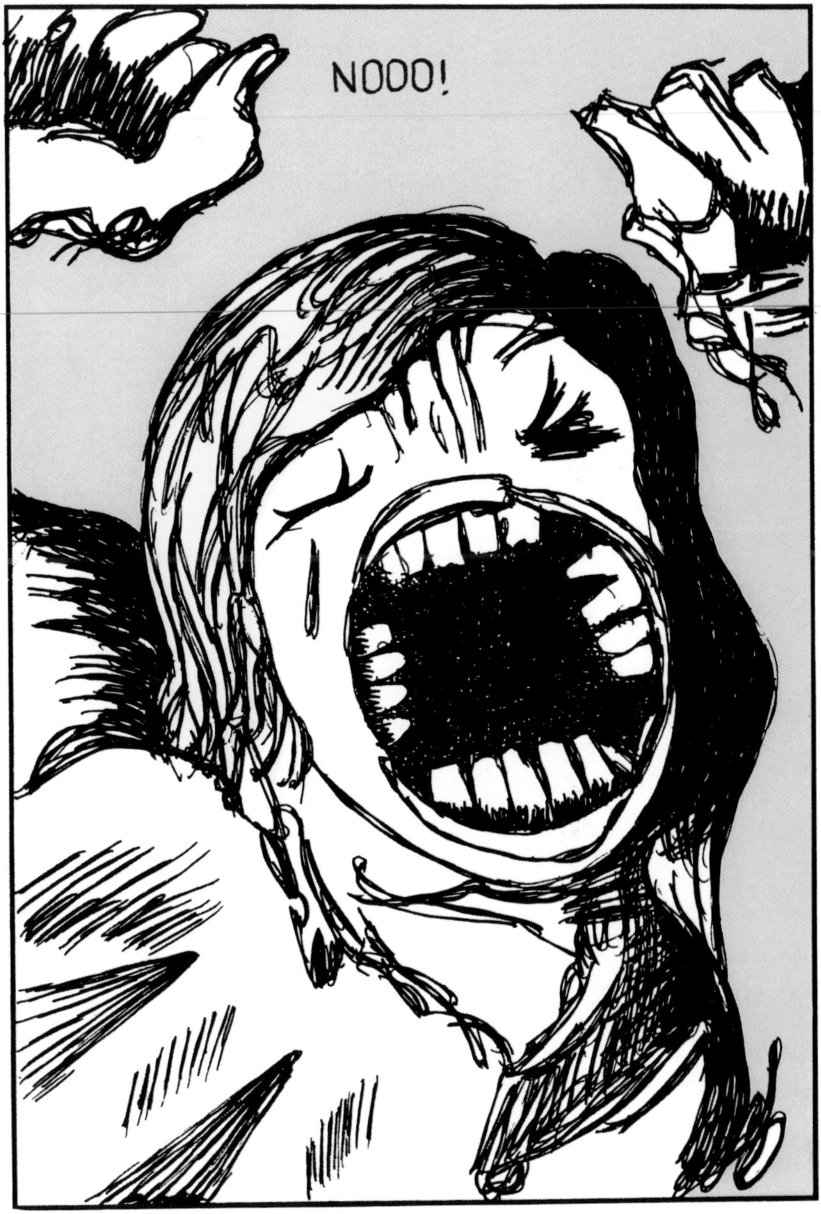
NOOO!

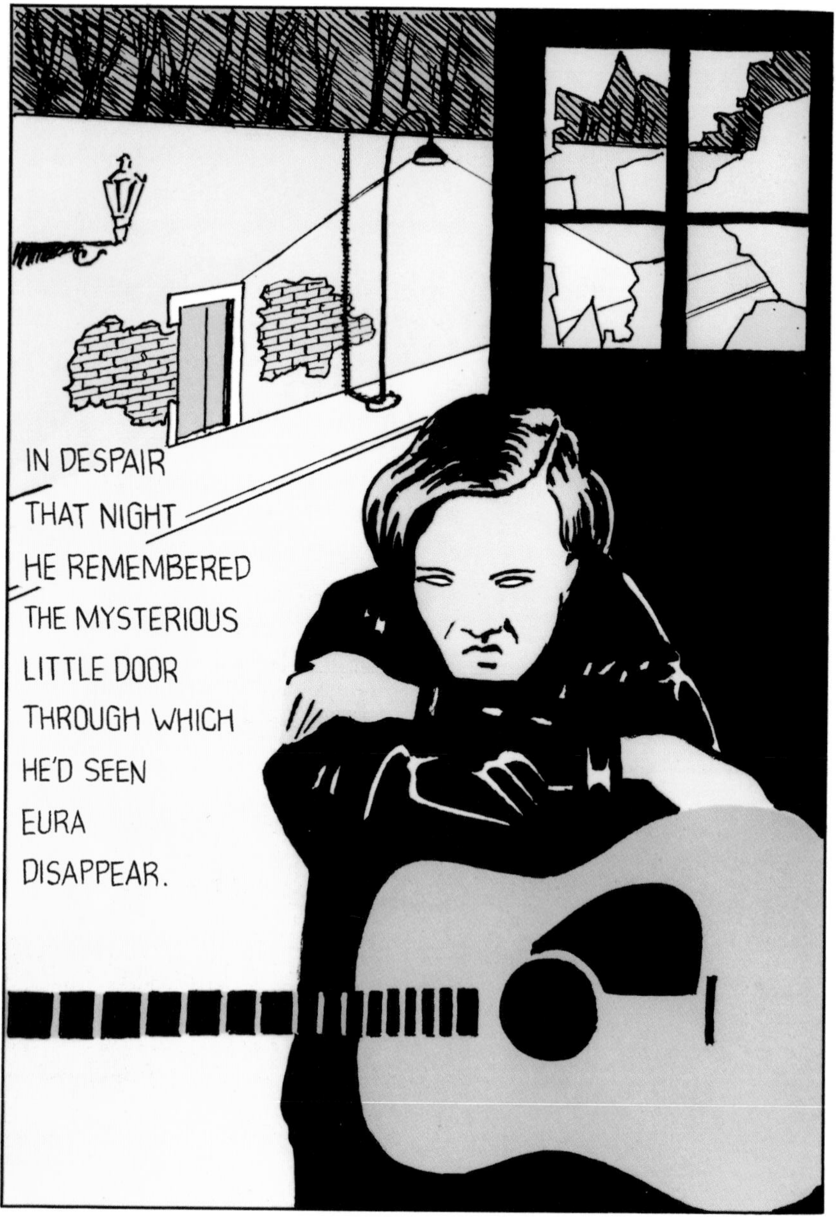
IN DESPAIR
THAT NIGHT
HE REMEMBERED
THE MYSTERIOUS
LITTLE DOOR
THROUGH WHICH
HE'D SEEN
EURA
DISAPPEAR.

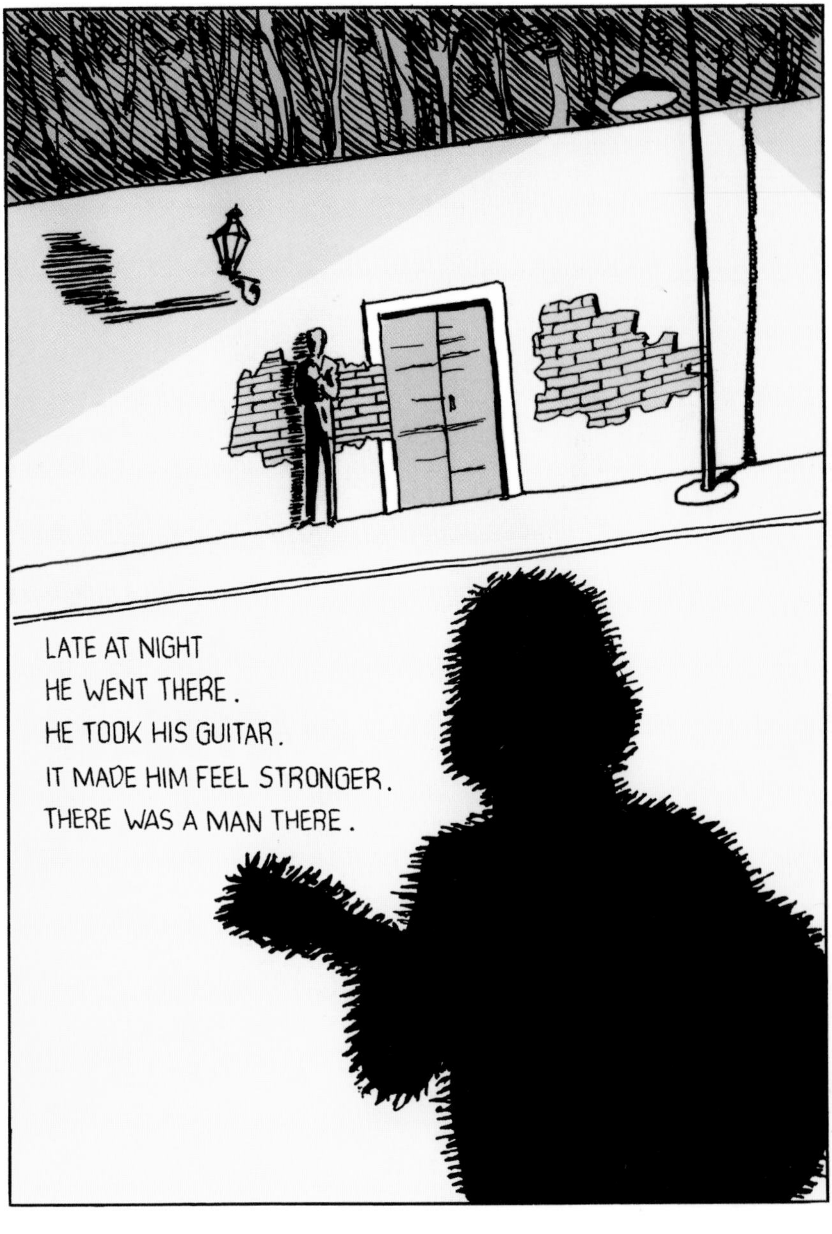
LATE AT NIGHT
HE WENT THERE.
HE TOOK HIS GUITAR.
IT MADE HIM FEEL STRONGER.
THERE WAS A MAN THERE.

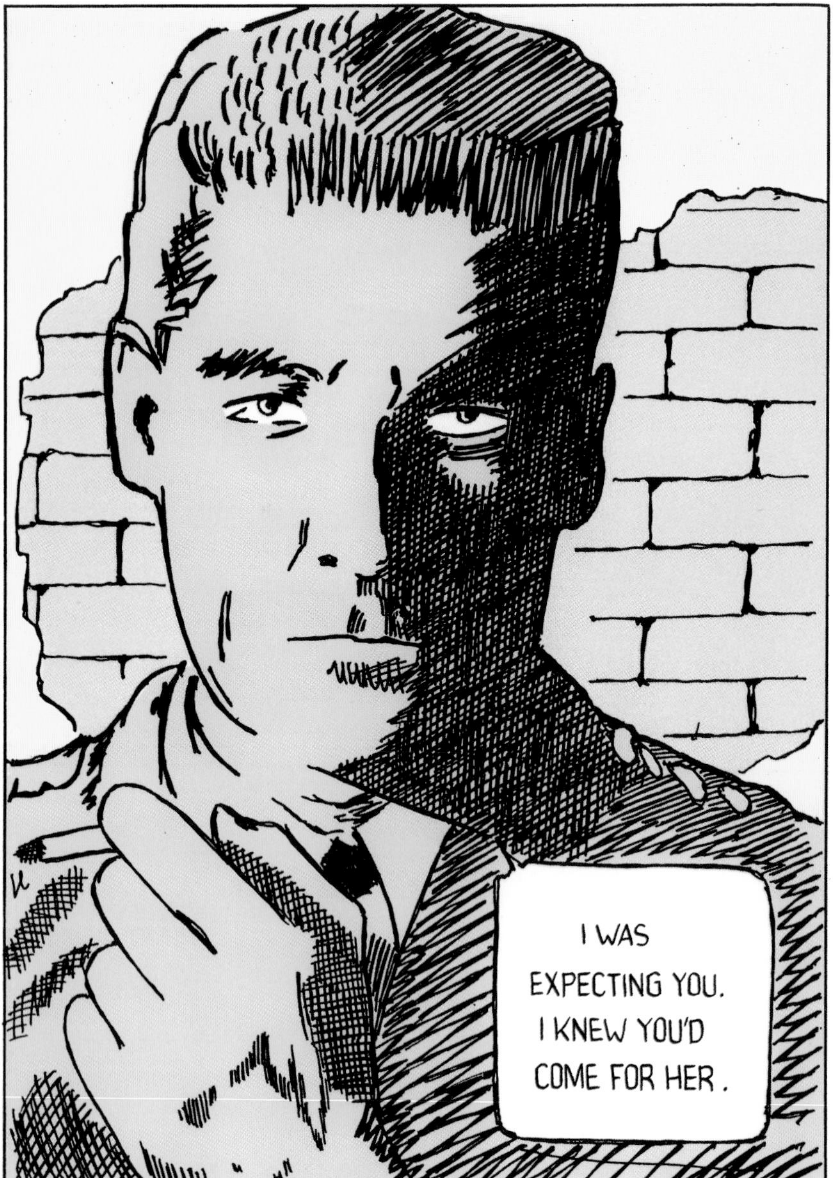
I WAS EXPECTING YOU. I KNEW YOU'D COME FOR HER.

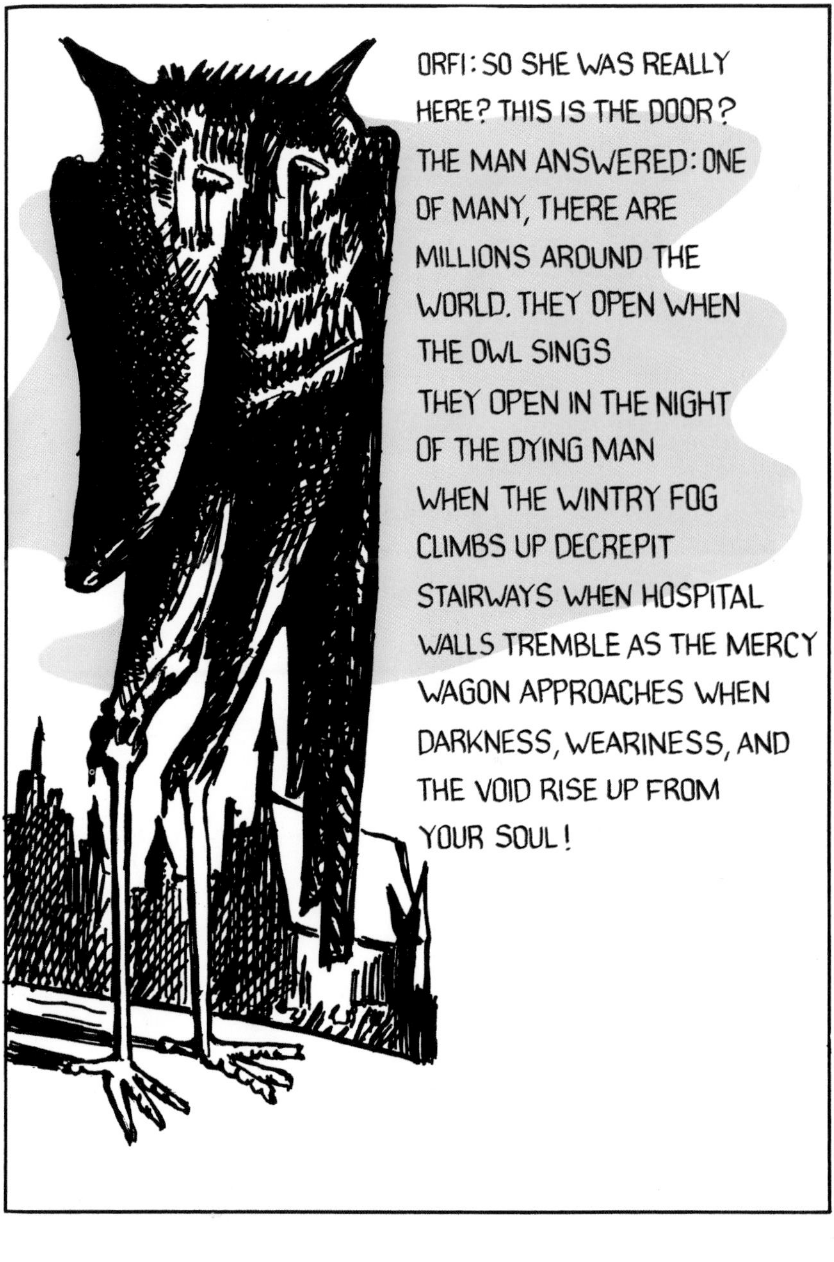
ORFI: SO SHE WAS REALLY HERE? THIS IS THE DOOR?
THE MAN ANSWERED: ONE OF MANY, THERE ARE MILLIONS AROUND THE WORLD. THEY OPEN WHEN THE OWL SINGS
THEY OPEN IN THE NIGHT OF THE DYING MAN
WHEN THE WINTRY FOG CLIMBS UP DECREPIT STAIRWAYS WHEN HOSPITAL WALLS TREMBLE AS THE MERCY WAGON APPROACHES WHEN DARKNESS, WEARINESS, AND THE VOID RISE UP FROM YOUR SOUL!

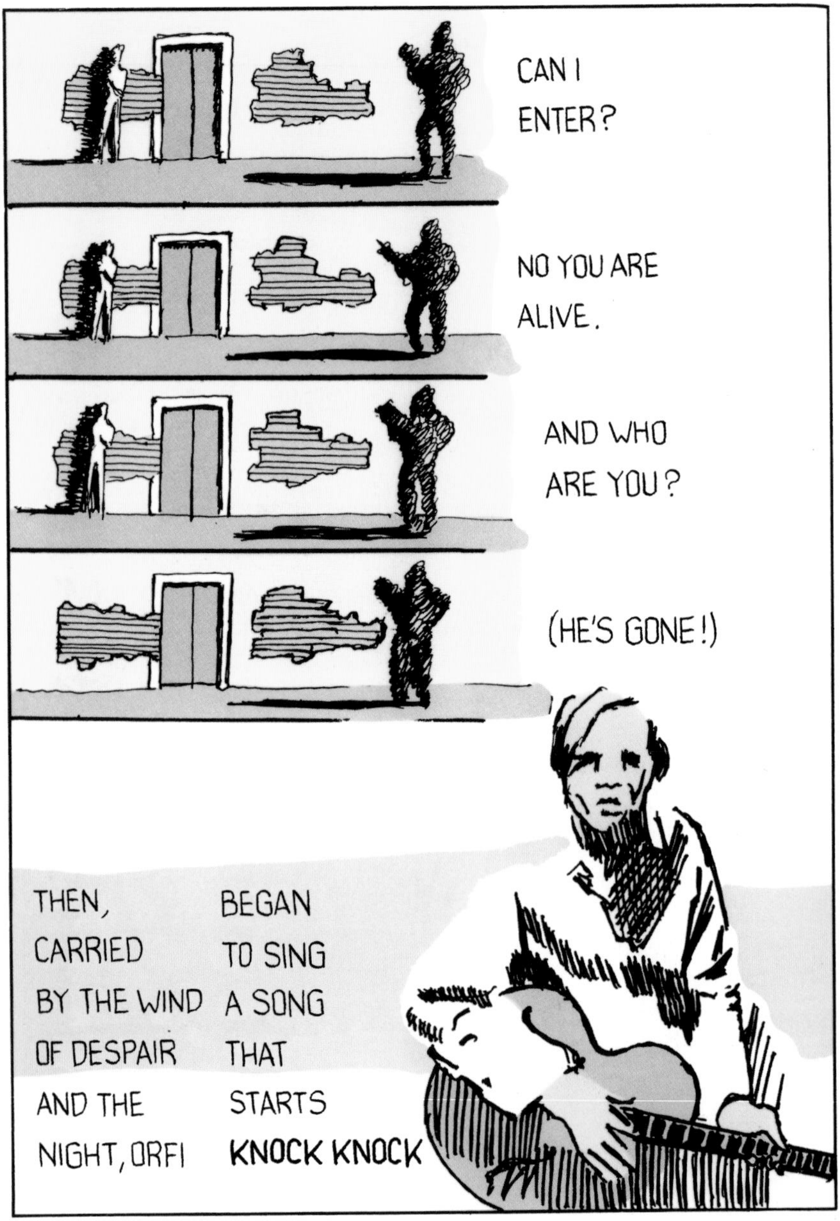
CAN I
ENTER?
NO YOU ARE
ALIVE.
AND WHO
ARE YOU?
(HE'S GONE!)
THEN,
CARRIED
BY THE WIND
OF DESPAIR
AND THE
NIGHT, ORFI
BEGAN
TO SING
A SONG
THAT
STARTS
KNOCK KNOCK

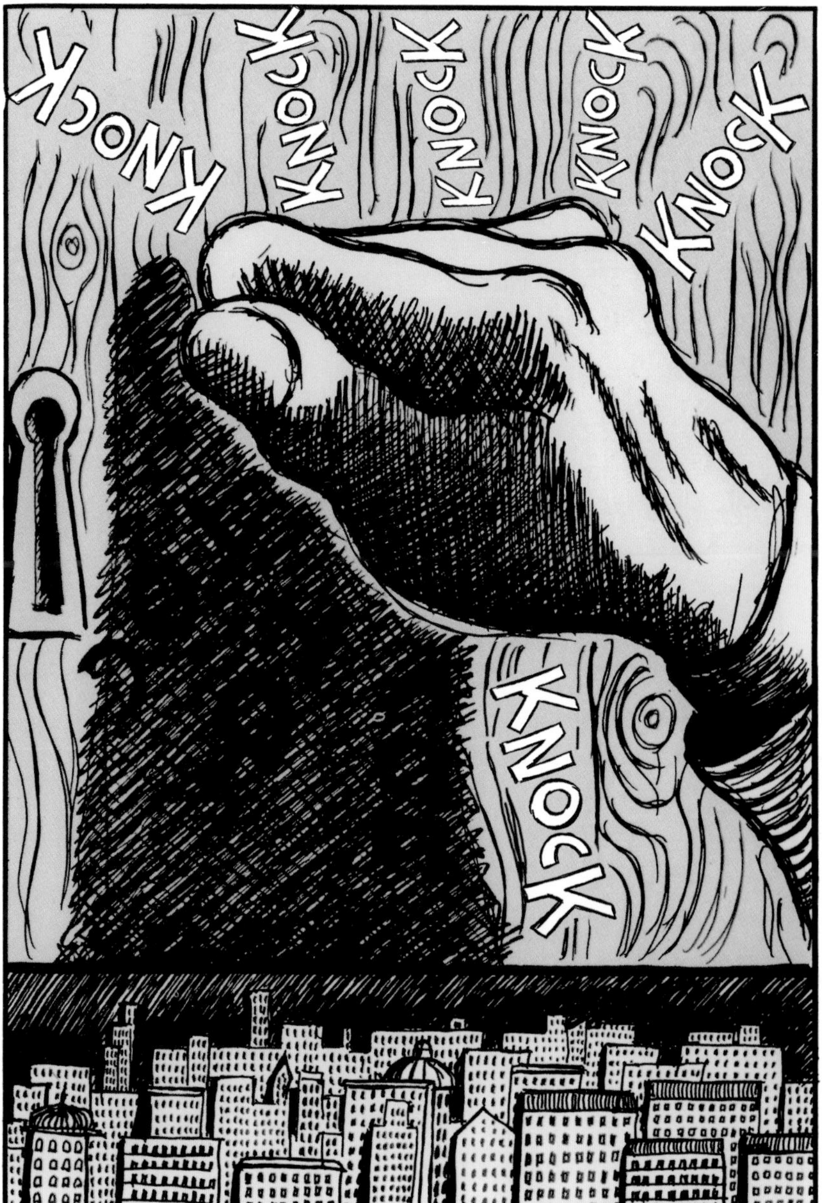
KNOCK
KNOCK
KNOCK
KNOCK
KNOCK
KNOCK

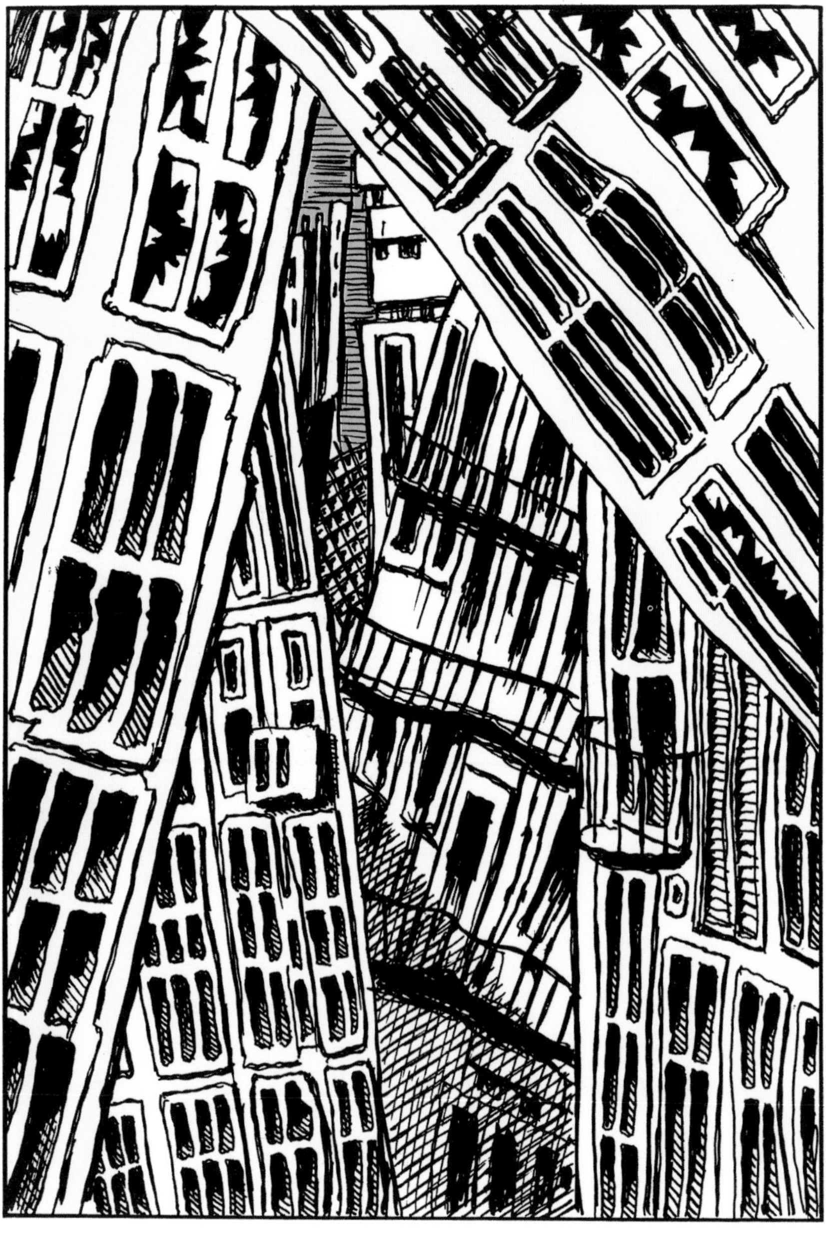

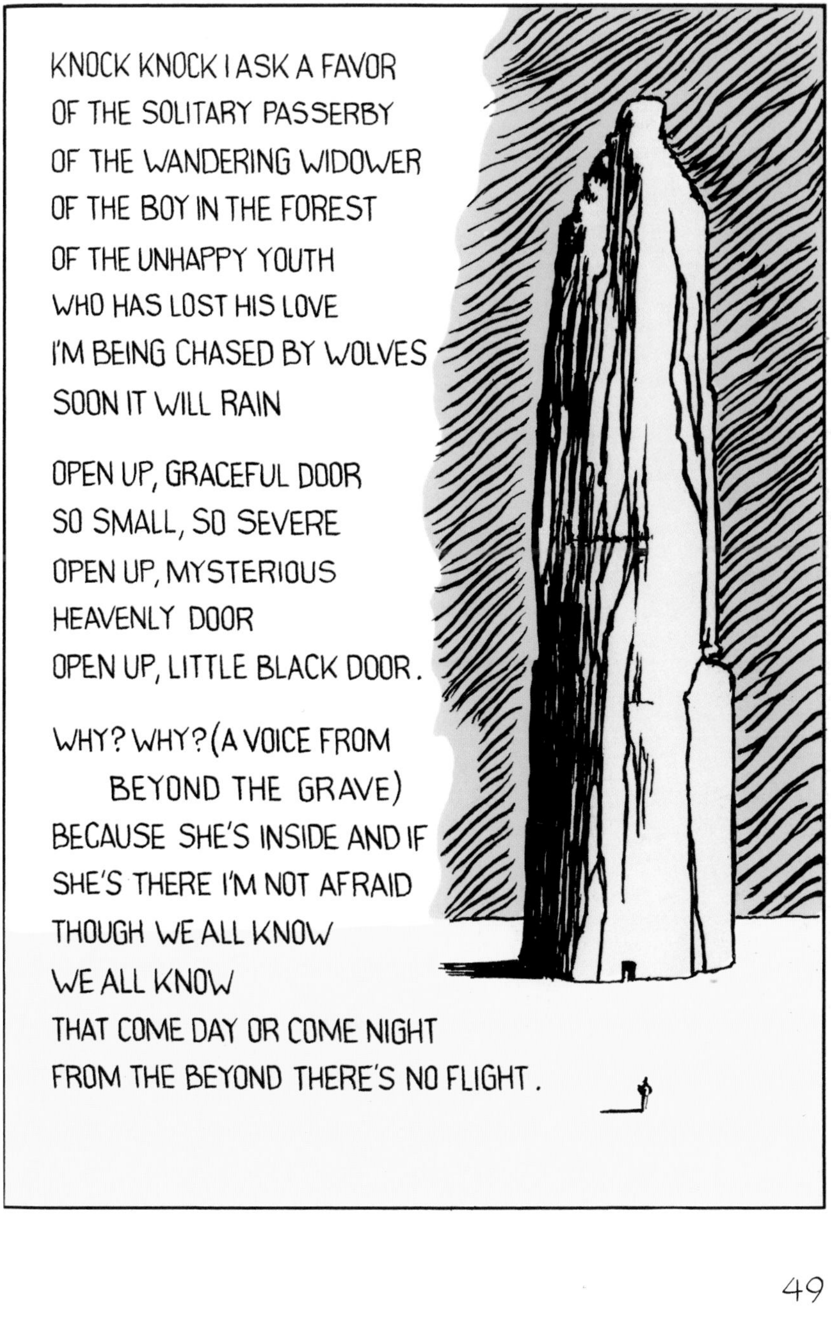
KNOCK KNOCK I ASK A FAVOR
OF THE SOLITARY PASSERBY
OF THE WANDERING WIDOWER
OF THE BOY IN THE FOREST
OF THE UNHAPPY YOUTH
WHO HAS LOST HIS LOVE
I'M BEING CHASED BY WOLVES
SOON IT WILL RAIN

OPEN UP, GRACEFUL DOOR
SO SMALL, SO SEVERE
OPEN UP, MYSTERIOUS
HEAVENLY DOOR
OPEN UP, LITTLE BLACK DOOR.

WHY? WHY? (A VOICE FROM
BEYOND THE GRAVE)
BECAUSE SHE'S INSIDE AND IF
SHE'S THERE I'M NOT AFRAID
THOUGH WE ALL KNOW
WE ALL KNOW
THAT COME DAY OR COME NIGHT
FROM THE BEYOND THERE'S NO FLIGHT.

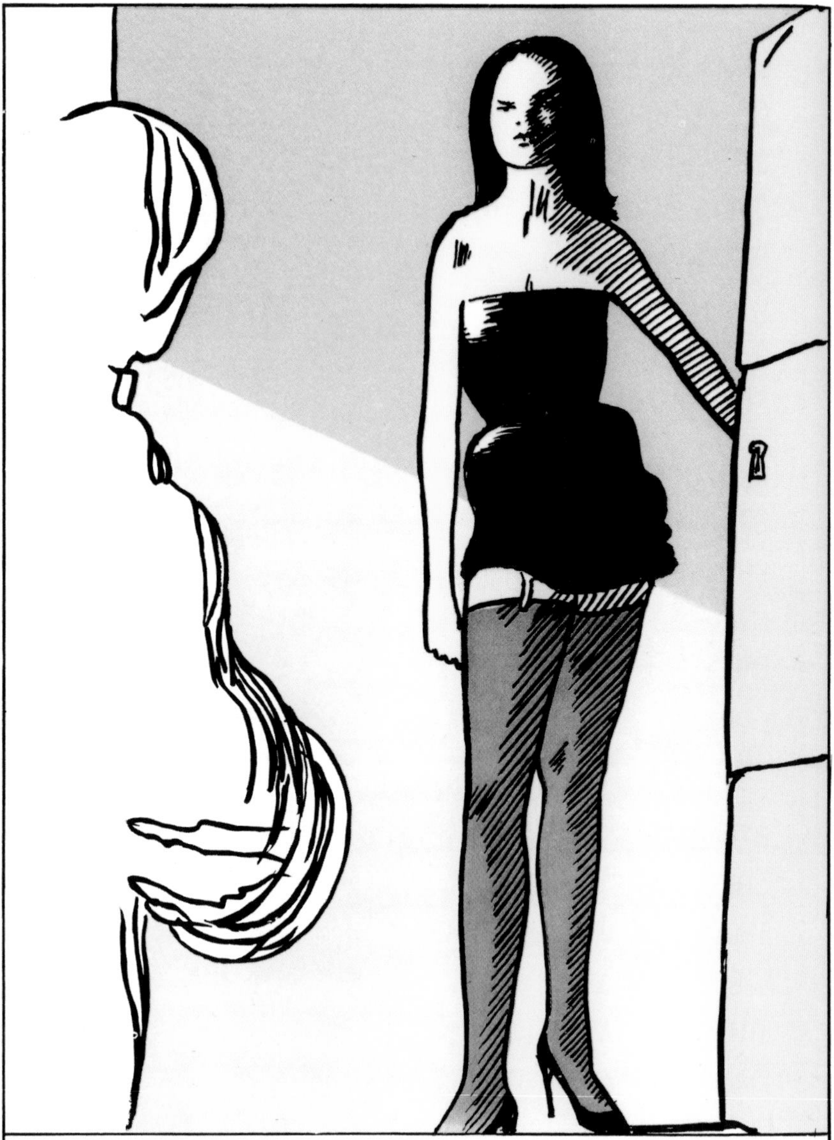

THE DOOR OPENED. A GIRL STOOD THERE.

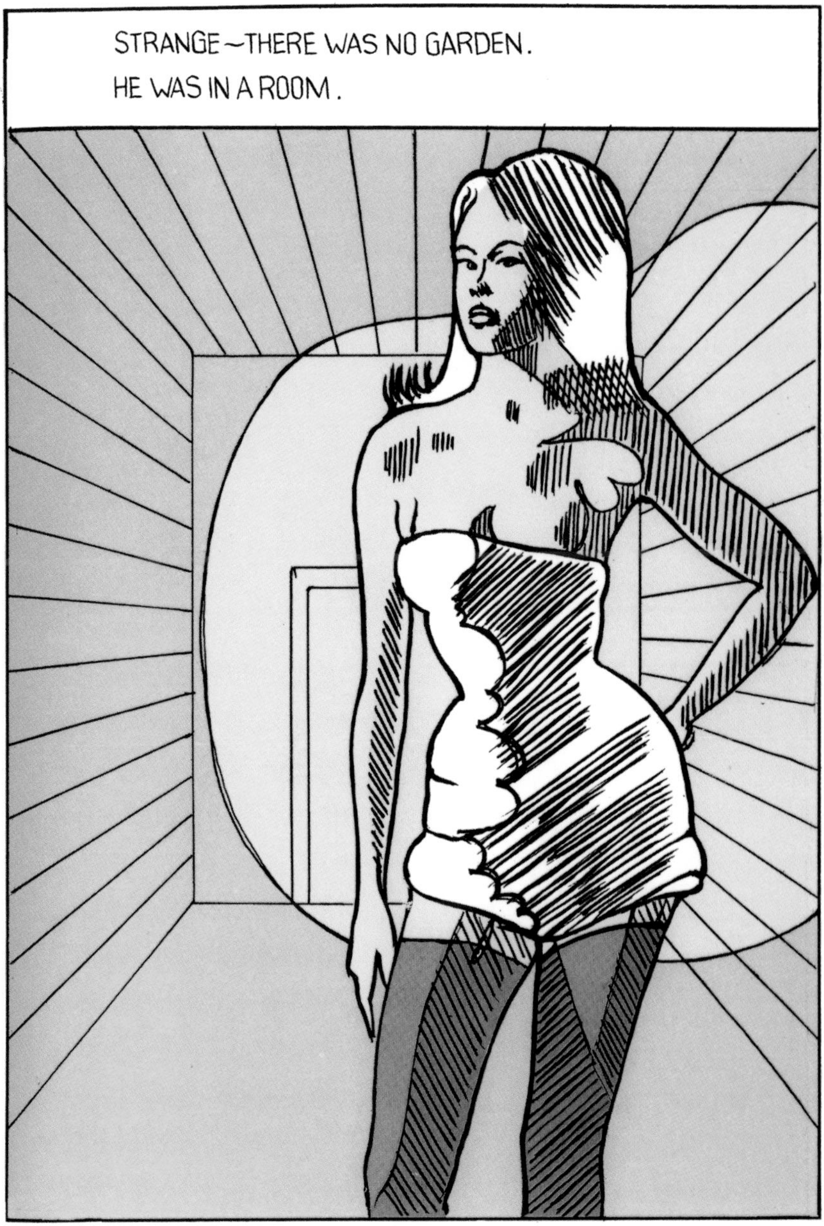
STRANGE—THERE WAS NO GARDEN.
HE WAS IN A ROOM.

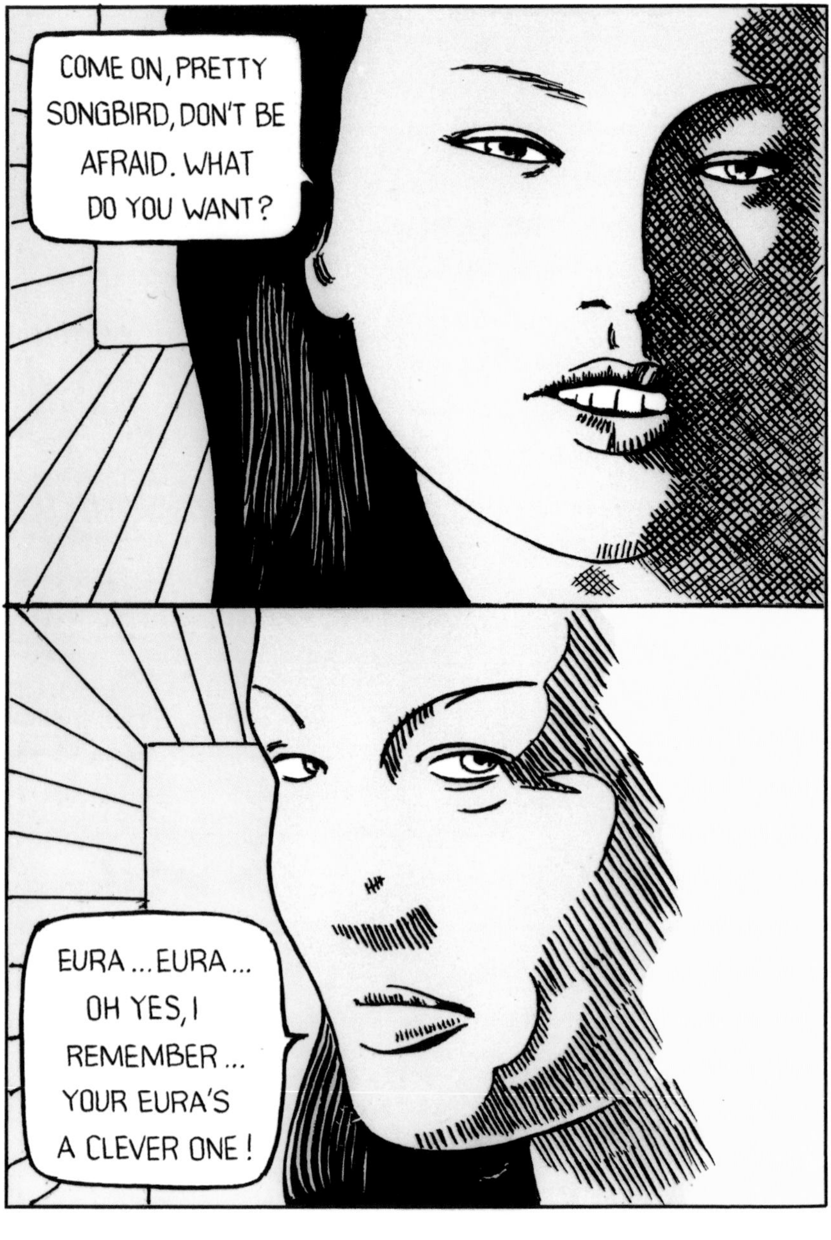
COME ON, PRETTY SONGBIRD, DON'T BE AFRAID. WHAT DO YOU WANT?
EURA ... EURA ... OH YES, I REMEMBER ... YOUR EURA'S A CLEVER ONE!

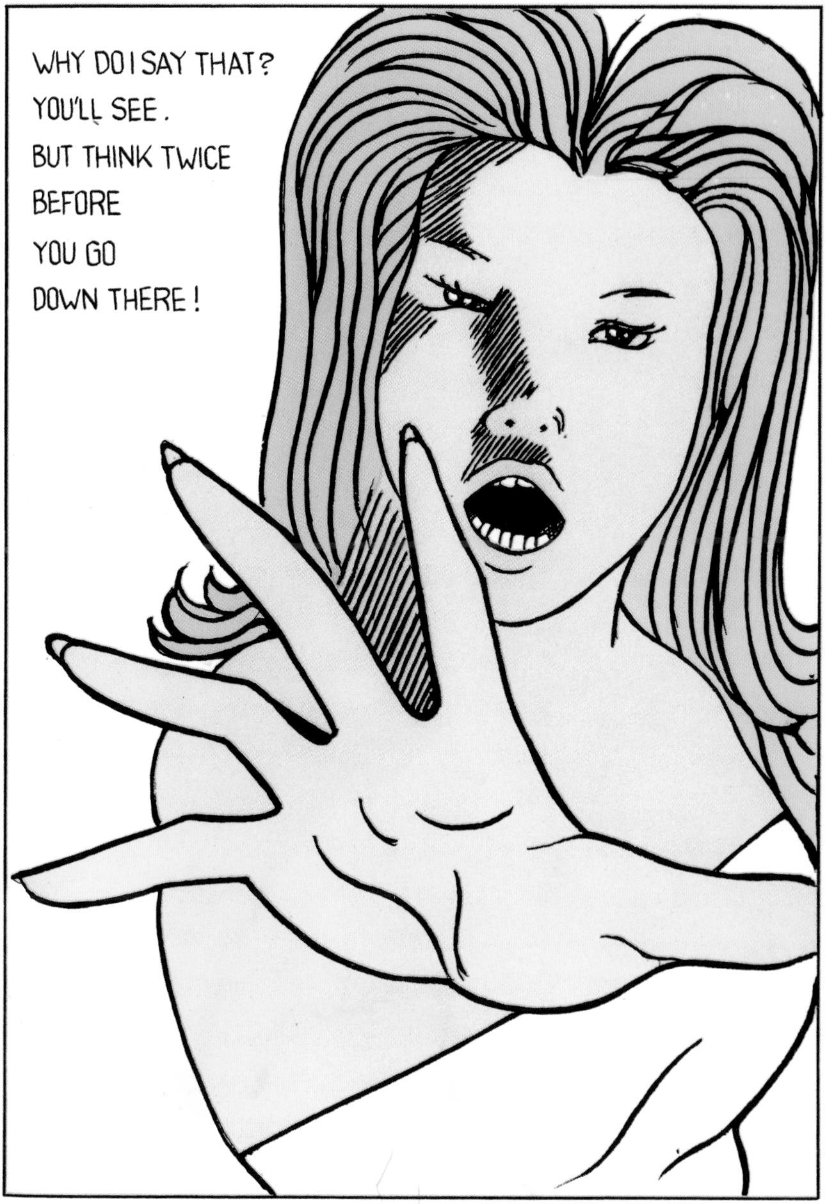
WHY DO I SAY THAT?
YOU'LL SEE.
BUT THINK TWICE
BEFORE
YOU GO
DOWN THERE!

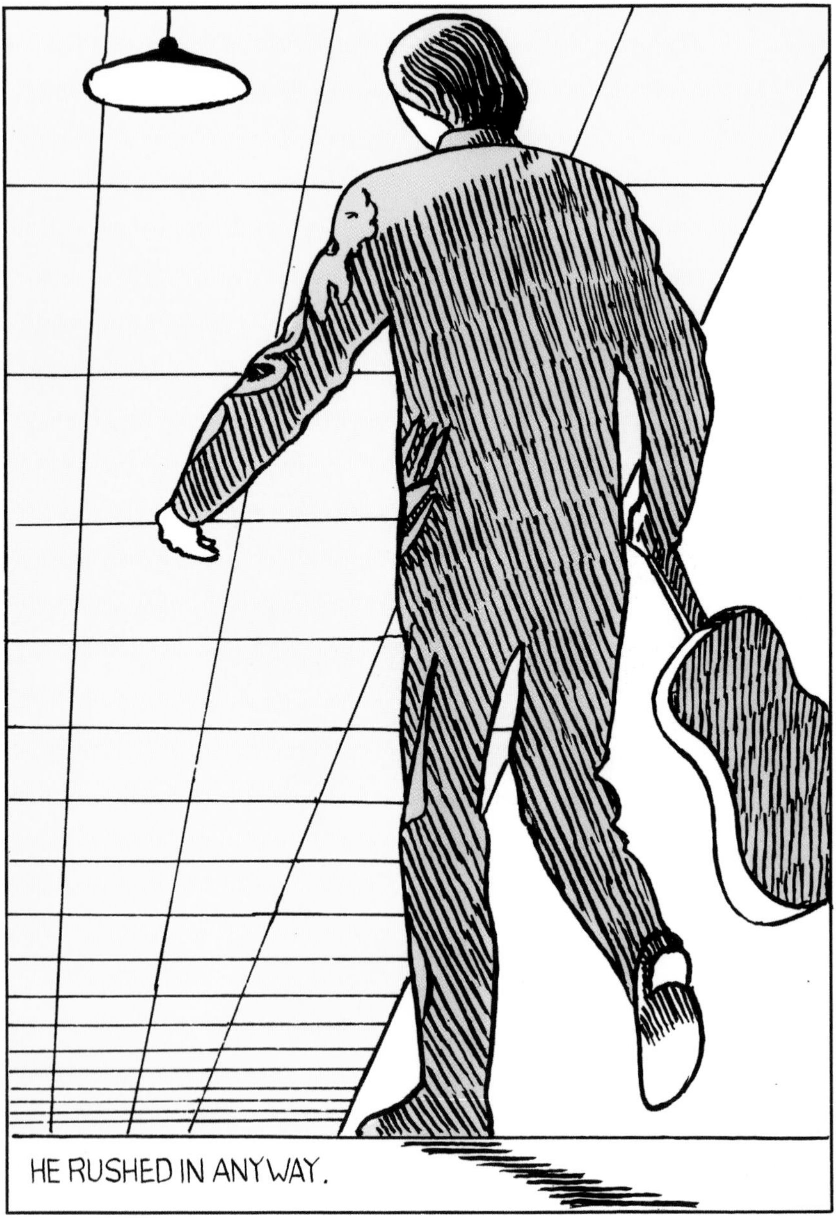
HE RUSHED IN ANYWAY.

THE DESCENT

DESCEND, BRAVE BOY, ORFI, DESCEND
STEPS, STAIRS. THE DESCENT IS EASY.
BUT WHAT THEN? WHAT ABOUT THE WAY BACK UP?
WILL YOU MAKE IT? WILL WE?
AND DOWN AT THE BOTTOM? DO YOU KNOW WHO'S WAITING?
ARE THEY EXPECTING YOU? IS SHE?

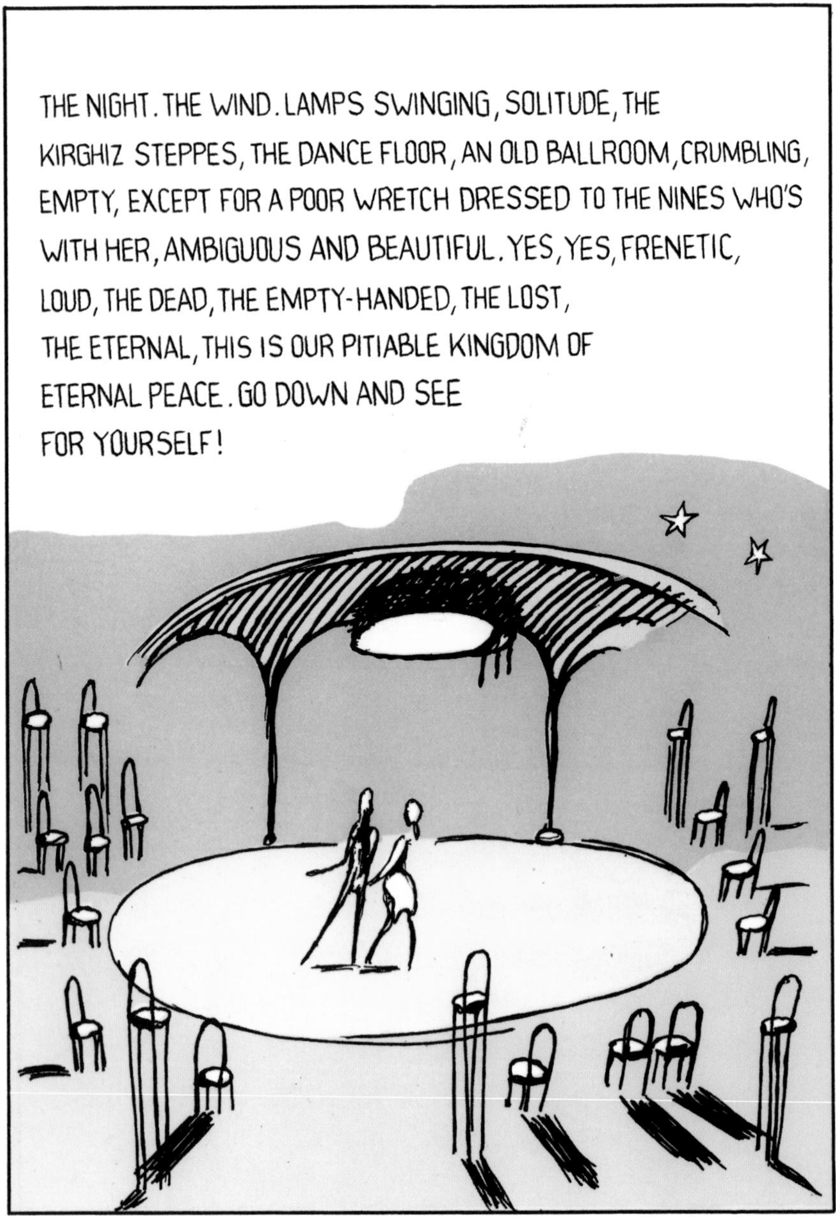
THE NIGHT. THE WIND. LAMPS SWINGING, SOLITUDE, THE KIRGHIZ STEPPES, THE DANCE FLOOR, AN OLD BALLROOM, CRUMBLING, EMPTY, EXCEPT FOR A POOR WRETCH DRESSED TO THE NINES WHO'S WITH HER, AMBIGUOUS AND BEAUTIFUL. YES, YES, FRENETIC, LOUD, THE DEAD, THE EMPTY-HANDED, THE LOST, THE ETERNAL, THIS IS OUR PITIABLE KINGDOM OF ETERNAL PEACE. GO DOWN AND SEE FOR YOURSELF!

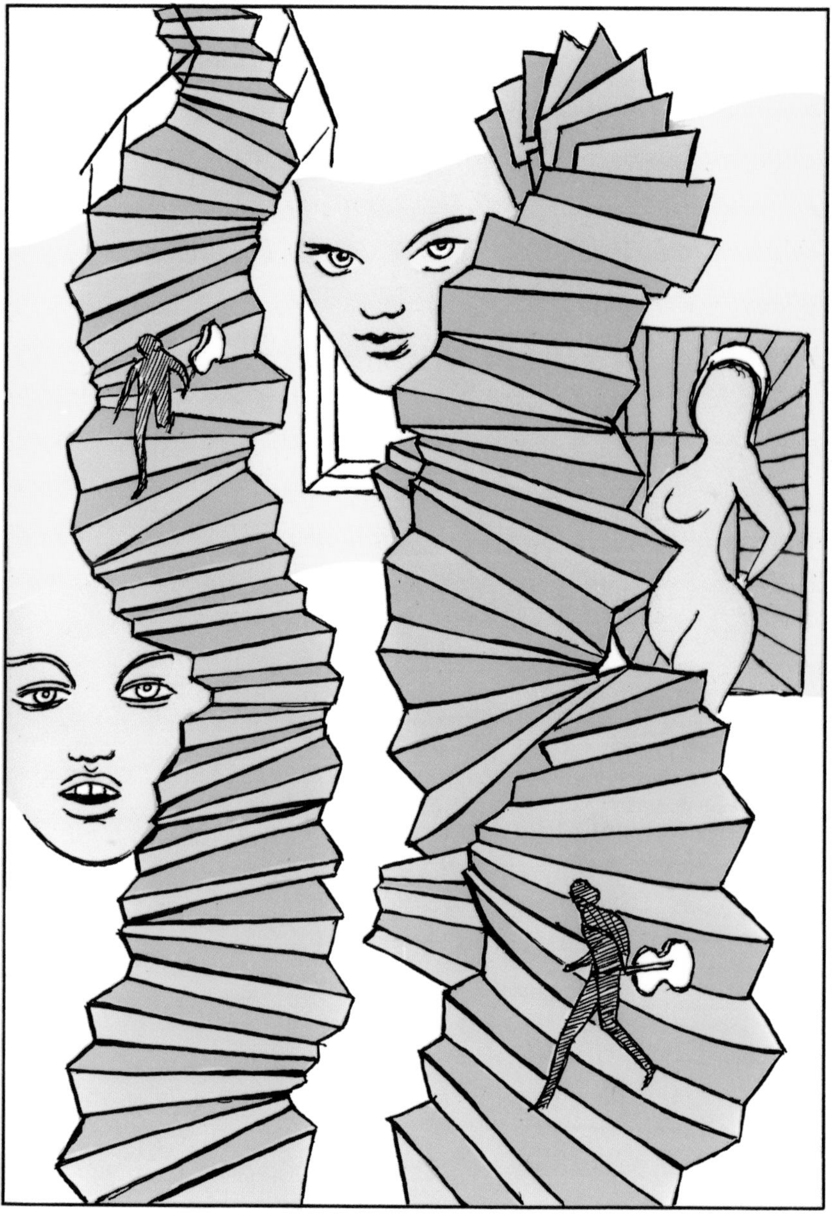

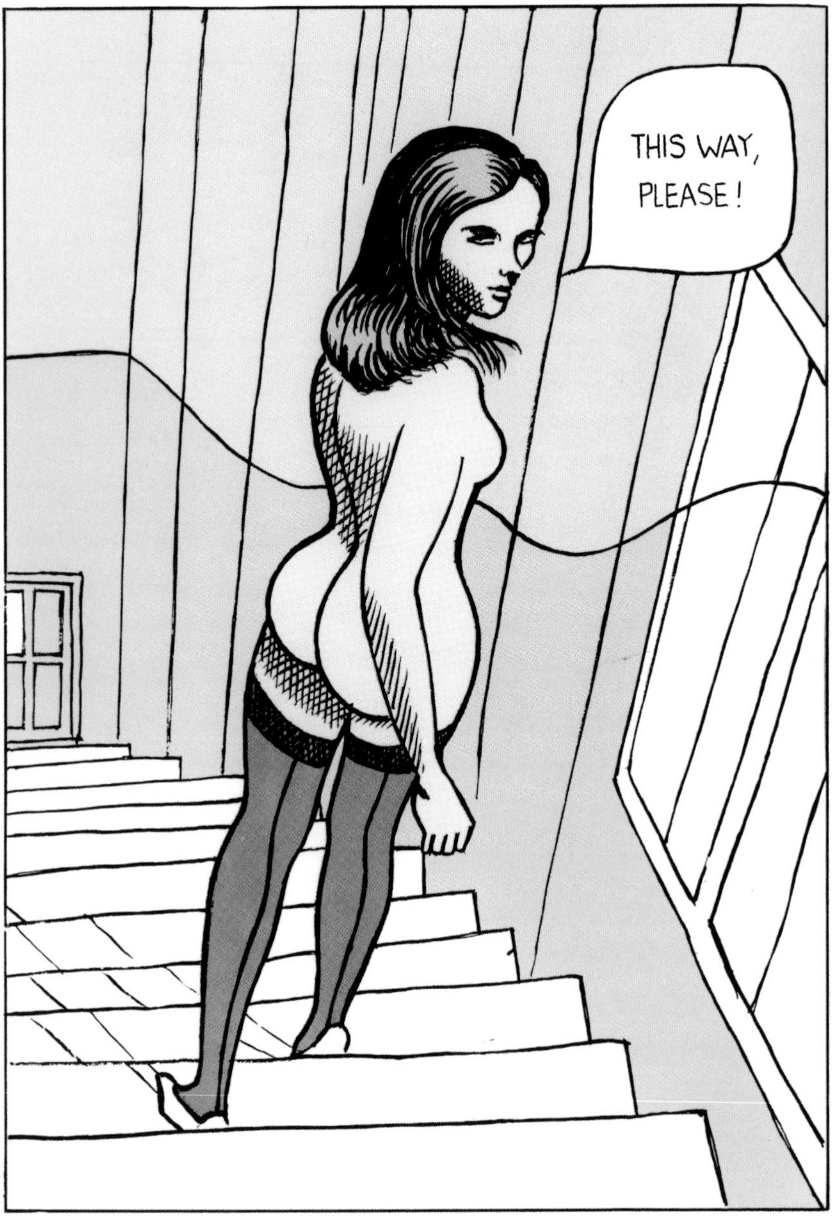
THIS WAY, PLEASE!

EXPLANATION OF THE AFTERLIFE

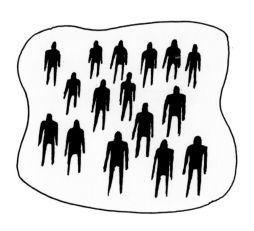

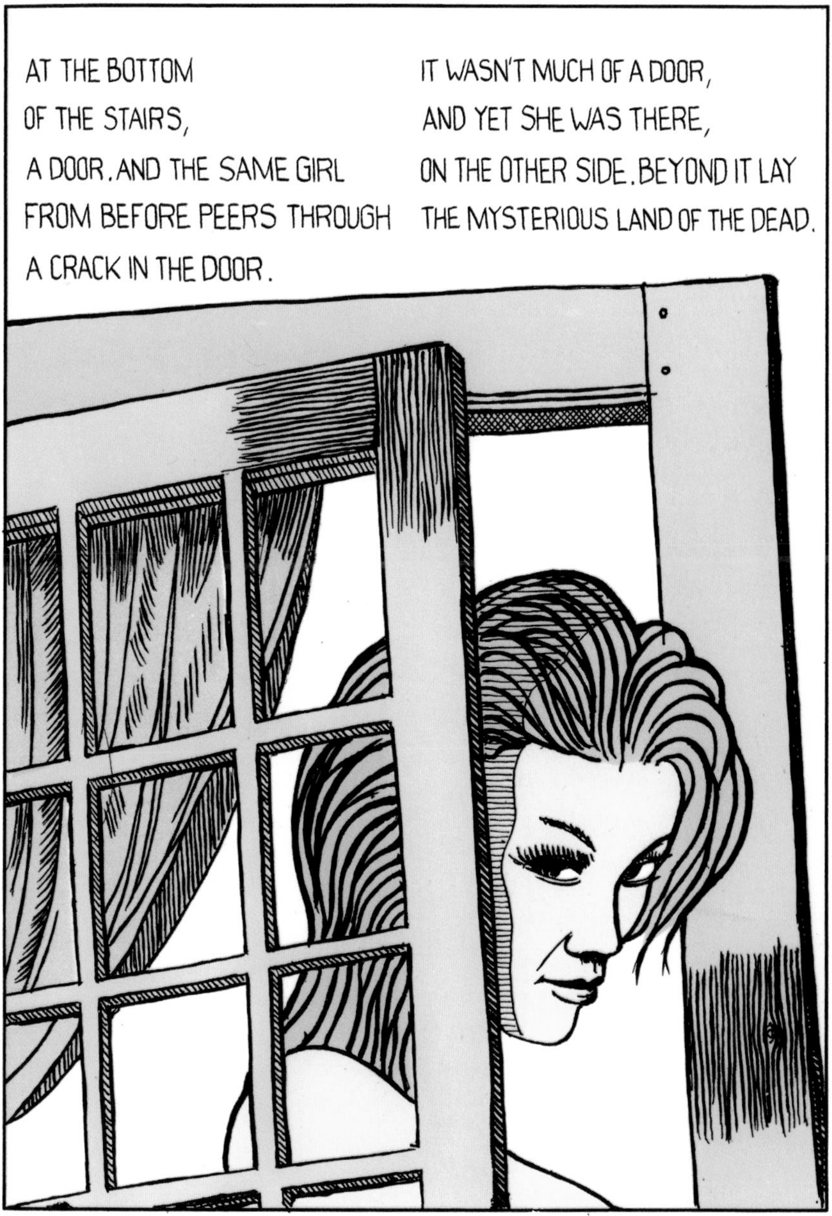
AT THE BOTTOM
OF THE STAIRS,
A DOOR. AND THE SAME GIRL
FROM BEFORE PEERS THROUGH
A CRACK IN THE DOOR.
IT WASN'T MUCH OF A DOOR,
AND YET SHE WAS THERE,
ON THE OTHER SIDE. BEYOND IT LAY
THE MYSTERIOUS LAND OF THE DEAD.

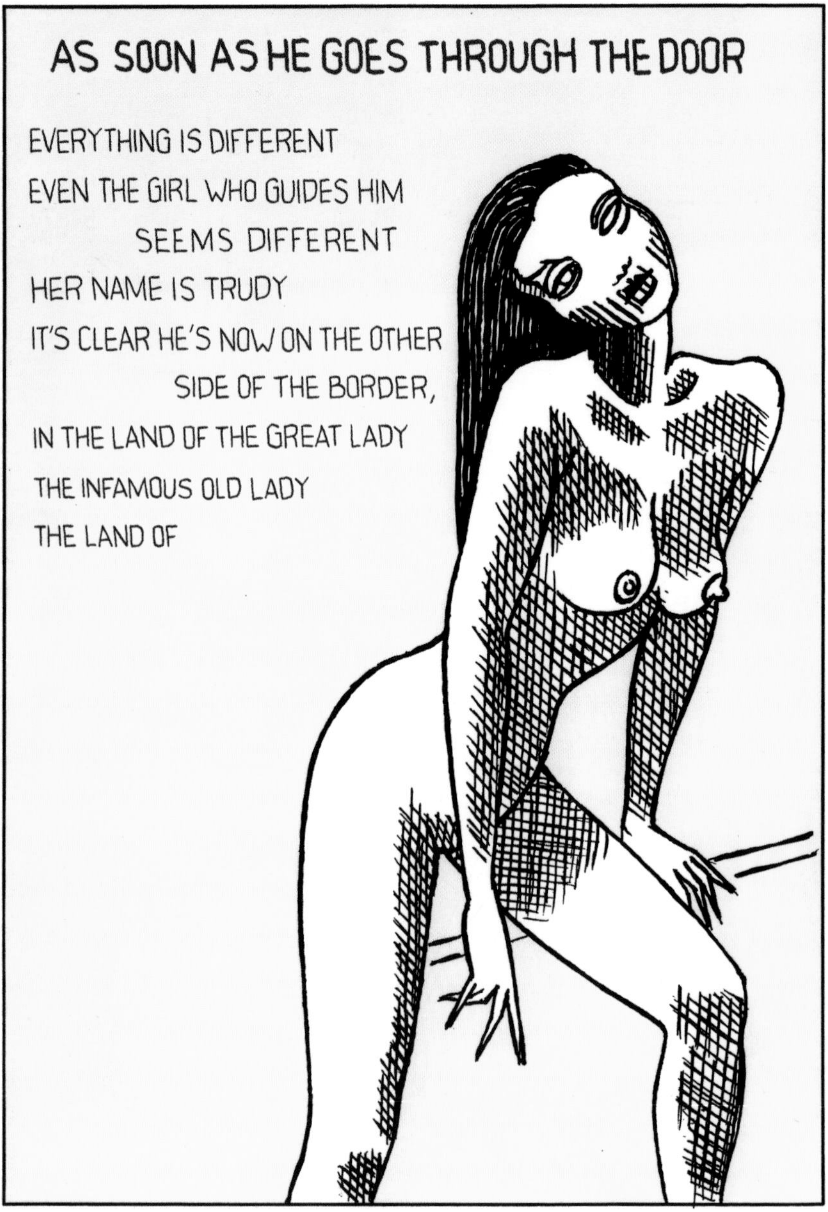
AS SOON AS HE GOES THROUGH THE DOOR
EVERYTHING IS DIFFERENT
EVEN THE GIRL WHO GUIDES HIM
SEEMS DIFFERENT
HER NAME IS TRUDY
IT'S CLEAR HE'S NOW ON THE OTHER
SIDE OF THE BORDER,
IN THE LAND OF THE GREAT LADY
THE INFAMOUS OLD LADY
THE LAND OF

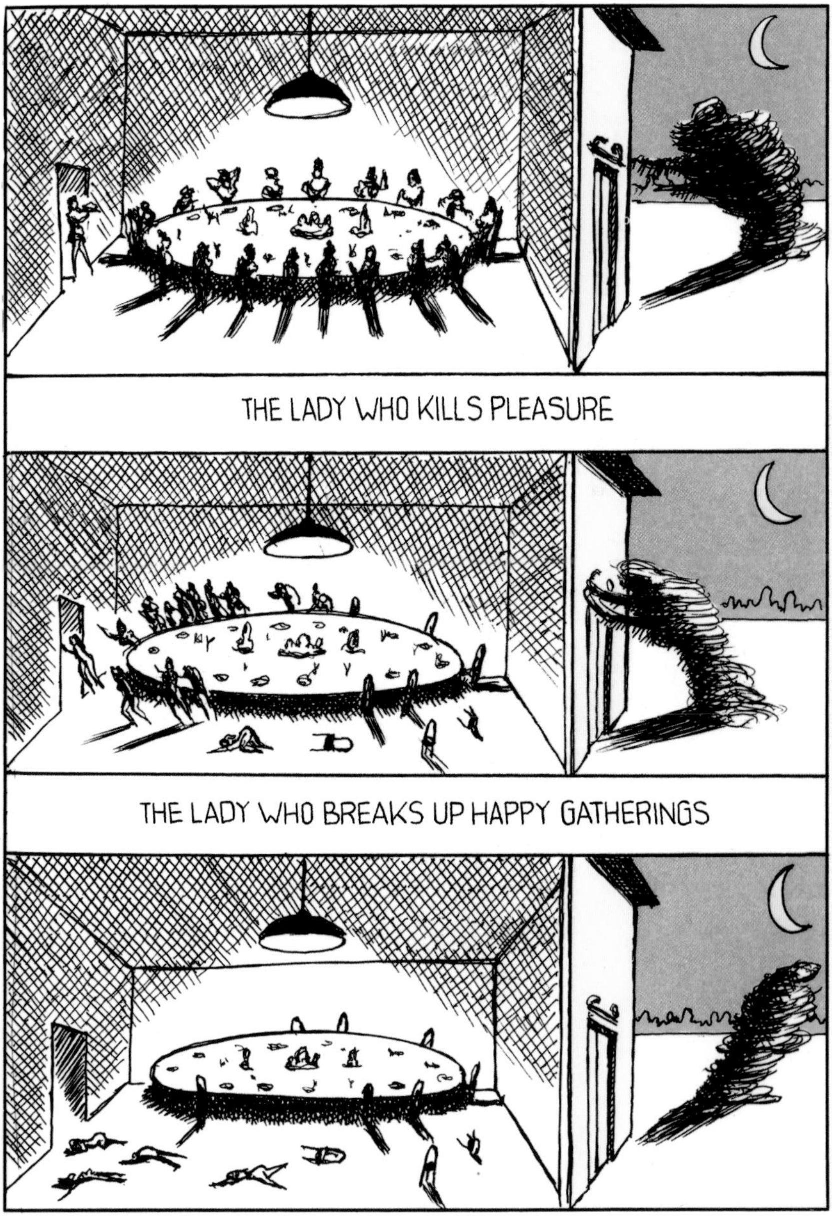
THE LADY WHO KILLS PLEASURE
THE LADY WHO BREAKS UP HAPPY GATHERINGS

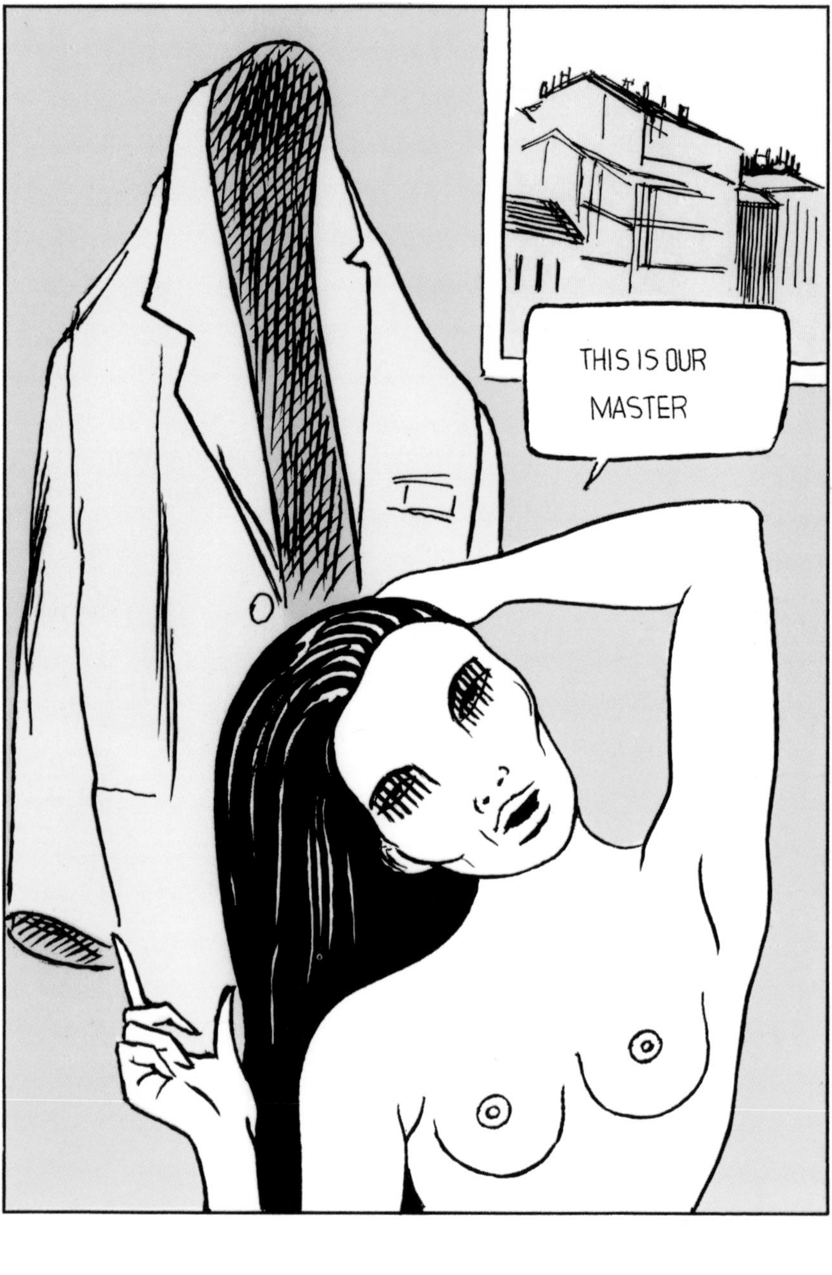
THIS IS OUR MASTER

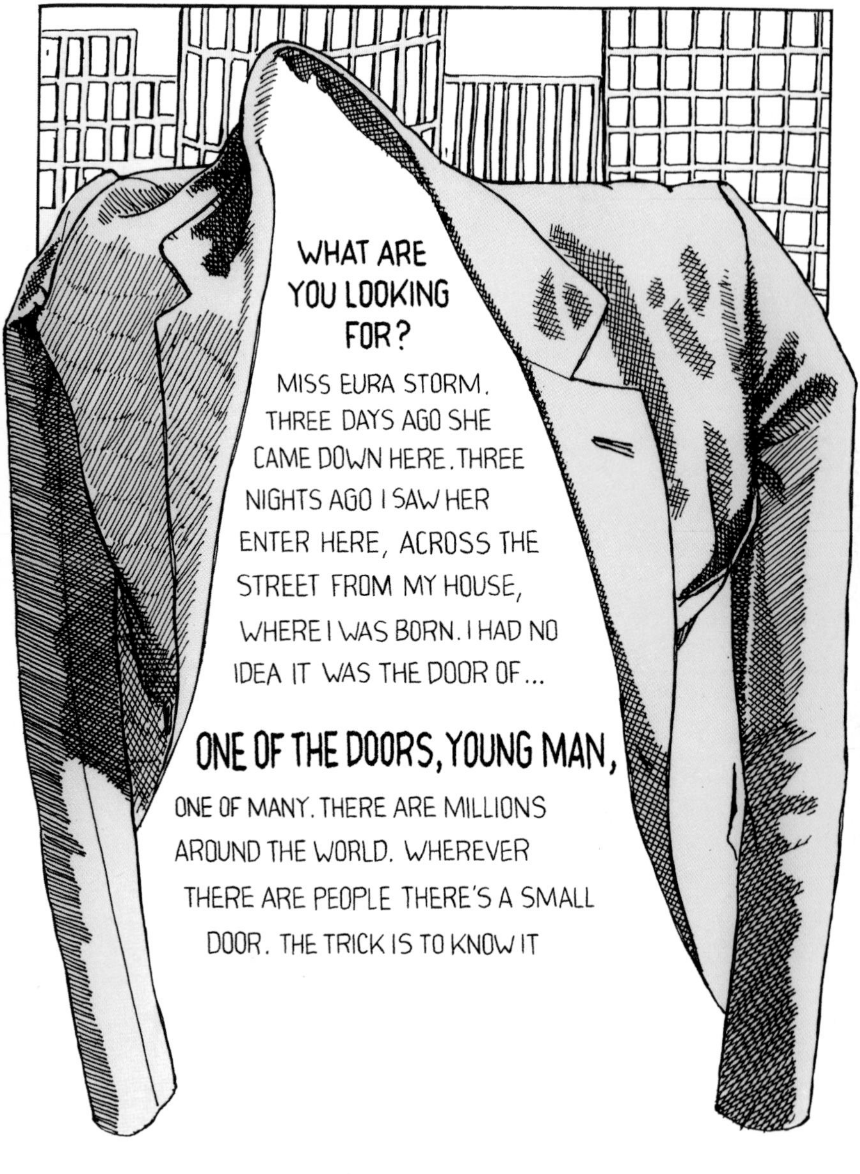
WHAT ARE YOU LOOKING FOR?
MISS EURA STORM. THREE DAYS AGO SHE CAME DOWN HERE. THREE NIGHTS AGO I SAW HER ENTER HERE, ACROSS THE STREET FROM MY HOUSE, WHERE I WAS BORN. I HAD NO IDEA IT WAS THE DOOR OF...
ONE OF THE DOORS, YOUNG MAN,
ONE OF MANY. THERE ARE MILLIONS AROUND THE WORLD. WHEREVER THERE ARE PEOPLE THERE'S A SMALL DOOR. THE TRICK IS TO KNOW IT

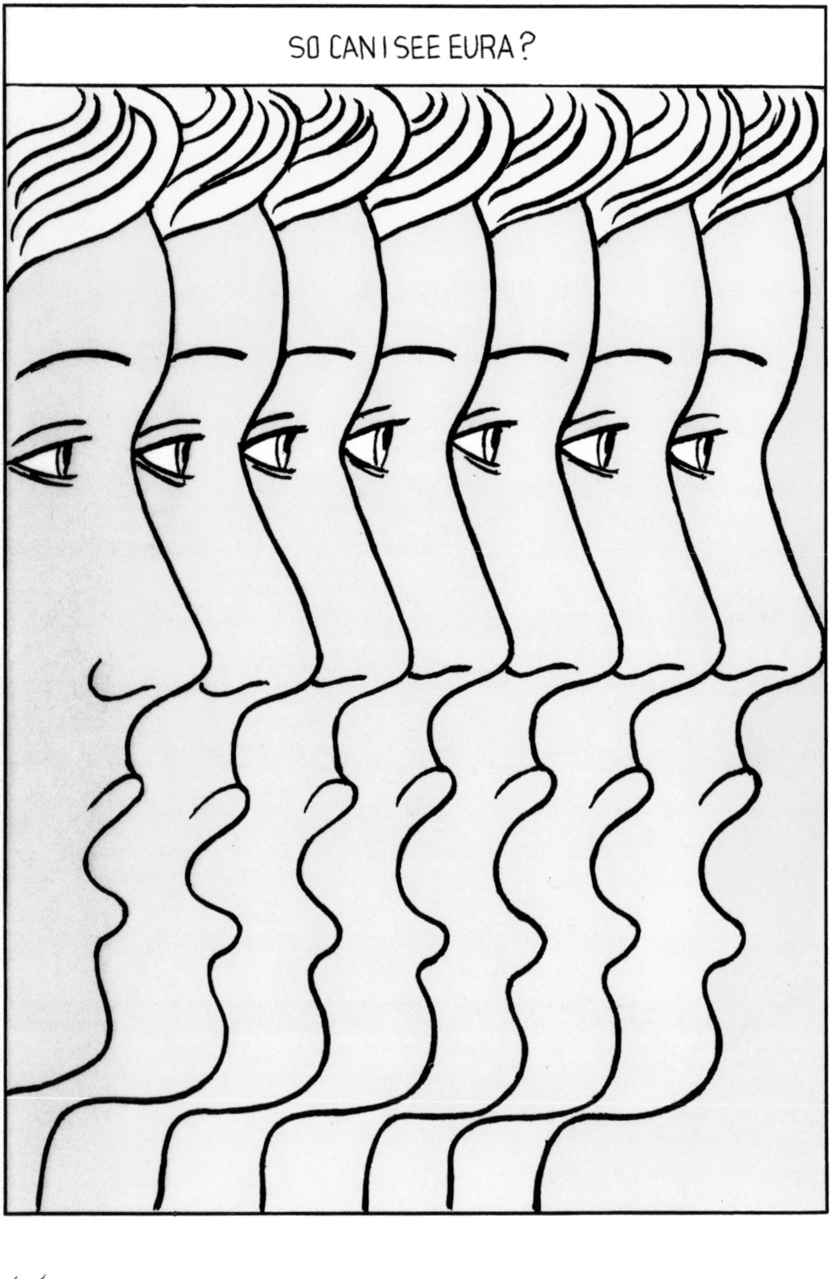
SO CAN I SEE EURA?

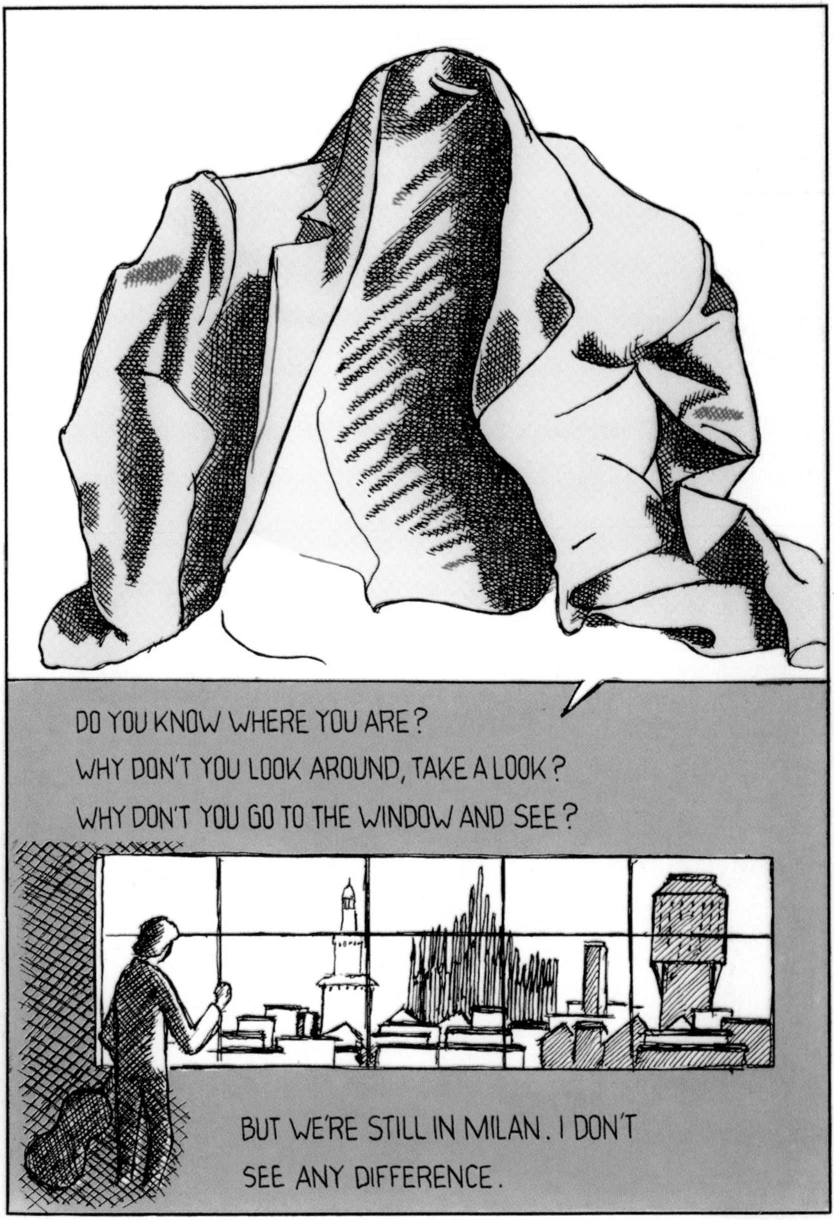
DO YOU KNOW WHERE YOU ARE?
WHY DON'T YOU LOOK AROUND, TAKE A LOOK?
WHY DON'T YOU GO TO THE WINDOW AND SEE?
BUT WE'RE STILL IN MILAN. I DON'T SEE ANY DIFFERENCE.

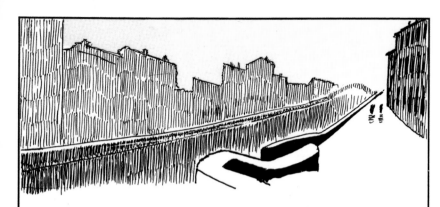

TO YOU, ORFI, IT'S MILAN, BECAUSE MILAN IS YOUR LIFE,
BUT TO ANOTHER IT'S ZAGREB, KARLSRUHE, PARANÁ.
OR DID YOU THINK IT WAS AS DANTE DESCRIBED IT?
WHAT DO YOU MEAN?
THE AFTERLIFE, PALE AVERNUS, I MEAN, DID YOU REALLY THINK
                                        IT CONTAINED ALL
THE MEN AND WOMEN WHO LIVED BEFORE, THE MILLIONS AND
                                        MILLIONS.
ALL THE CIVILIZATIONS OF THE DISTANT AGES,
                IS THAT WHAT YOU IMAGINED?
ALL OF THEM TOGETHER IN THE VALLEY OF JEHOSHAPHAT?
NO, THERE'S NOT ENOUGH ROOM.
NO, NO, EACH MAN TAKES HIS OWN WORLD WITH HIM.
I IMAGINE THAT'S ENOUGH FOR HIM.
ESPECIALLY SINCE HERE TIME STANDS STILL
THE CLOCKS GO ON TICKING BUT TIME STANDS STILL
THE RIVERS FLOW BUT TIME STANDS STILL
IT'S ALWAYS THE SAME DAY.

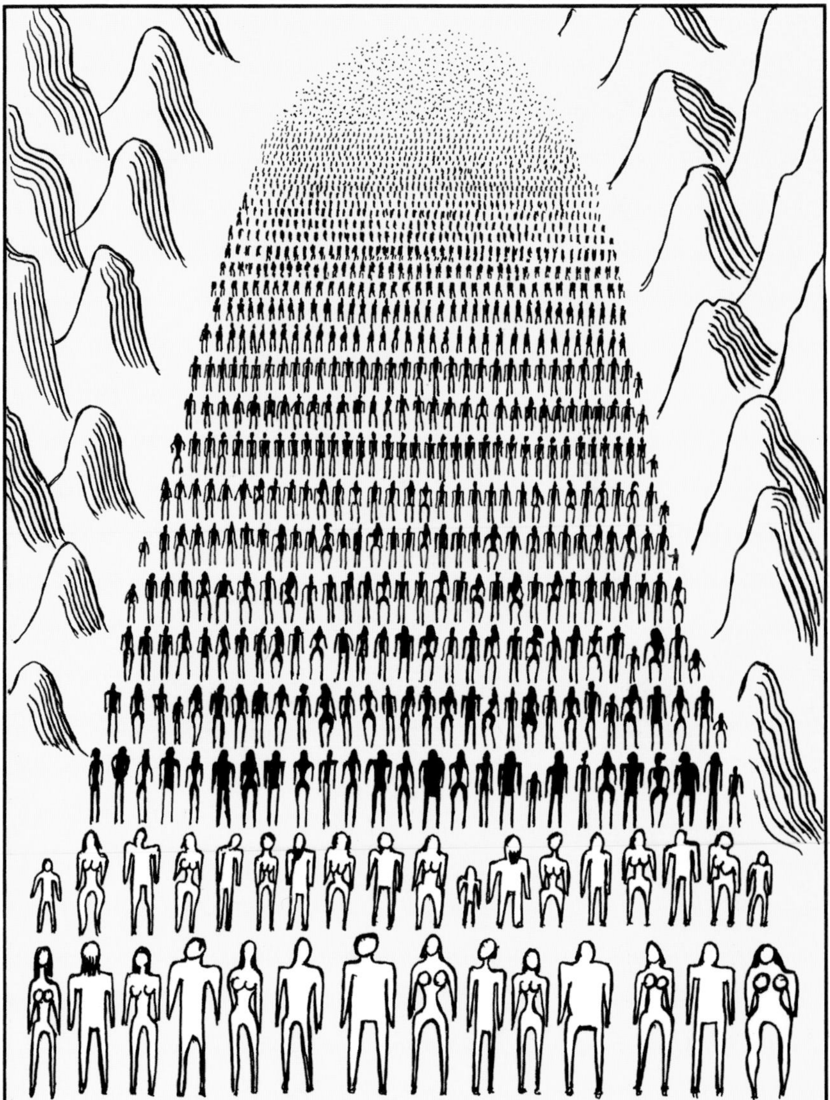
ALL TOGETHER IN THE VALLEY OF JEHOSHAPHAT?

WHAT PURPOSE WOULD IT SERVE

FOR TIME TO PASS,

DAY AFTER DAY, YEAR AFTER YEAR ?

ETERNITY IS LIKE A STONE

        BUT YOU CAN'T SEE THE DIFFERENCE.

        THE CARS, THE HOUSES, THE PEOPLE.

        THEY WALK, TALK, SMOKE, LAUGH.

YES. PERHAPS THEY LAUGH LESS THAN YOU DO,

REMEMBER, THEY'RE IMMORTAL,

THEY WILL NEVER LEAVE HERE.

OF COURSE EVERYTHING IS IN WORKING ORDER.

EVERYTHING IS IN WORKING ORDER

BONES VEINS NERVES EVERYTHING WORKS

THEY MOVE EAT DRINK ETCETERA

THEY LIVE, ALMOST.

YES, THEY'RE PRACTICALLY TRANSPARENT, IT'S TRUE,

PLUS THEY NO LONGER HAVE HOPE

THAT MOST MALICIOUS OF TORMENTS

THEY SUFFER NO PAIN

NO HOSPITALS, FUNERALS, CEMETARIES, OR GRAVES.

THEY'RE LUCKY, WOULDN'T YOU SAY ?

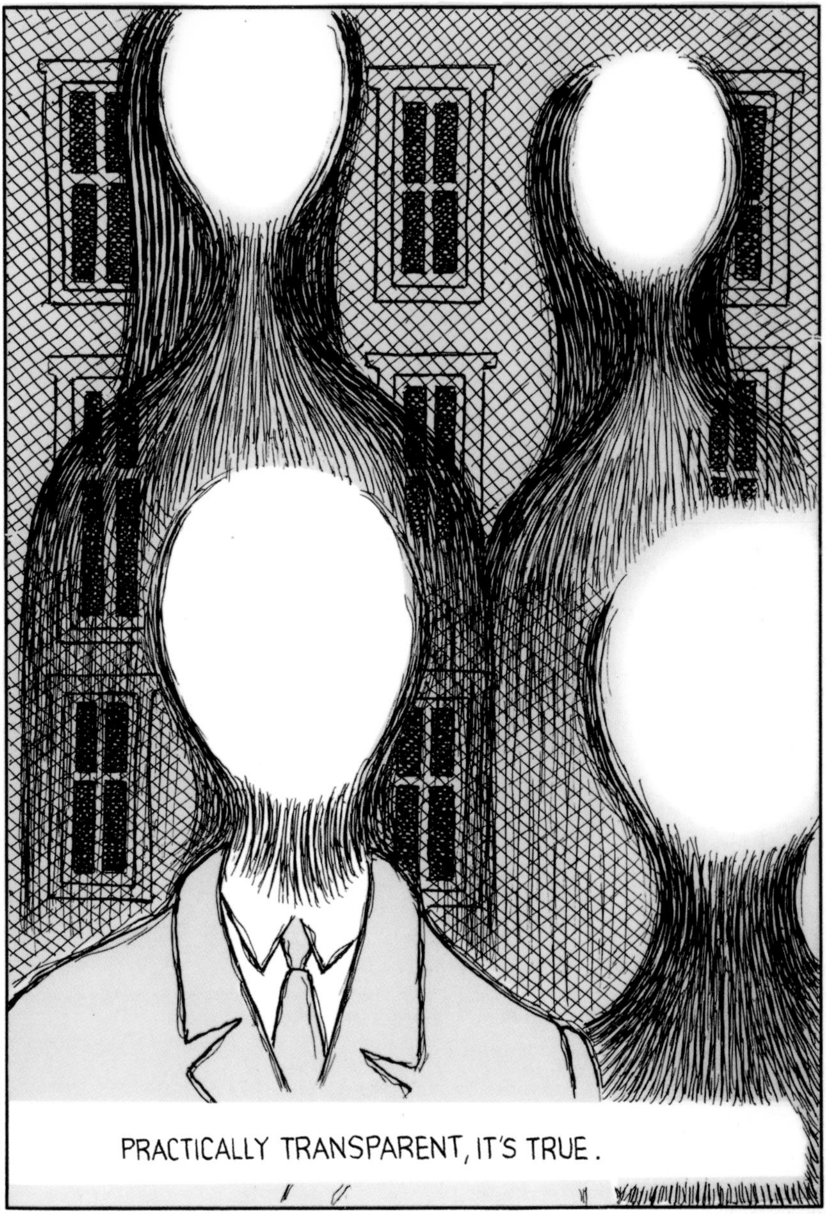
PRACTICALLY TRANSPARENT, IT'S TRUE.

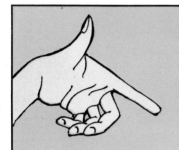

BUT WHO ARE YOU?

I WAS JUST LIKE YOU
CAME DOWN FROM ABOVE BY CHANCE
A LITTLE DOOR ACCIDENTALLY LEFT OPEN,
                    THAT WAS ALL
THEY CAJOLED ME
STAY STAY WE'LL MAKE YOU GREAT WE'LL
                    GIVE YOU POWER
(THE LIVING ARE HELD IN HIGH ESTEEM
                    DOWN HERE)
SO I BECAME A GUARDIAN DEMON
NOT REALLY A DEMON MORE LIKE
A PROTECTOR, A SENTINEL, A SUPERVISOR.
I WAS IN CHARGE, DID AS I SAW FIT
UNTIL TIME CAUGHT UP WITH ME.
I GREW OLD, PERHAPS I DIED, WHO KNOWS.
GOD, HOW MUCH TIME HAS PASSED!
OF COURSE I WOULDN'T MIND GOING BACK.

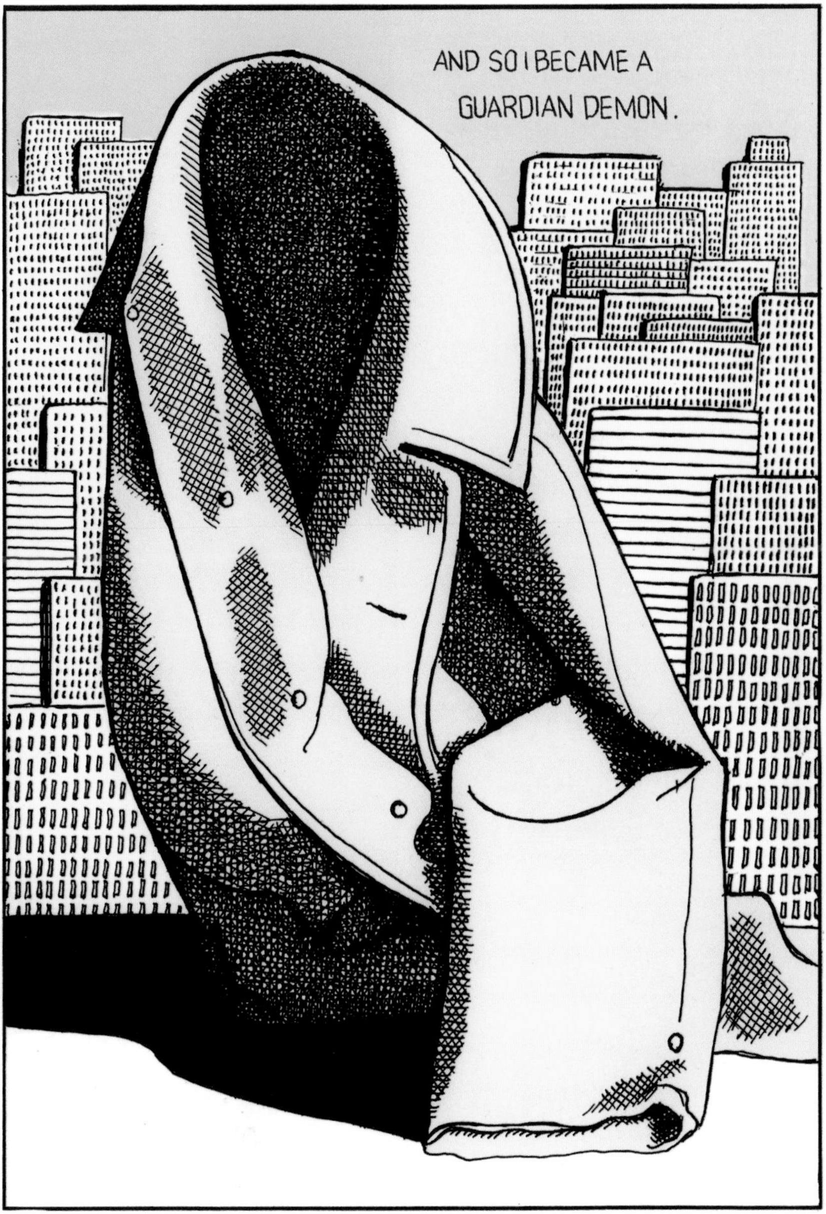
AND SO I BECAME A
GUARDIAN DEMON.

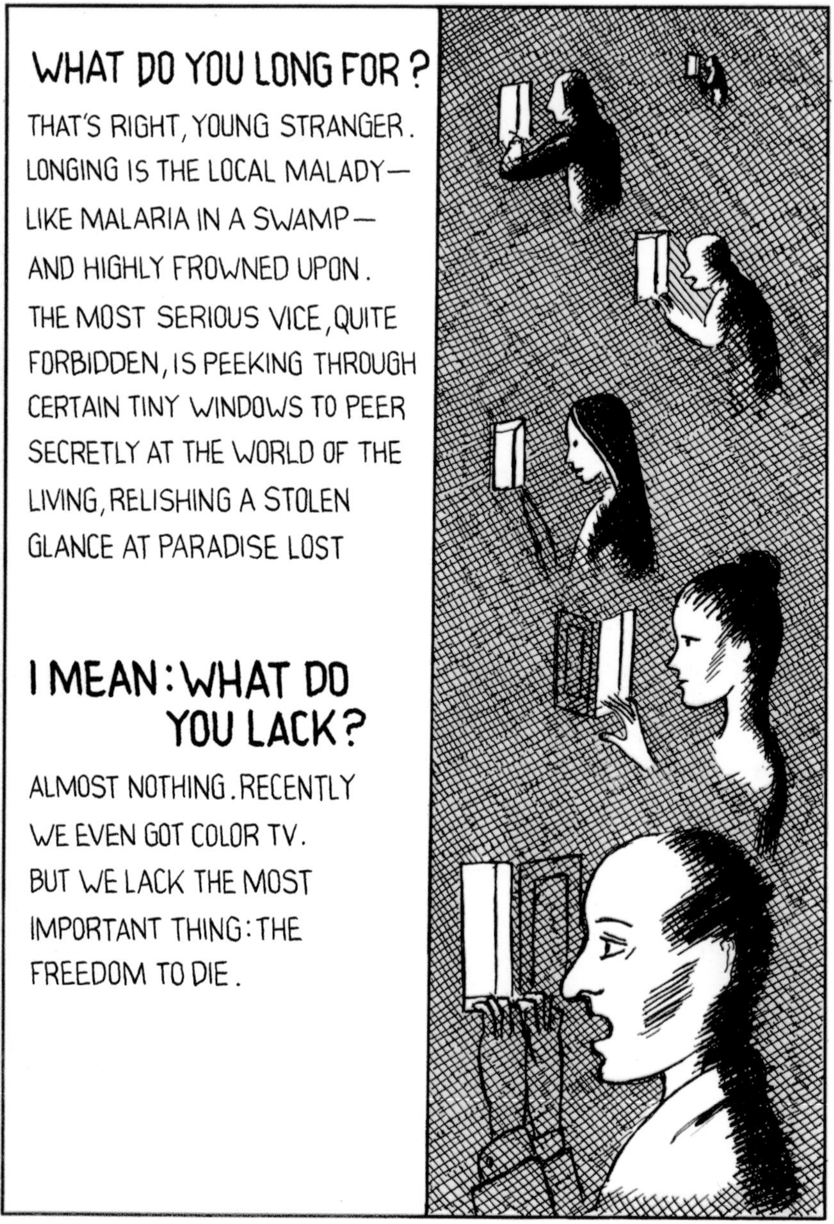
WHAT DO YOU LONG FOR?
THAT'S RIGHT, YOUNG STRANGER. LONGING IS THE LOCAL MALADY— LIKE MALARIA IN A SWAMP— AND HIGHLY FROWNED UPON. THE MOST SERIOUS VICE, QUITE FORBIDDEN, IS PEEKING THROUGH CERTAIN TINY WINDOWS TO PEER SECRETLY AT THE WORLD OF THE LIVING, RELISHING A STOLEN GLANCE AT PARADISE LOST
I MEAN: WHAT DO YOU LACK?
ALMOST NOTHING. RECENTLY WE EVEN GOT COLOR TV. BUT WE LACK THE MOST IMPORTANT THING: THE FREEDOM TO DIE.

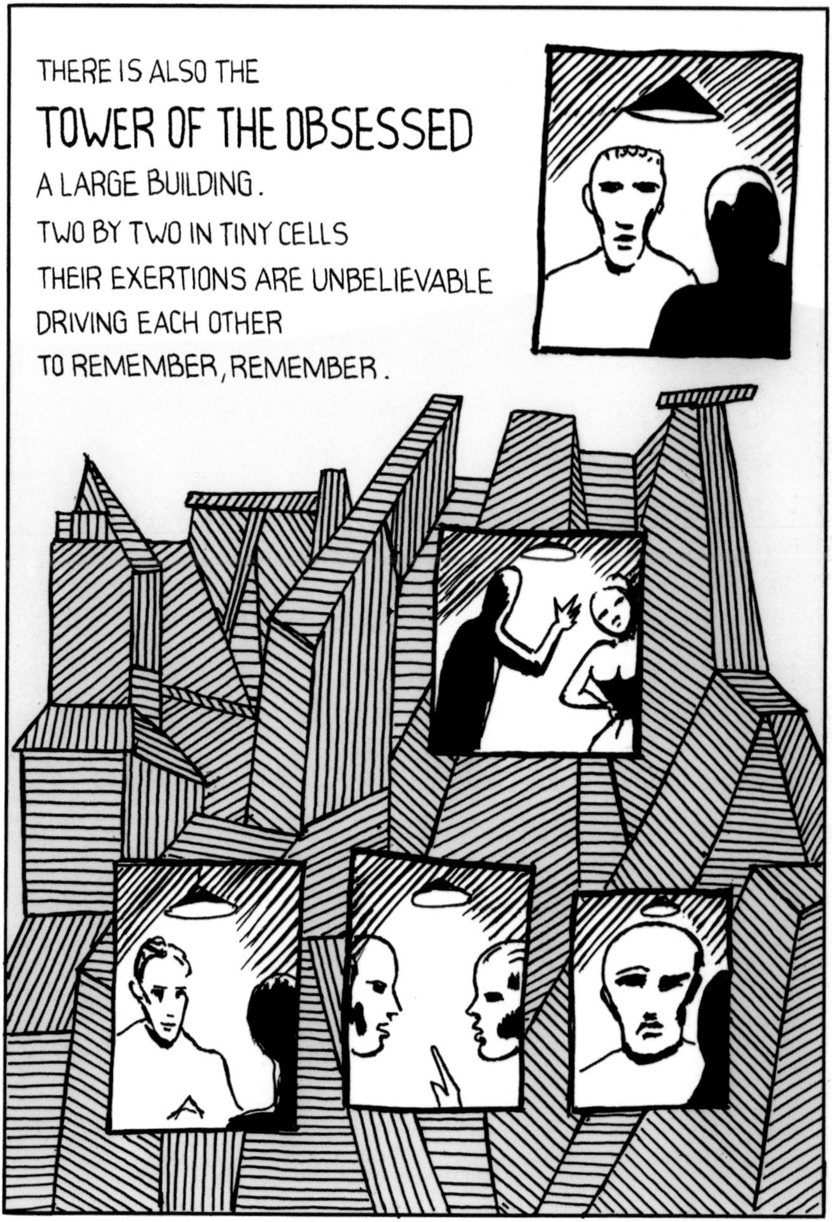
THERE IS ALSO THE
TOWER OF THE OBSESSED
A LARGE BUILDING.
TWO BY TWO IN TINY CELLS
THEIR EXERTIONS ARE UNBELIEVABLE
DRIVING EACH OTHER
TO REMEMBER, REMEMBER.

DO YOU REMEMBER WHEN LATE AT NIGHT
AT THE FRONT DOOR OF YOUR HOUSE
WITH THE MOON SETTING BEHIND THE ROOFS OF MILAN,
YOUR FRIEND SAID: ISN'T IT TERRIBLE, ALL OF THIS,
LIFE WORK MONEY SUCCESS LOVE?
YES YES YOU ANSWERED.
AND AT THE END OF IT ALL DEATH?
WOULDN'T YOU RATHER PUT A BULLET THROUGH YOUR HEAD?
YES, YES, YOU ANSWERED, YOU DIDN'T KNOW
THAT THIS DREAD WAS ITSELF BEAUTY, LIGHT
THE SALT OF LIFE.
AND NATURALLY YOU FORGOT
SLEEP, ALCOHOL, YOUTH,
YOU PUT IT OFF.
HERE TOO FRIENDS WALK EACH OTHER HOME
TAKING TURNS
TALKING ON AND ON,
EVEN IF IT IS FORBIDDEN,
REMEMBERING, REMEMBERING.
OH THE DREAD IS GONE, THE NIGHTMARES, THE ANGUISH,
                                    THE INJUSTICE
HERE EVERYONE IS HEALTHY, EQUAL, CONTENT.
OH, SWEET UNHAPPINESS!

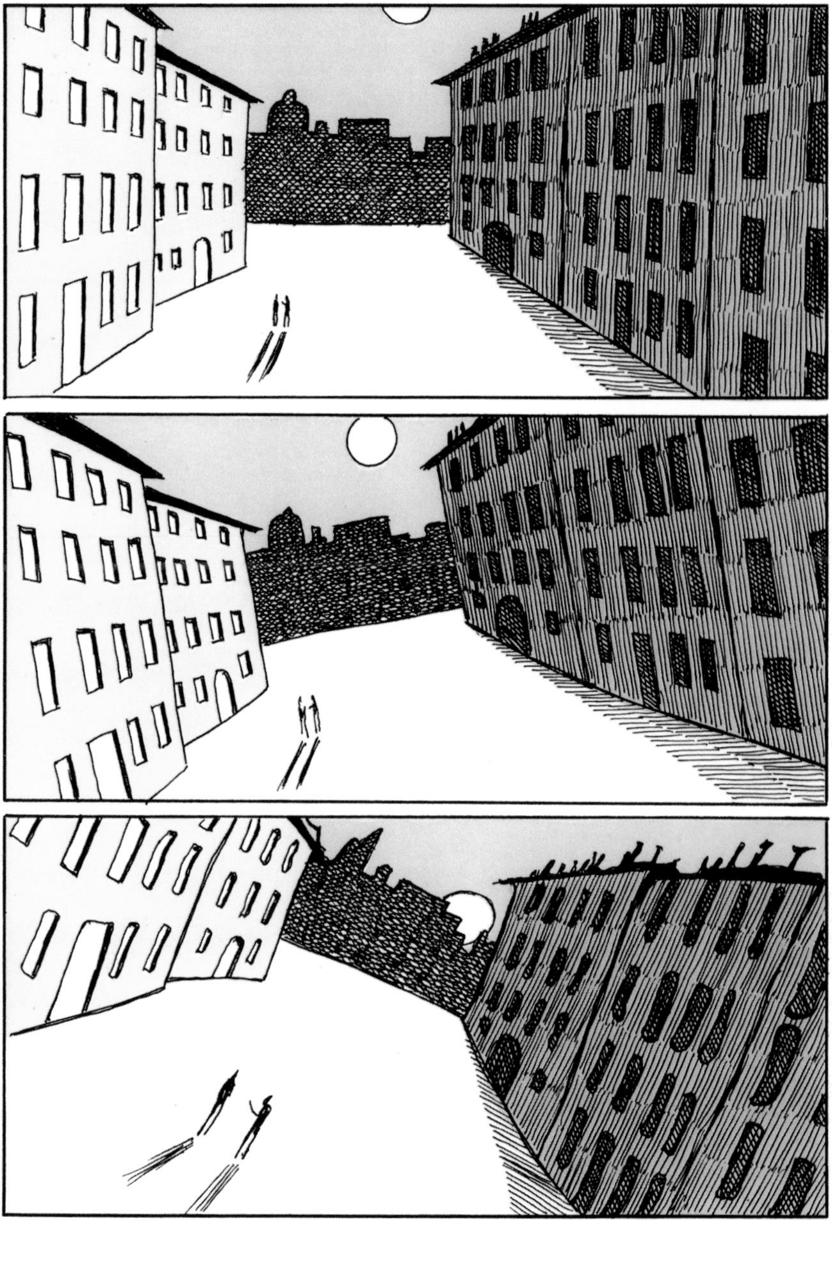

DO YOU HAVE STARS HERE ?

YES, OF COURSE, BUT THEY SHINE WITH A STEADY LIGHT,
THEY DO NOT SHIMMER AS THEY DO UP THERE.

AND WIND? AND STORMS?

WE HAVE WIND, AND STORMS, BUT NO FEAR.

AND NIGHT ?

YES, WE HAVE NIGHT, BUT NOT THE ANCIENT NIGHT WITH ITS SHADOWS,
MURKY ALLEYS CRIMES AND CRIMINAL TEMPTATIONS
THE DISTANT LANTERN AND THE BREEZE THAT MAKES IT SWAY,
THE CREAKING FOOTSTEPS IN THE HALL MEAN NOTHING AND

                           THE FAR-OFF BELL
THE FAR-OFF VOICE CALLING OUT OVER THE ROOFTOPS
THE HOWLING DOGS
IN THE VAST COUNTRYSIDE BENEATH THE GLOW OF THE MOON
MEAN NOTHING NOR DOES THE WHITE DESERTED ROAD THAT FADES
BEYOND THE HILL AT SUNSET
BECAUSE ON THE OTHER SIDE THERE IS NO UNKNOWN
NO DARKNESS, NO END, NO FINAL SEPARATION, NO FAREWELL.

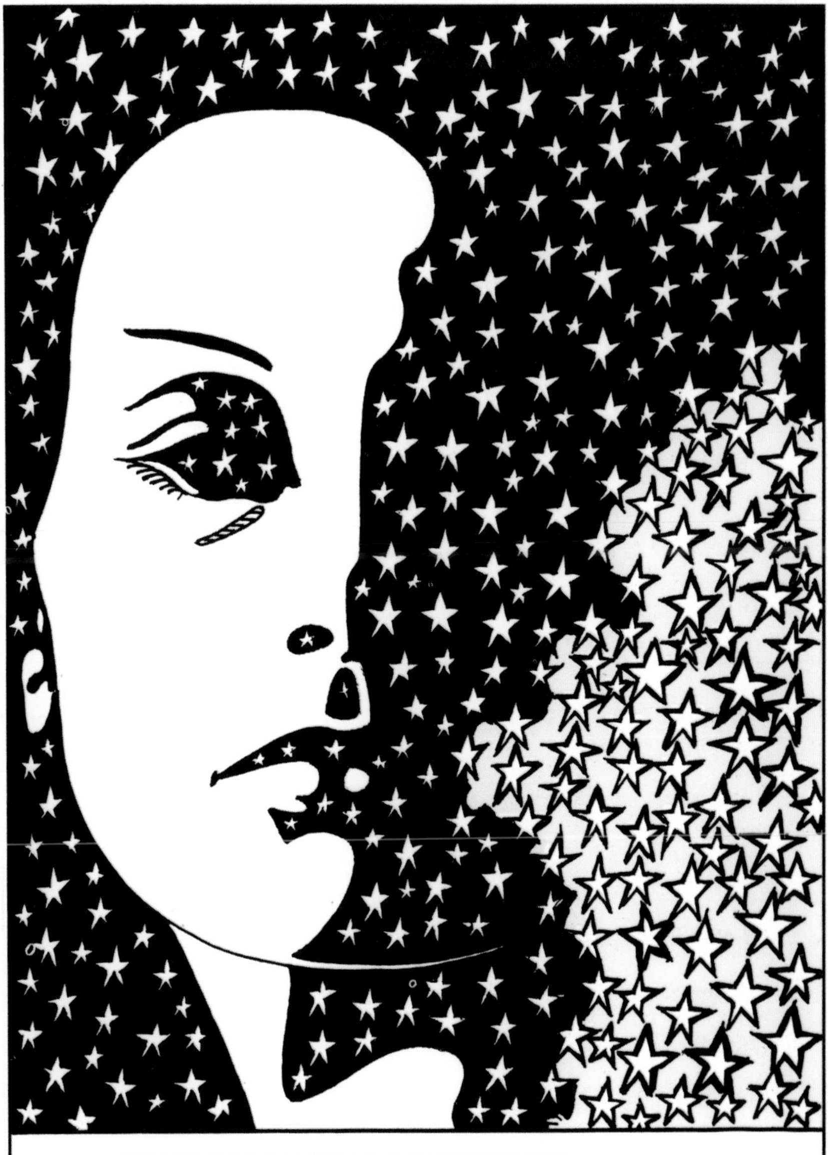
...THEY DO NOT SHIMMER AS THEY DO UP THERE

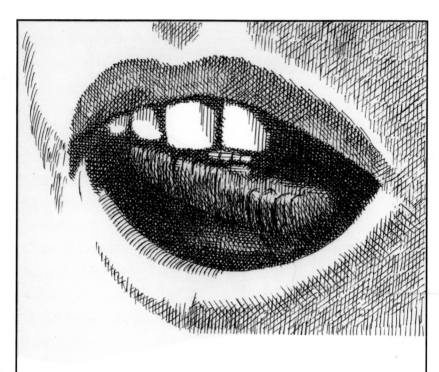

AND LOVE?

OBVIOUSLY NO CHILDREN ARE BORN HERE

AND NATURE NO LONGER NEEDS

ITS ANCIENT MARVELOUS WILES

TO ENSURE THE PROPAGATION OF THE SPECIES

IT NO LONGER AROUSES

IN THE DARKEST CORNERS OF HUMAN FANTASY

ITS MARVELOUS TEMPTATIONS.

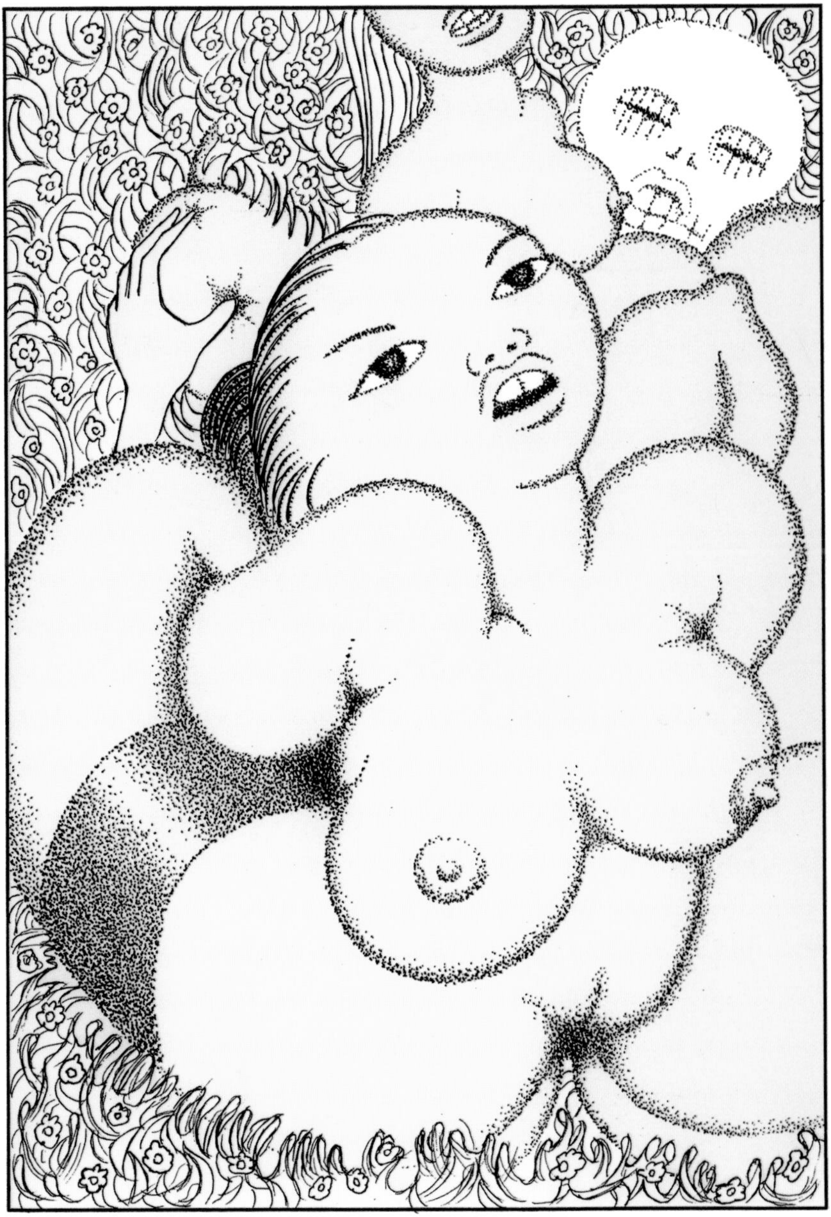

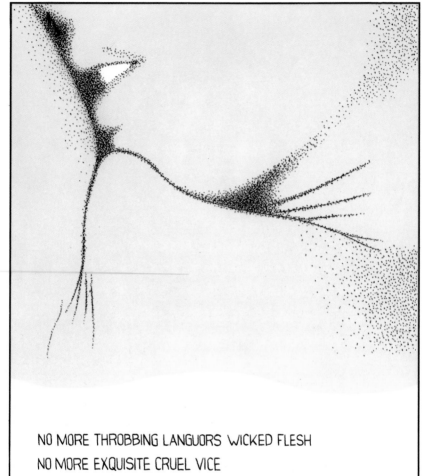

NO MORE THROBBING LANGUORS WICKED FLESH
NO MORE EXQUISITE CRUEL VICE
MOUTHS THAT TOMORROW...
TENDER NOTHINGS AS FLEETING AS FLOWERS.
INSTEAD AN INCONQUERABLE DULLNESS
SAMENESS, PREDICTABILITY, BOREDOM.

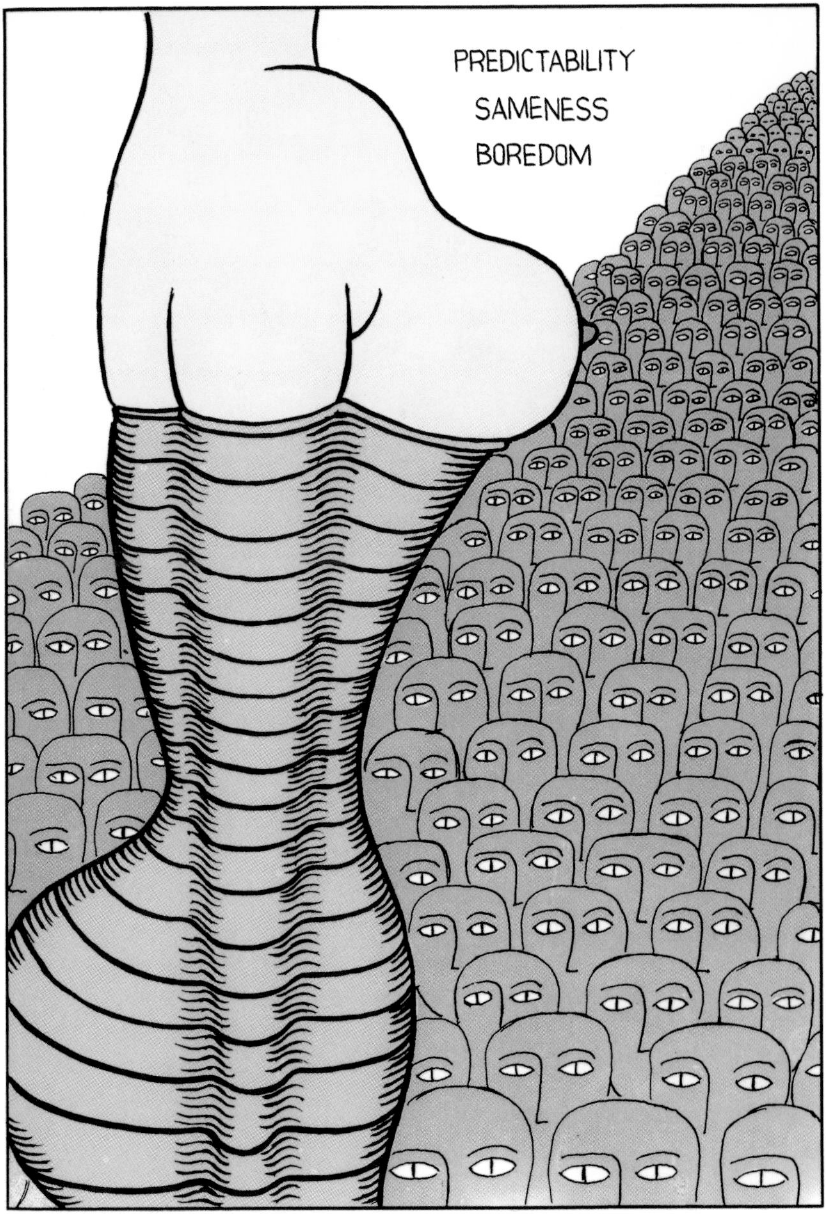
PREDICTABILITY
SAMENESS
BOREDOM

HERE, DEPRIVED
OF BURNING DESIRE, MEN
STILL HAVE VAGUE MEMORIES
OF THE SWEET SENSATION, BUT CANNOT REKINDLE IT
ALONE, AND IF THEY MEET SOMEONE
WHO FOR A MOMENT
REAWAKENS THE THRILL DEEP IN THEIR BONES
THE ORGASM, THE OBSESSION
THAT ONCE DROVE THEM WILD,
THEY'RE GRATEFUL.

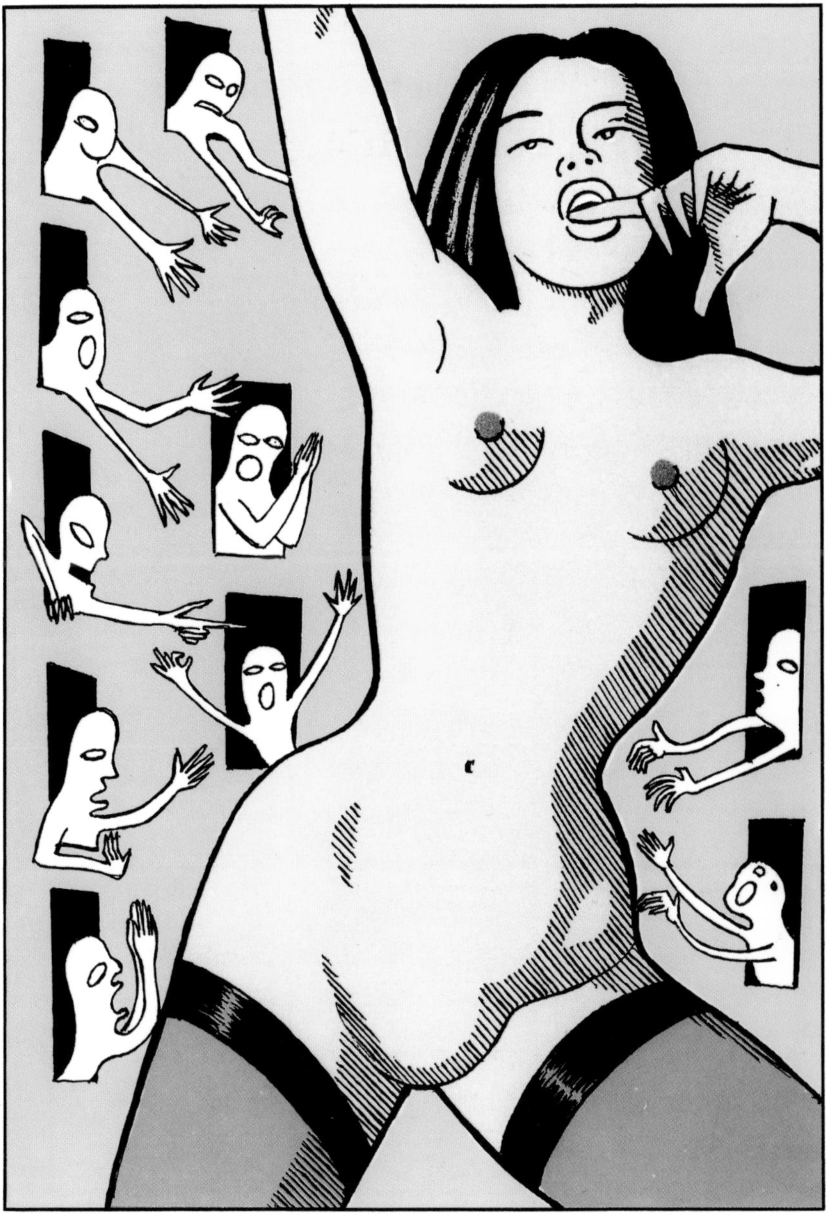

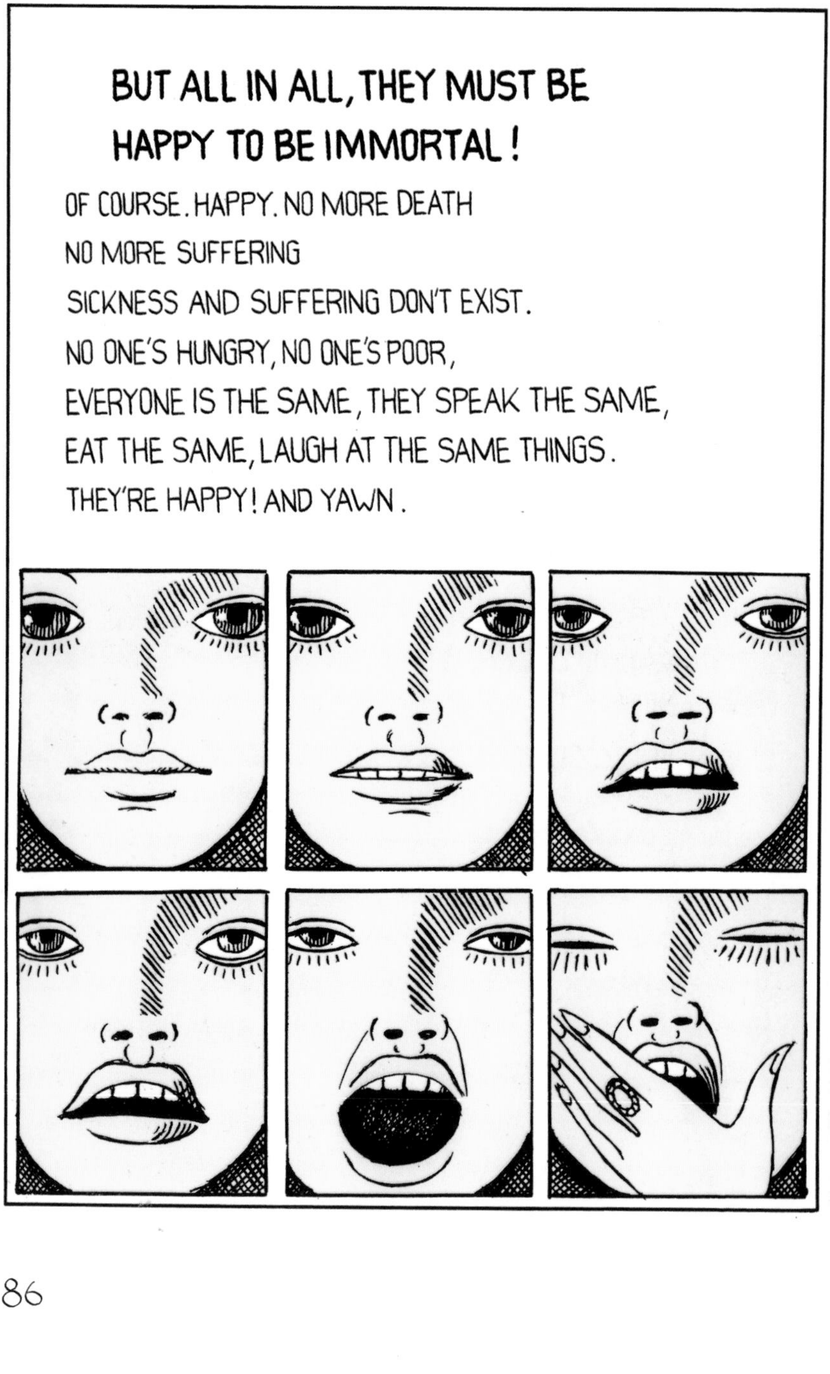
BUT ALL IN ALL, THEY MUST BE
HAPPY TO BE IMMORTAL!
OF COURSE. HAPPY. NO MORE DEATH
NO MORE SUFFERING
SICKNESS AND SUFFERING DON'T EXIST.
NO ONE'S HUNGRY, NO ONE'S POOR,
EVERYONE IS THE SAME, THEY SPEAK THE SAME,
EAT THE SAME, LAUGH AT THE SAME THINGS.
THEY'RE HAPPY! AND YAWN.

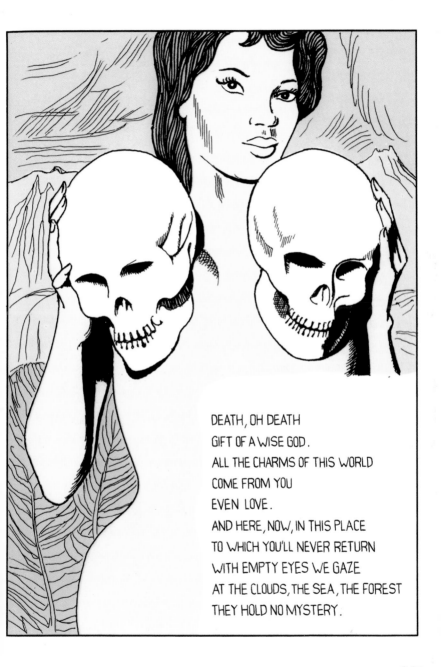

DEATH, OH DEATH
GIFT OF A WISE GOD.
ALL THE CHARMS OF THIS WORLD
COME FROM YOU
EVEN LOVE.
AND HERE, NOW, IN THIS PLACE
TO WHICH YOU'LL NEVER RETURN
WITH EMPTY EYES WE GAZE
AT THE CLOUDS, THE SEA, THE FOREST
THEY HOLD NO MYSTERY.

87

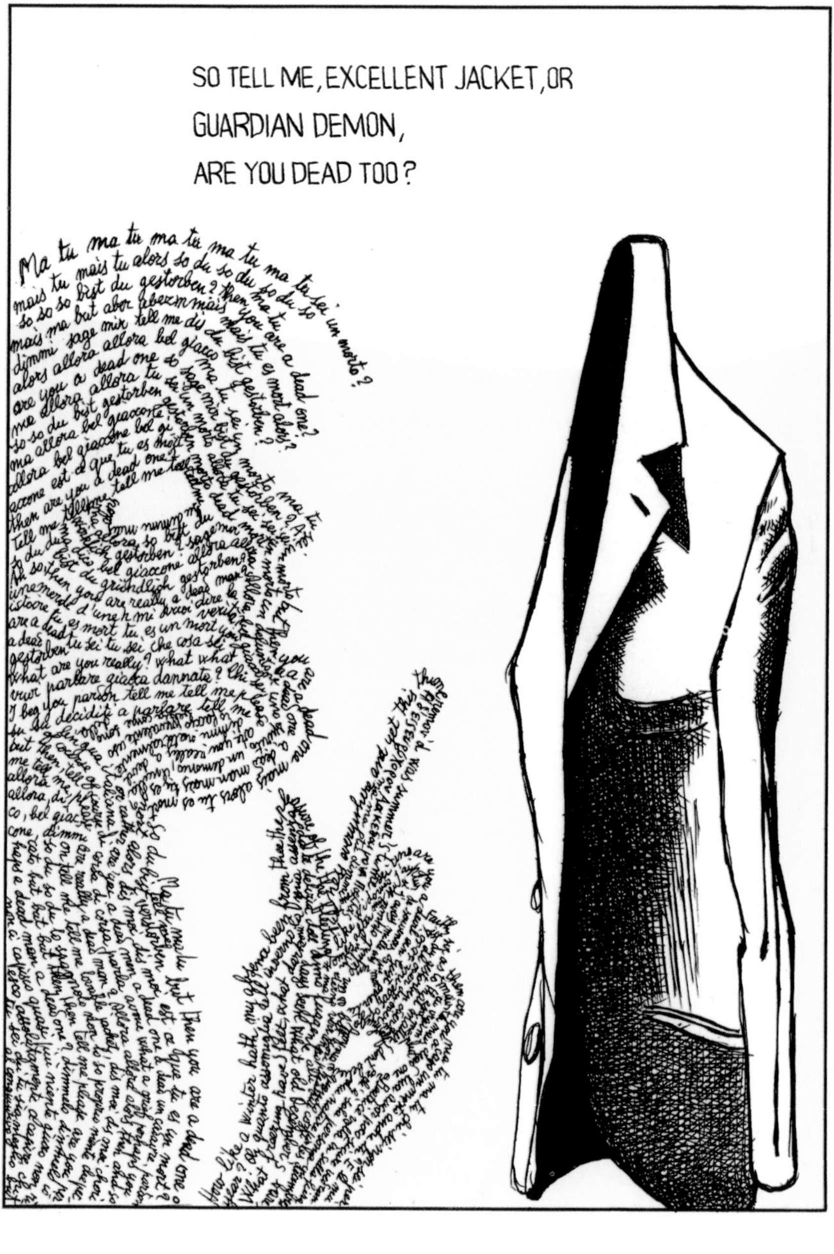
SO TELL ME, EXCELLENT JACKET, OR
GUARDIAN DEMON,
ARE YOU DEAD TOO?

TRUTH IS, I'M NOT QUITE SURE.

YOU SEE, UP THERE WHERE YOU COME FROM I WALKED ALL NIGHT

UNDER THE RAIN, UNDER THE BURNING SUN, IN THE SNOW, IN

THE MUD, IN THE MARSHES

I TRUDGED EVERY NIGHT OF THE MONTH

NIGHT AND DAY FOR A YEAR, FOR MANY YEARS, A WHOLE LIFE

IT WAS CONSTANT SUFFERING, TOIL, ALWAYS LOOKING TO TOMORROW

NOW I TRY TO REMEMBER, BUT I CAN'T

I CAN'T REMEMBER WHAT WAS GOOD ABOUT IT.

NOW IT ALL SEEMS SENSELESS.

CAN YOU TELL ME WHAT IT WAS ?

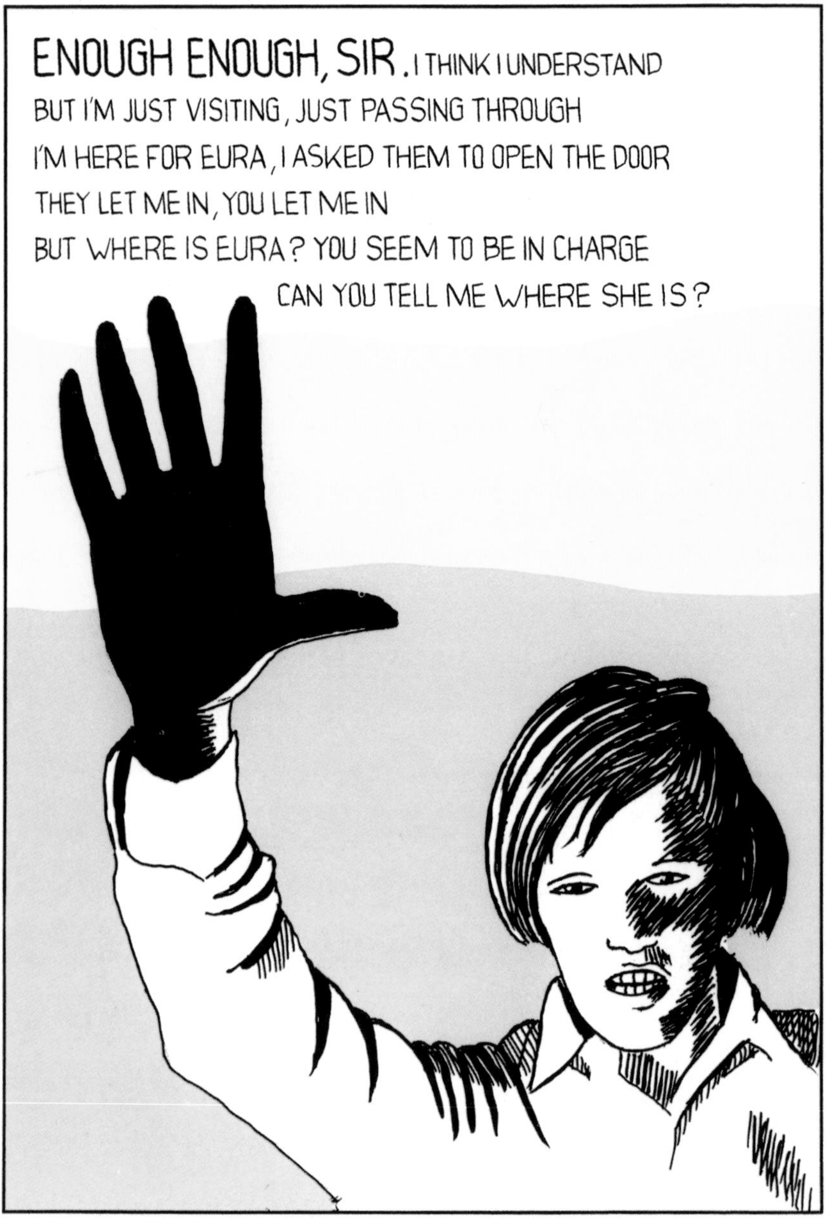
ENOUGH ENOUGH, SIR. I THINK I UNDERSTAND
BUT I'M JUST VISITING, JUST PASSING THROUGH
I'M HERE FOR EURA, I ASKED THEM TO OPEN THE DOOR
THEY LET ME IN, YOU LET ME IN
BUT WHERE IS EURA? YOU SEEM TO BE IN CHARGE
CAN YOU TELL ME WHERE SHE IS?

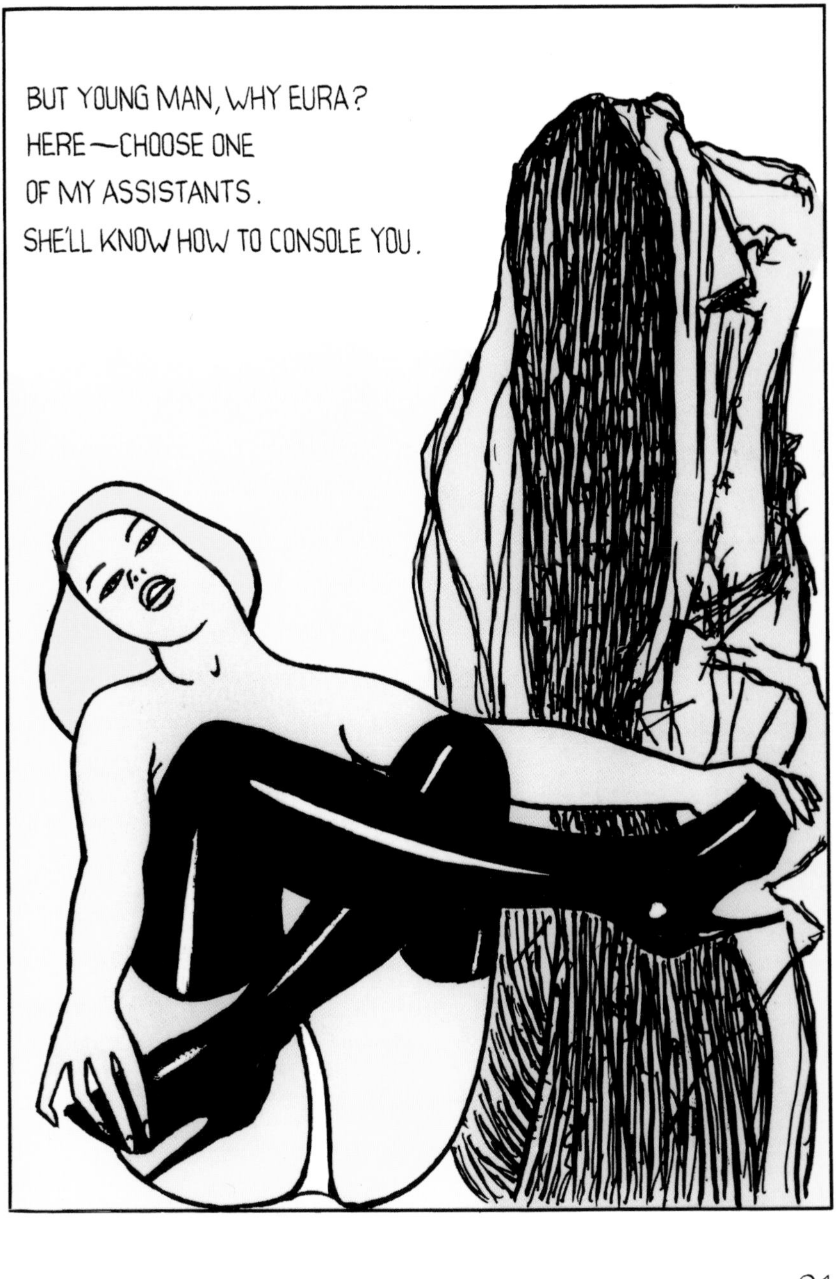
BUT YOUNG MAN, WHY EURA?
HERE—CHOOSE ONE
OF MY ASSISTANTS.
SHE'LL KNOW HOW TO CONSOLE YOU.

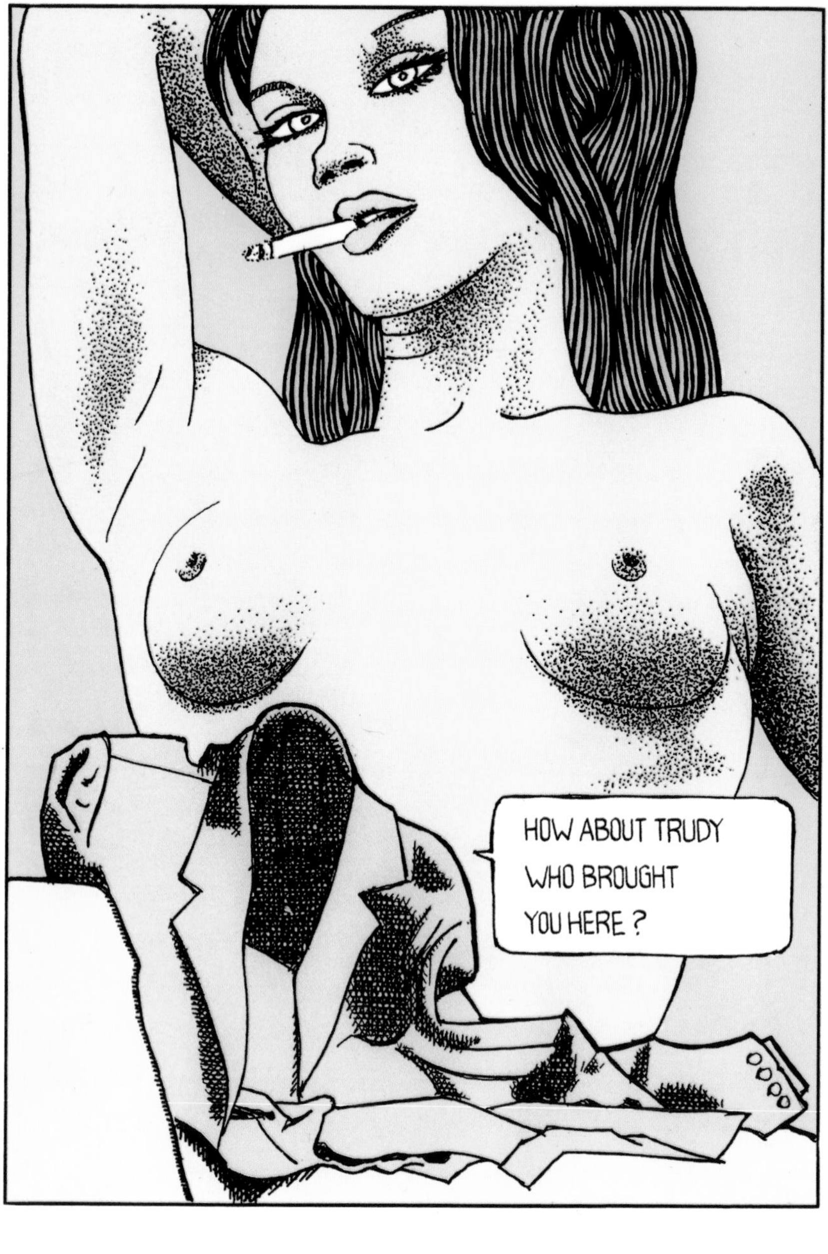
HOW ABOUT TRUDY WHO BROUGHT YOU HERE ?

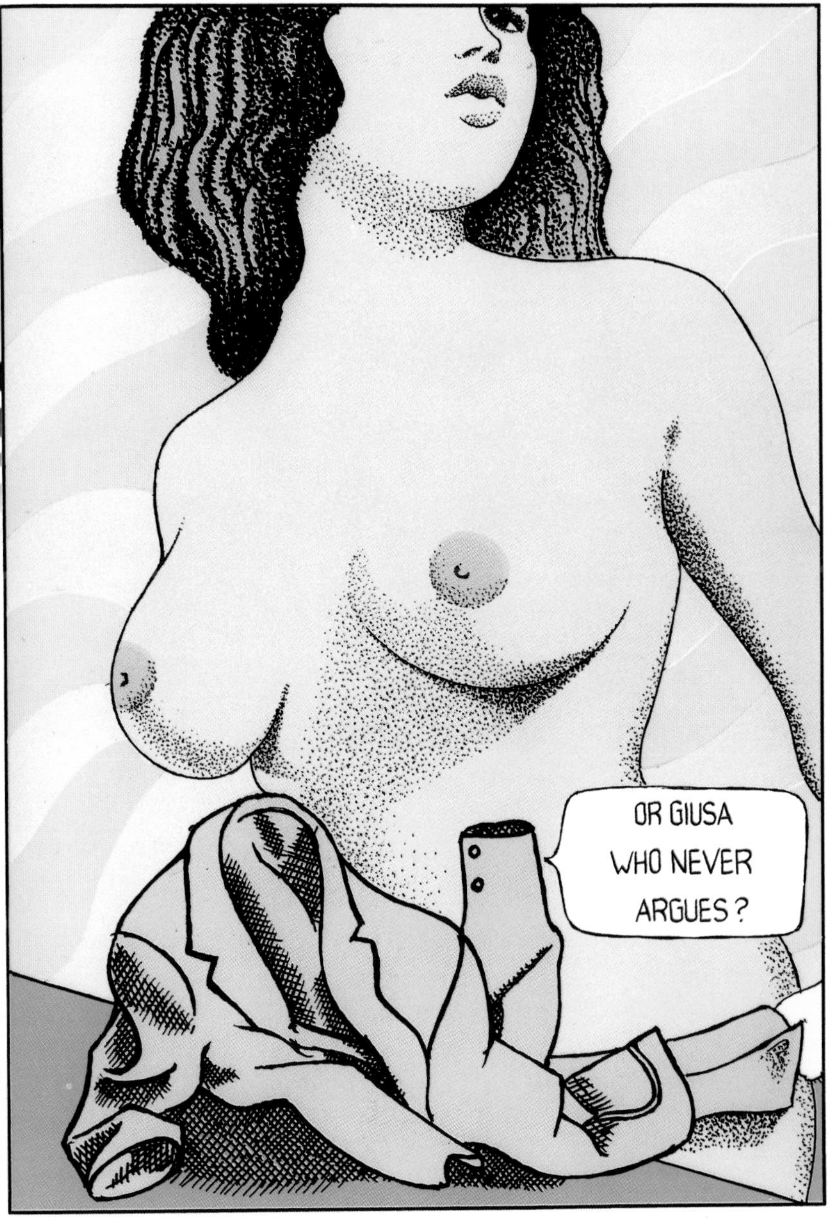
OR GIUSA WHO NEVER ARGUES ?

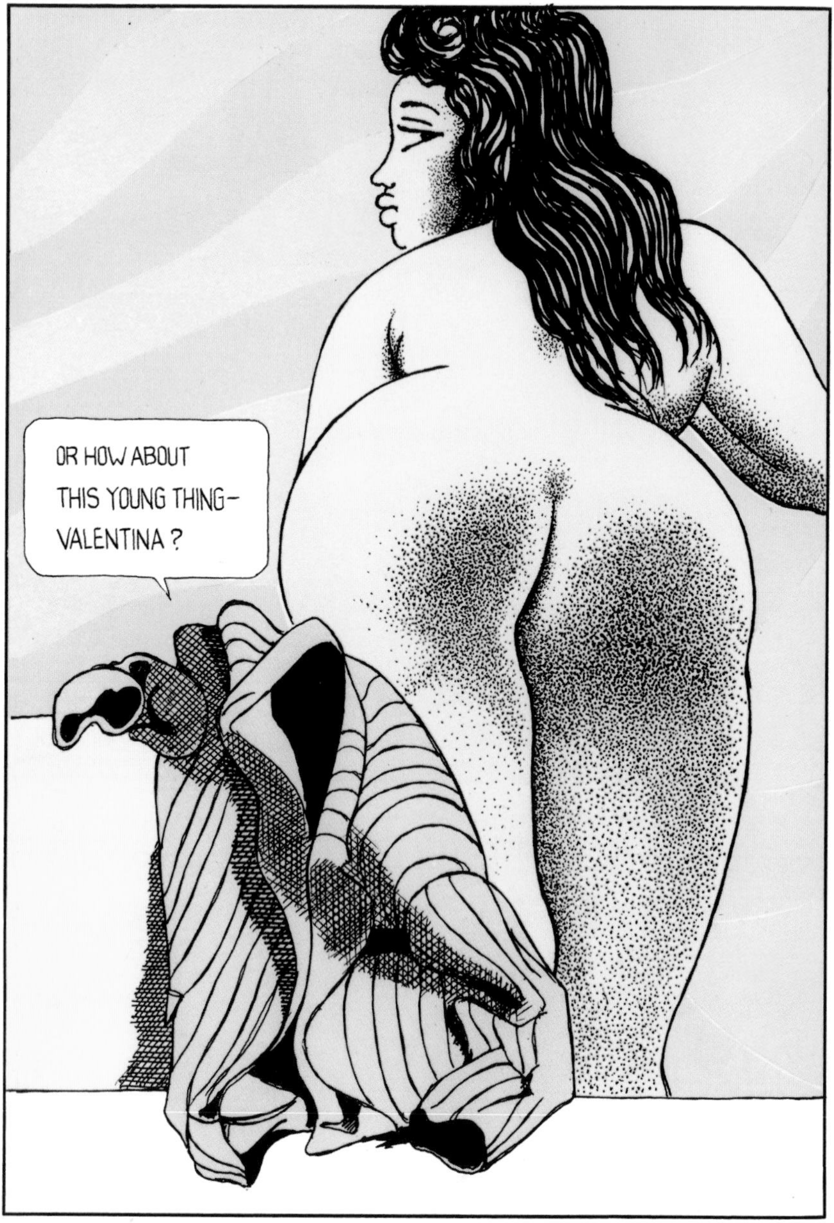
OR HOW ABOUT THIS YOUNG THING– VALENTINA ?

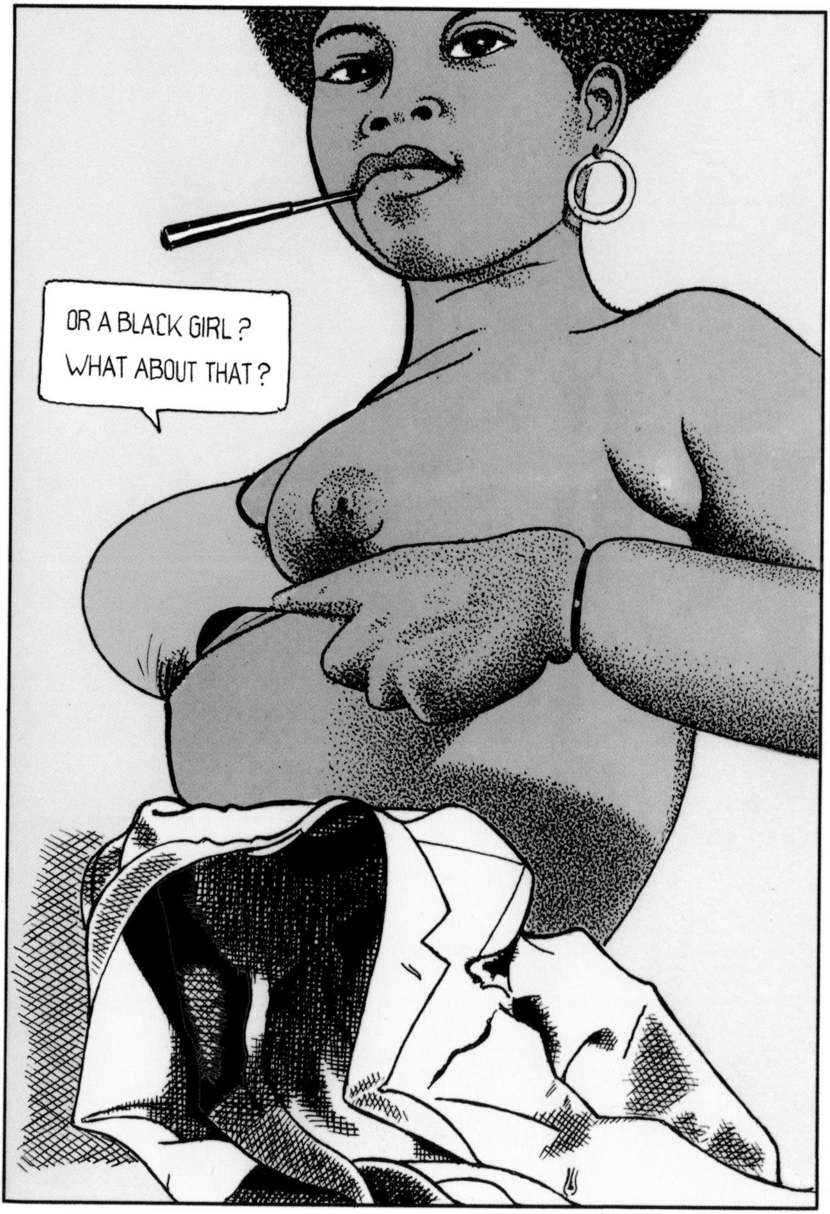
OR A BLACK GIRL? WHAT ABOUT THAT?

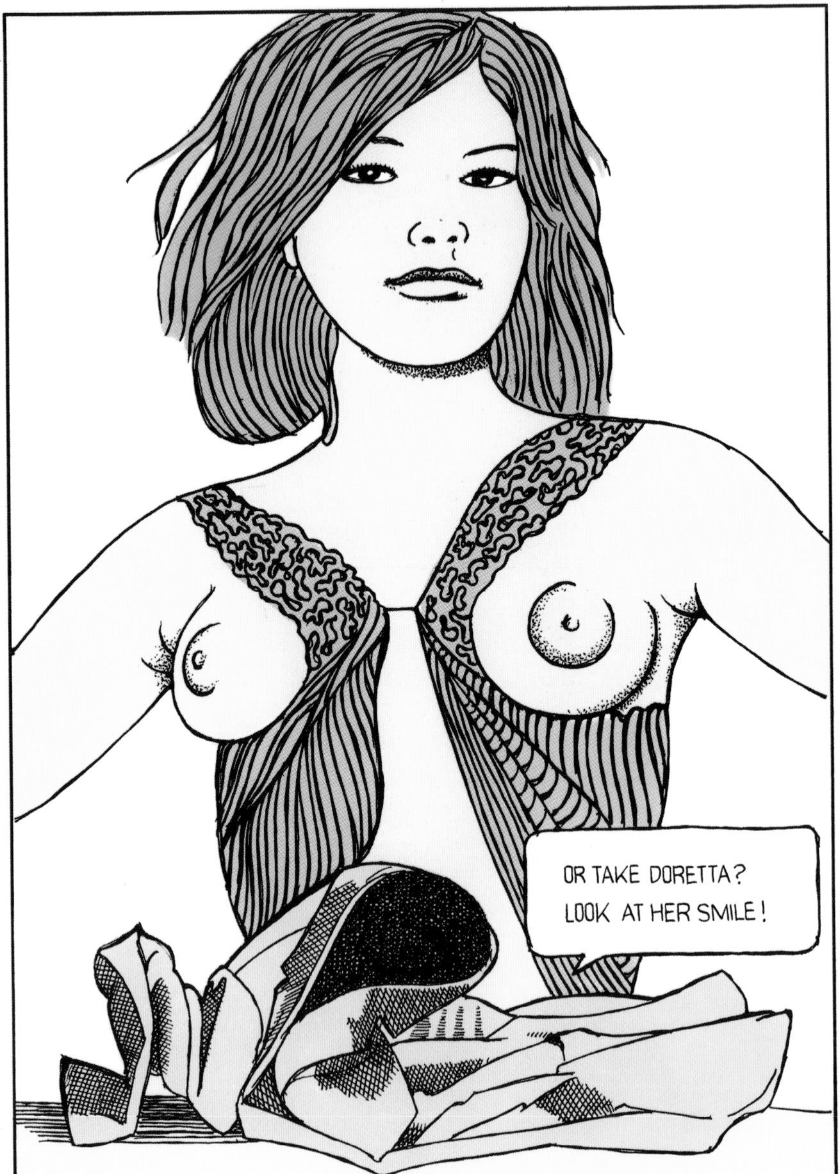
OR TAKE DORETTA? LOOK AT HER SMILE!

ORFI'S SONGS

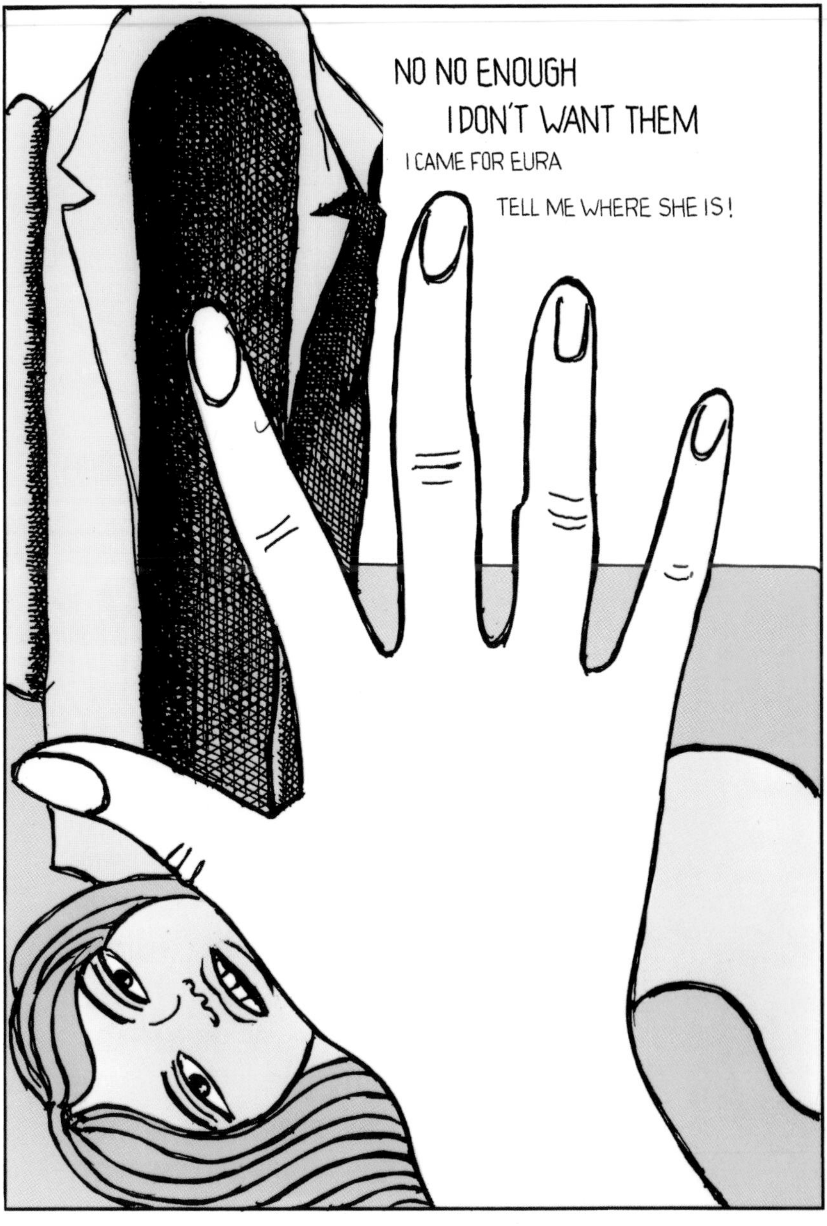
NO NO ENOUGH
I DON'T WANT THEM
I CAME FOR EURA
TELL ME WHERE SHE IS!

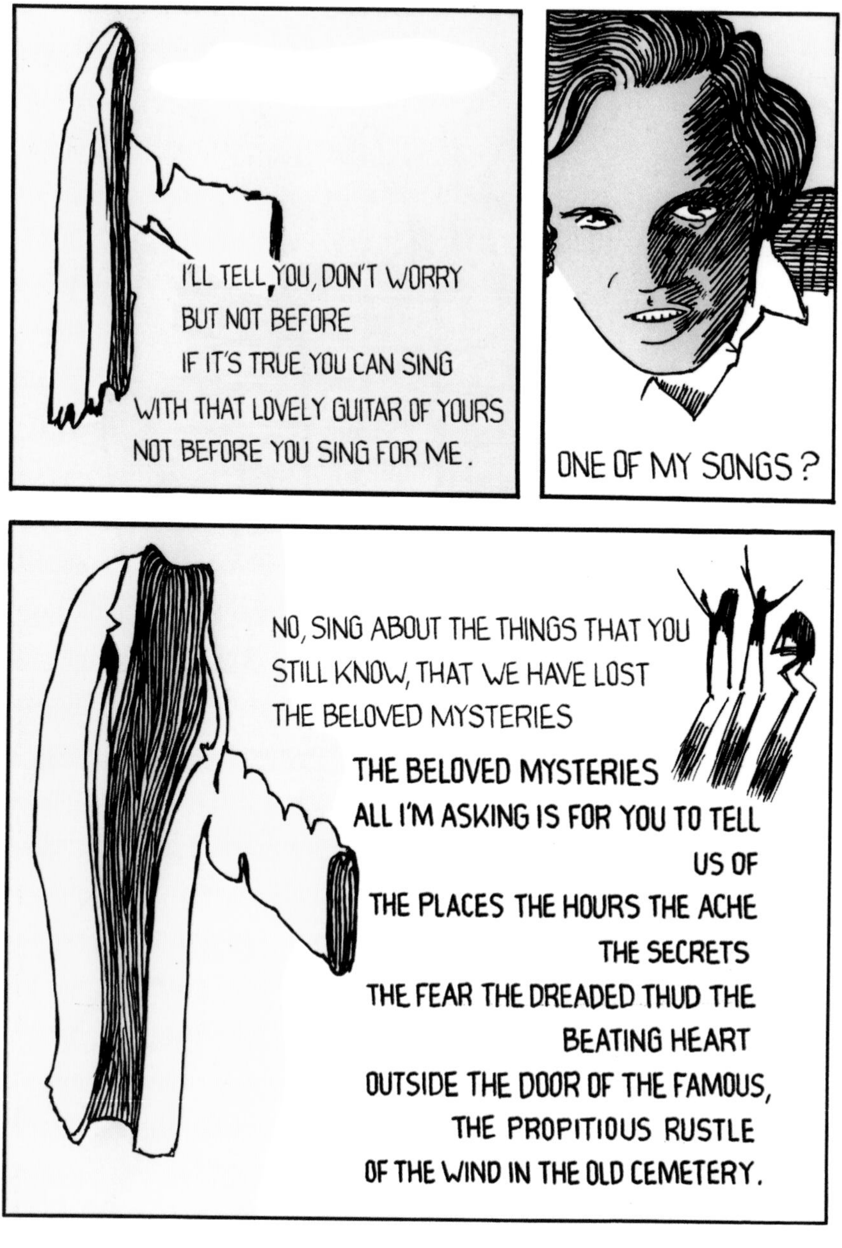
I'LL TELL YOU, DON'T WORRY
BUT NOT BEFORE
IF IT'S TRUE YOU CAN SING
WITH THAT LOVELY GUITAR OF YOURS
NOT BEFORE YOU SING FOR ME.
ONE OF MY SONGS?
NO, SING ABOUT THE THINGS THAT YOU
STILL KNOW, THAT WE HAVE LOST
THE BELOVED MYSTERIES
THE BELOVED MYSTERIES
ALL I'M ASKING IS FOR YOU TO TELL
US OF
THE PLACES THE HOURS THE ACHE
THE SECRETS
THE FEAR THE DREADED THUD THE
BEATING HEART
OUTSIDE THE DOOR OF THE FAMOUS,
THE PROPITIOUS RUSTLE
OF THE WIND IN THE OLD CEMETERY.

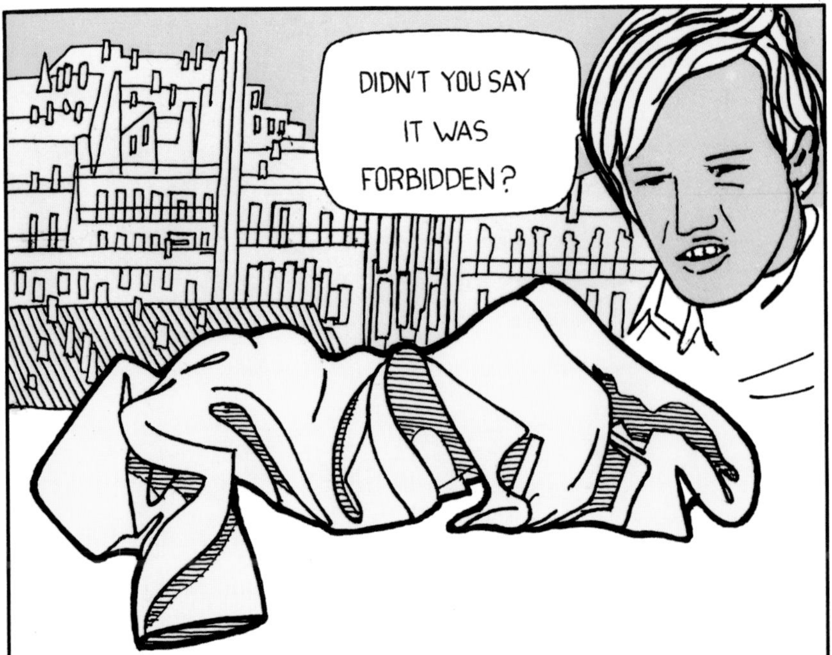
DIDN'T YOU SAY IT WAS FORBIDDEN?

DON'T WORRY YOUNG MAN
I'M AN OLD DEMON PRETTY CORRUPT AND KHRUSHCHEVIAN,
ONCE A LORD OF THE REALM
NOW DEMOTED TO BORDER GUARD.
DON'T WORRY MY FRIEND,
NO ONE WILL HEAR,
THE BIG BOSS WON'T HEAR,
THE NEW BOSS IS SORT OF A
MANAGERIAL DIRECTORIAL EXECUTIVE ROBOT
HE'D NEVER IMAGINE ...

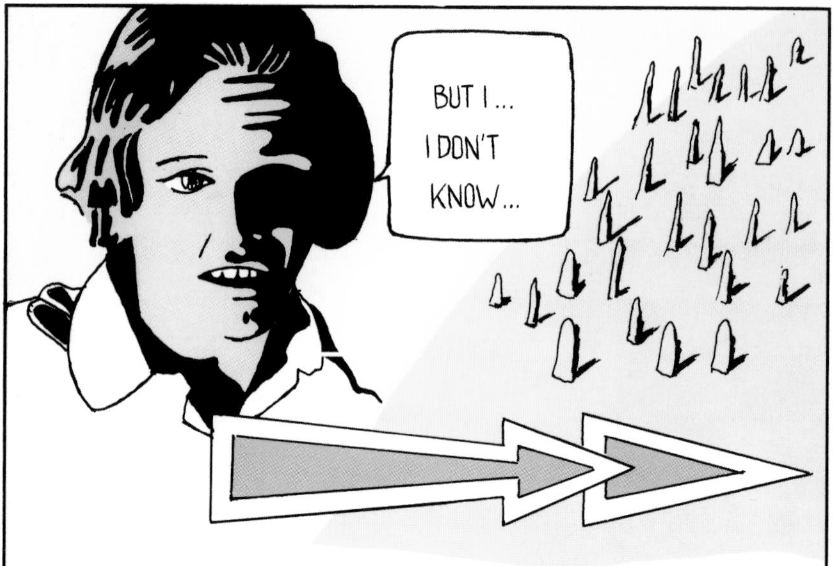
BUT I...
I DON'T
KNOW...

OH YES, YOU DO, STANDING THERE WITH YOUR GUITAR.
YOU KNOW JUST WHAT I MEAN.
YOUR CHILDHOOD MEMORIES,
AT NIGHT THE GHOSTS STRANGE THOUGHTS THE FUNNEL OF TIME,
YOUR FIRST INTIMATIONS
OF WHAT AWAITED YOU AT THE END OF THE ROAD
JUST TAKEN, THE SUN STILL SHINING,
AND ALL AROUND MEADOWS TREES AND LOVE,
THEN DESPAIR, SEPULCHRAL FEARS,
DIVINE AND MORTAL TERROR. DAMN IT, I DON'T HAVE TO
EXPLAIN THESE CRUEL THINGS TO YOU.
COME ON, SING, WE'RE ALL EARS.

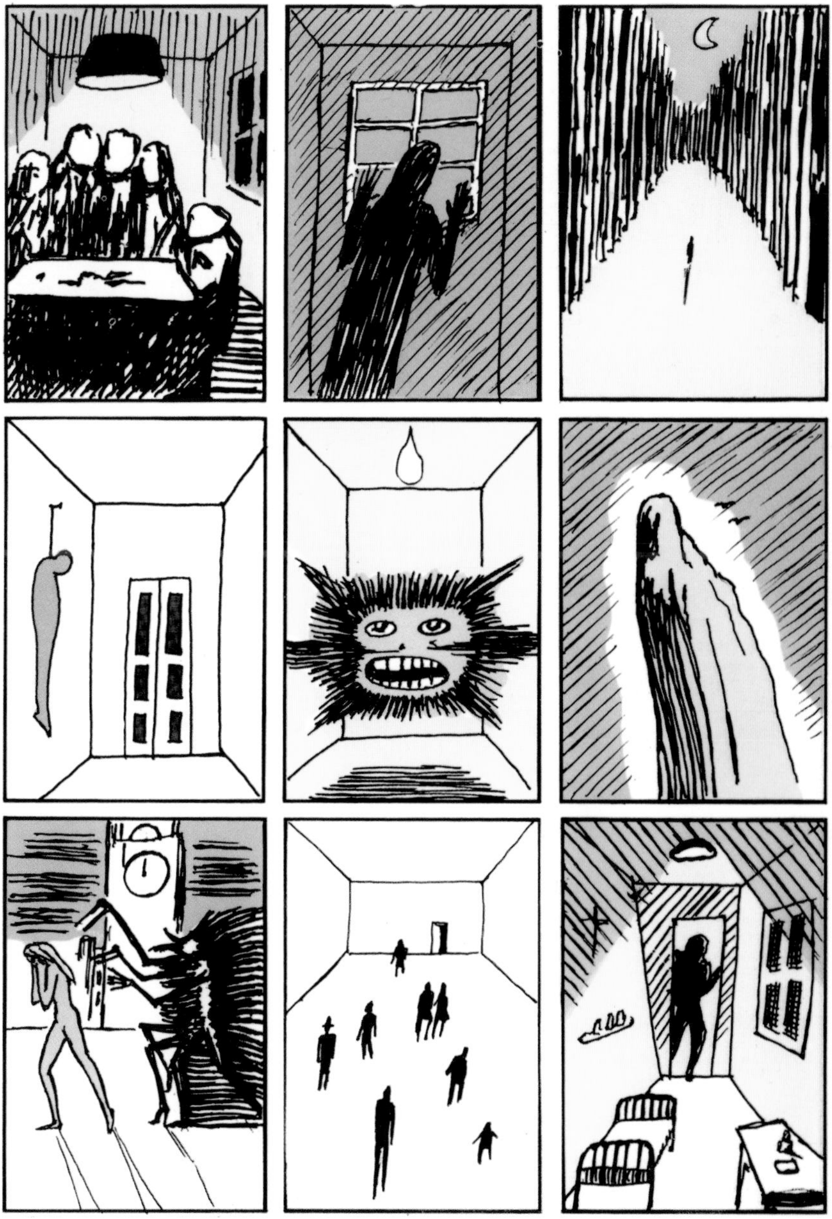

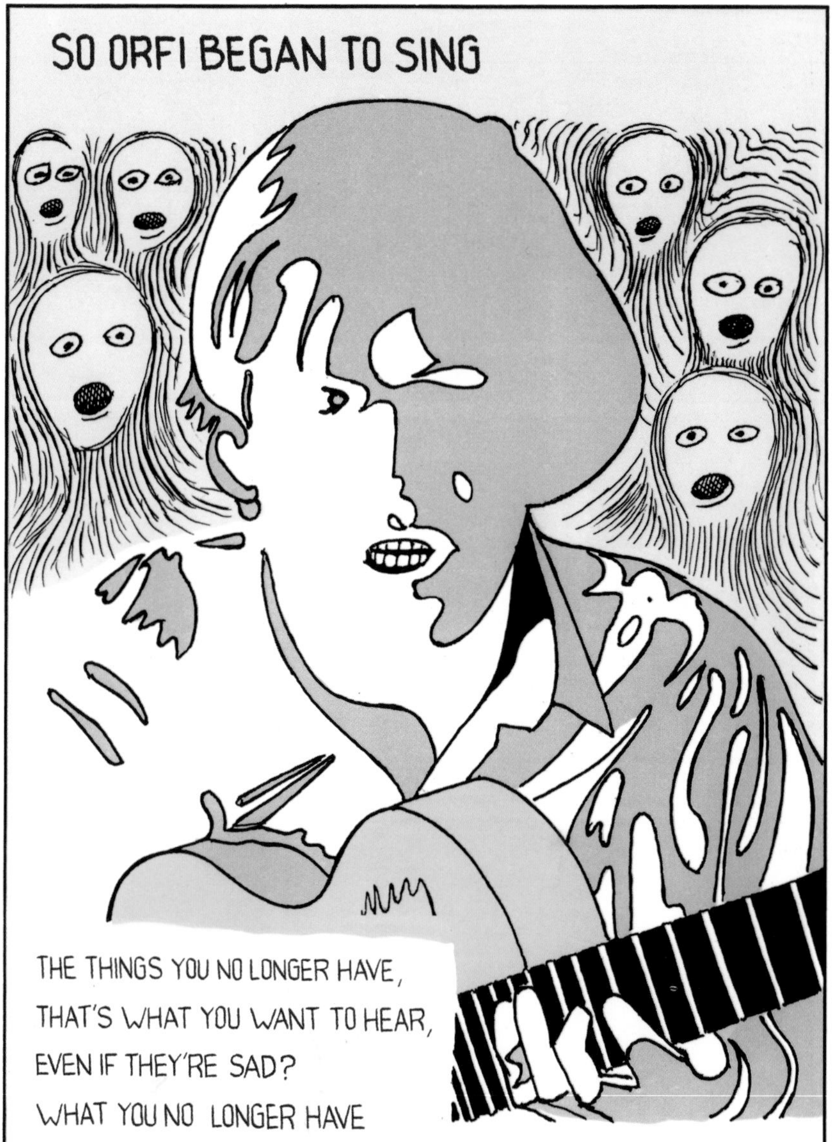
SO ORFI BEGAN TO SING
THE THINGS YOU NO LONGER HAVE,
THAT'S WHAT YOU WANT TO HEAR,
EVEN IF THEY'RE SAD?
WHAT YOU NO LONGER HAVE
BECAUSE DOWN HERE THERE'S NO FINAL EXIT.

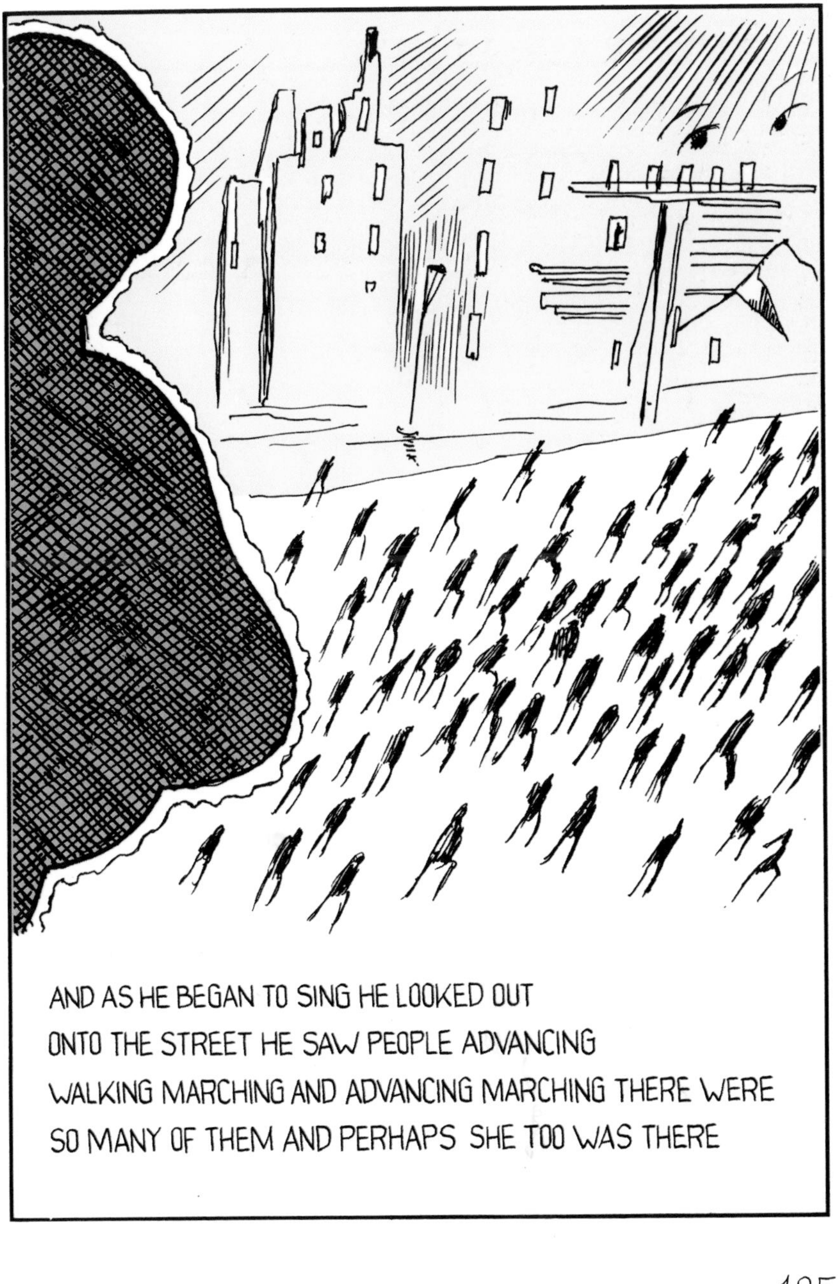
AND AS HE BEGAN TO SING HE LOOKED OUT
ONTO THE STREET HE SAW PEOPLE ADVANCING
WALKING MARCHING AND ADVANCING MARCHING THERE WERE
SO MANY OF THEM AND PERHAPS SHE TOO WAS THERE

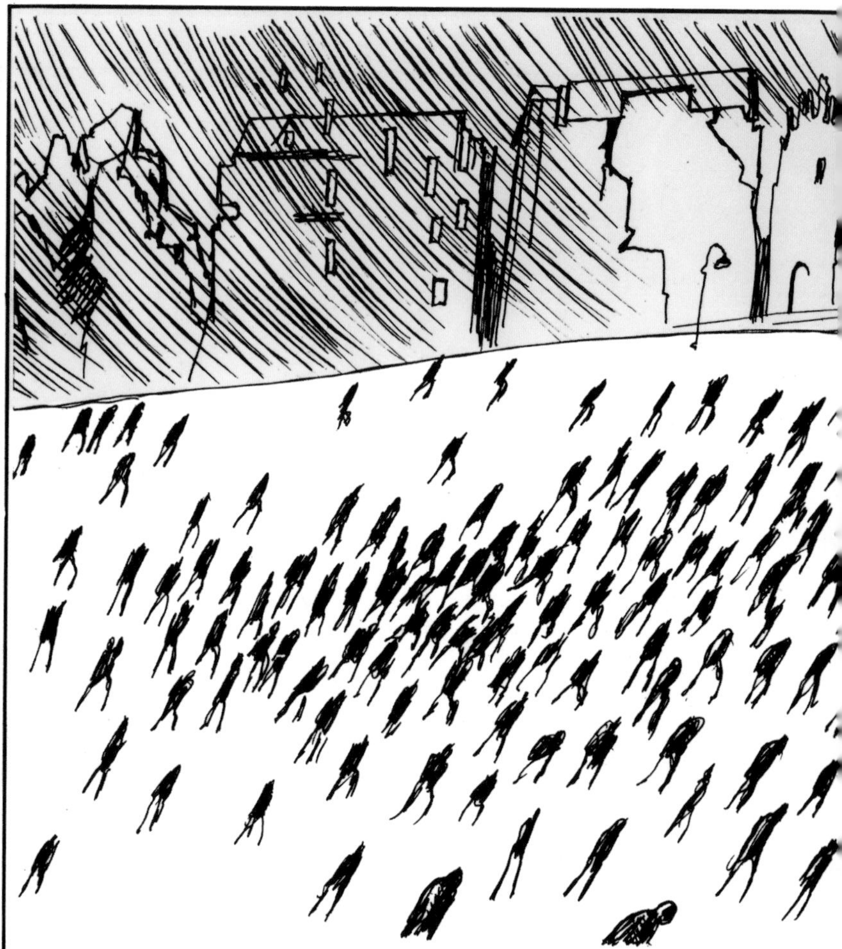
POOR AND RICH ALL DRAWN FORWARD
THEY DIDN'T SUFFER EXACTLY THEY WERE JUST HOP HOP
JUST EMPTY BECAUSE THEY WERE JUST MARCHING, WALKING
WALKING ALONG BUT THE ROAD HAD NO END

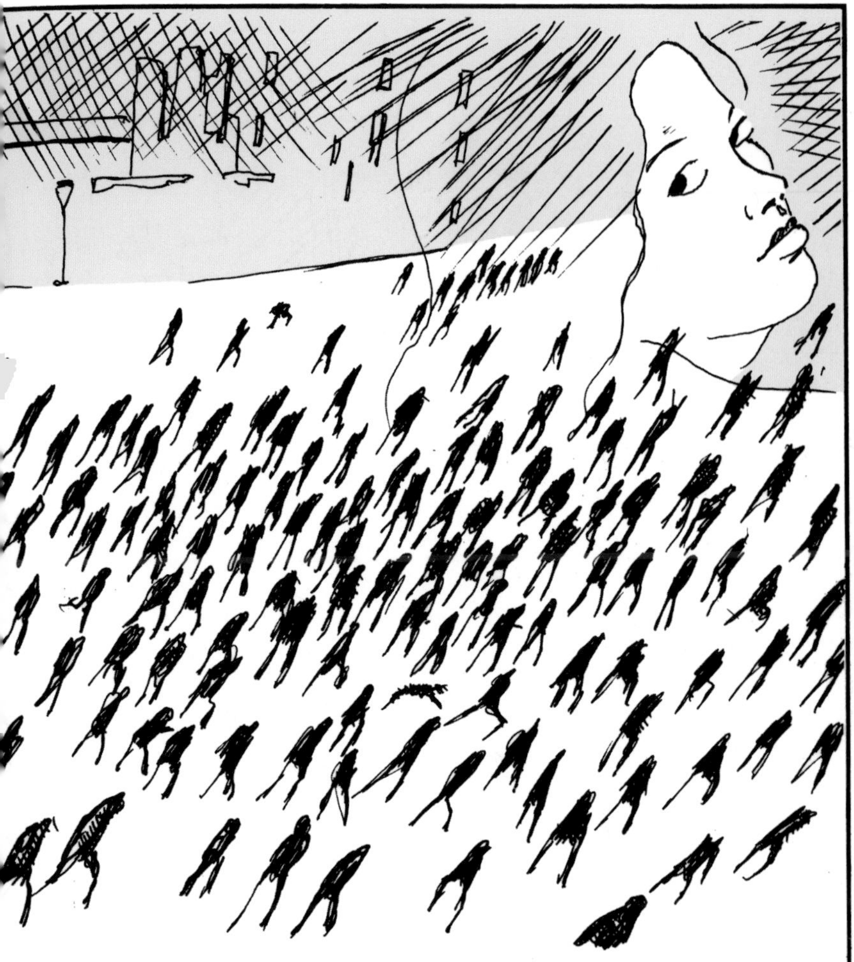
IT WOULD NEVER END THERE WAS NO
EXIT YOU UNDERSTAND NO EXIT
AT LAST HOP HOP THE ROAD
HAD NO END THEY WERE DEAD!

HE BEGAN TO SING:

DO YOU REMEMBER THE HOURS THE VOICES
THAT STIRRED YOU WHEN YOU WERE ABOVE
AND THE ETERNAL THOUGHT THE ACCURSED THOUGHT
YOU NOW PINE FOR,
                    DELICIOUS DEATH?

WHEN
    IN THE DESERTED COURTYARD
    OF HIS EXISTENCE
    A MAN SEES RISING
    OVER THE TERRACES AND WALLS
    THE IMMENSE BLACK MOON.

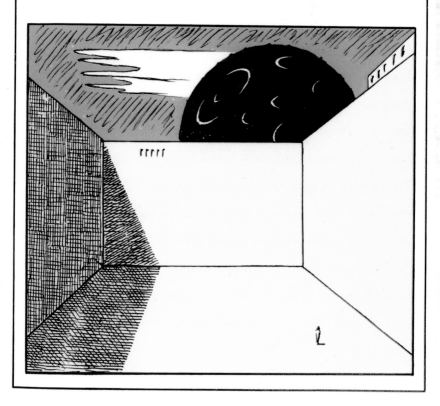

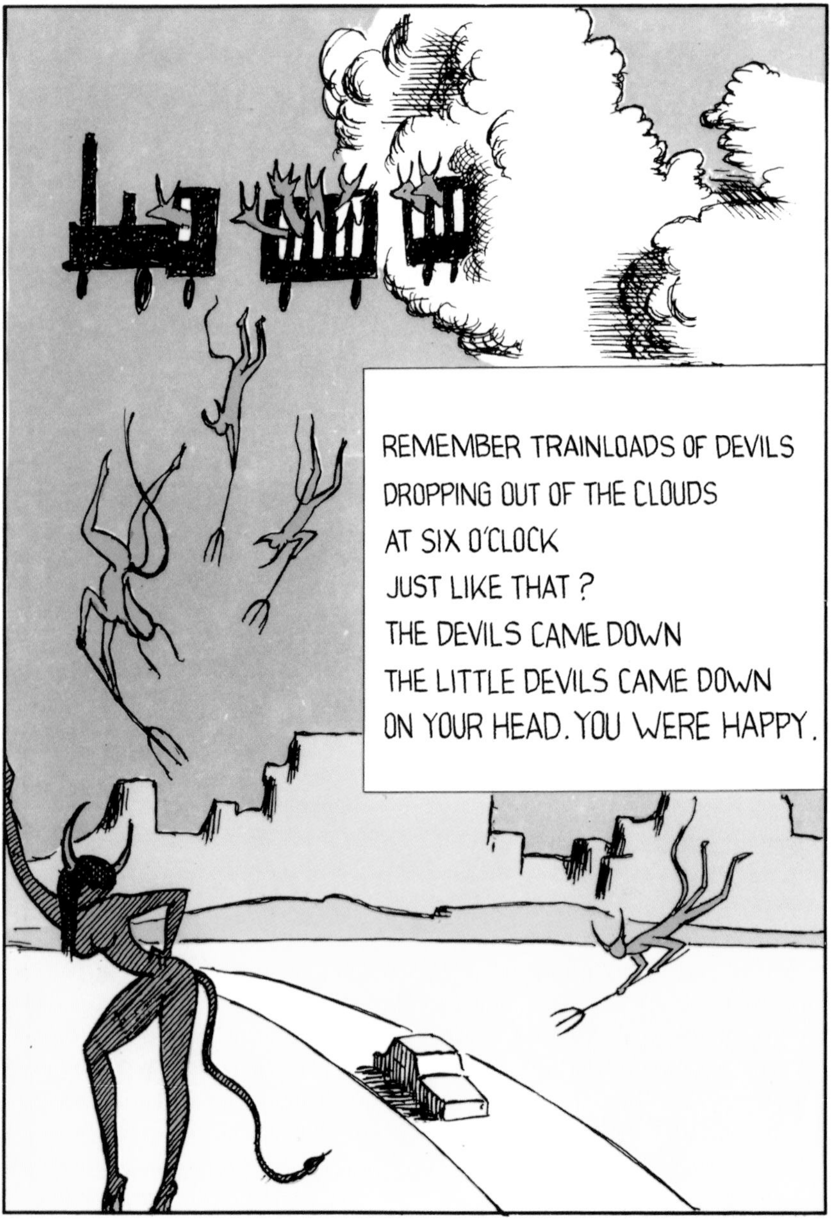
REMEMBER TRAINLOADS OF DEVILS
DROPPING OUT OF THE CLOUDS
AT SIX O'CLOCK
JUST LIKE THAT ?
THE DEVILS CAME DOWN
THE LITTLE DEVILS CAME DOWN
ON YOUR HEAD. YOU WERE HAPPY.

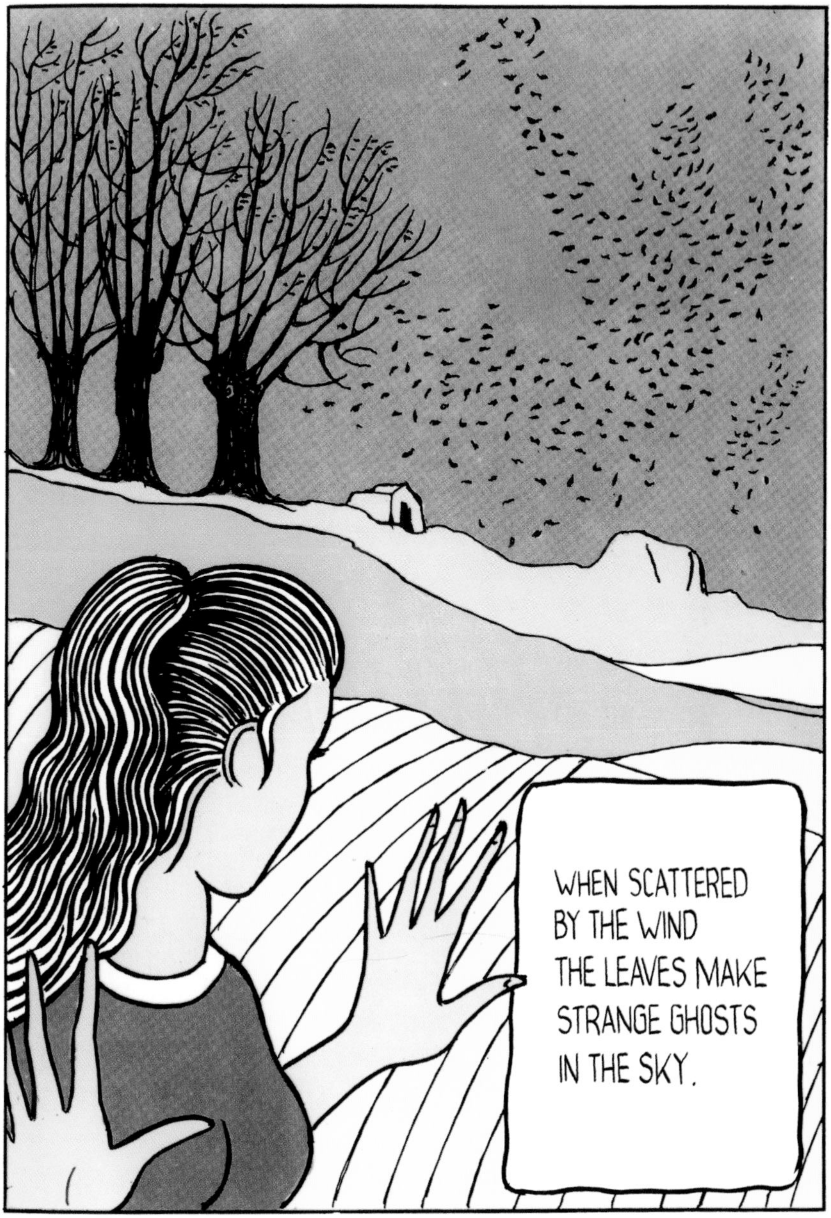
WHEN SCATTERED BY THE WIND THE LEAVES MAKE STRANGE GHOSTS IN THE SKY.

WHEN
STRANGE NOISES COME FROM ANCIENT DESERTED ROOMS.

WHEN THE AUTUMNAL SORCERERS TRAIL THEIR LONG DARK SHADOWS THROUGH THE GARDENS OF JOY.

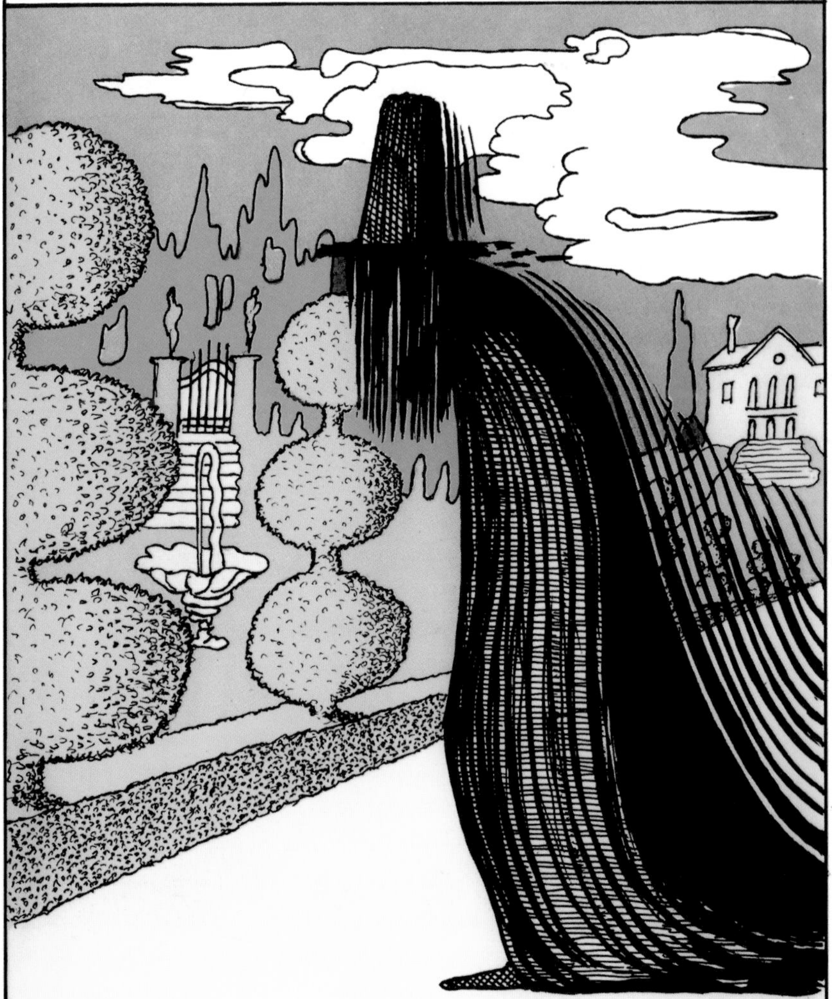

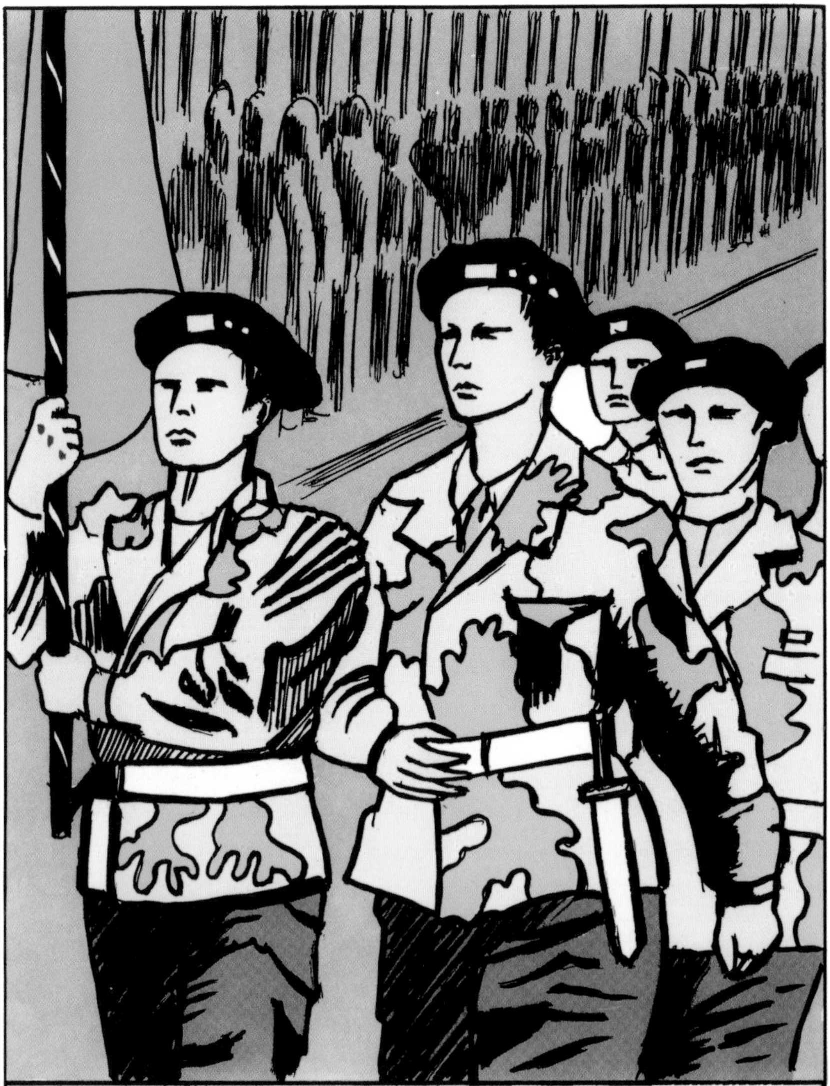
WHEN MARCHING TOWARD CERTAIN VICTORY
THE SOLDIERS SING.

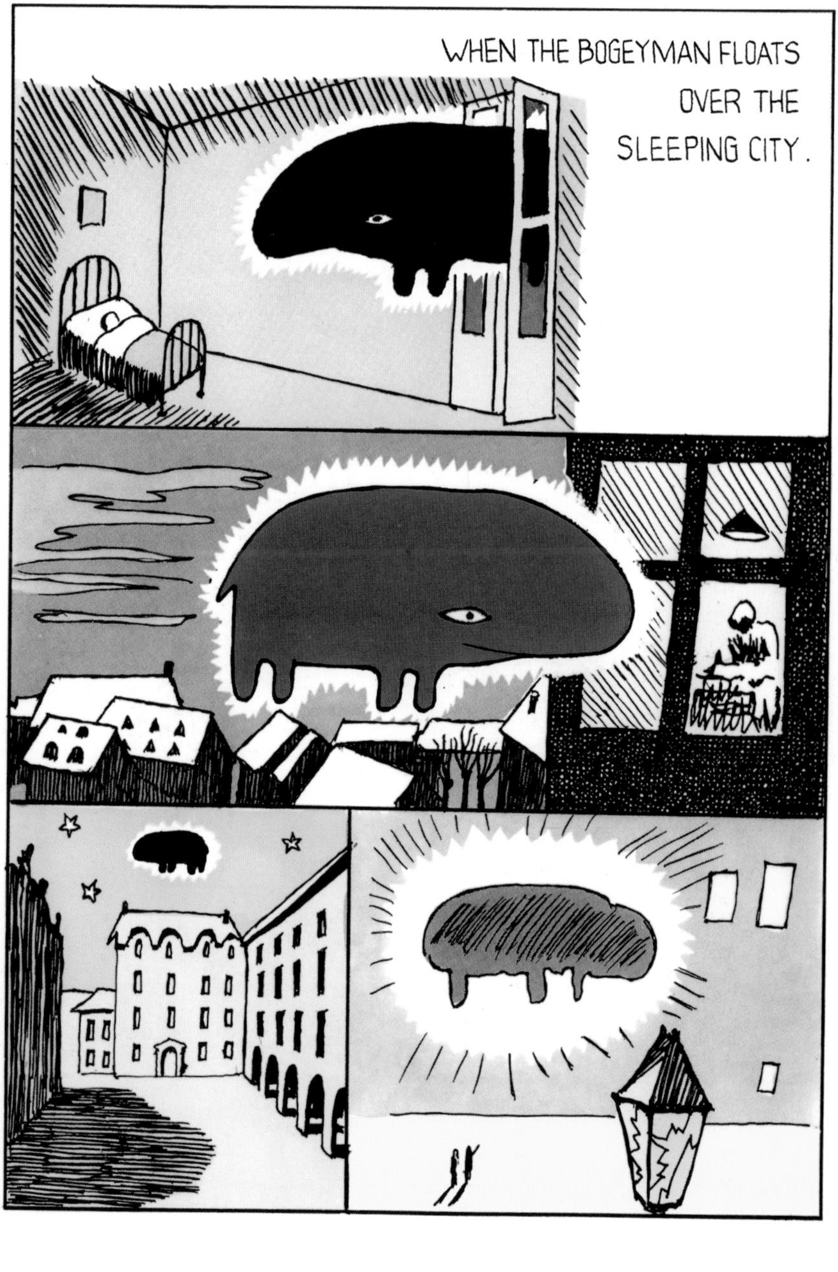
WHEN THE BOGEYMAN FLOATS OVER THE SLEEPING CITY.

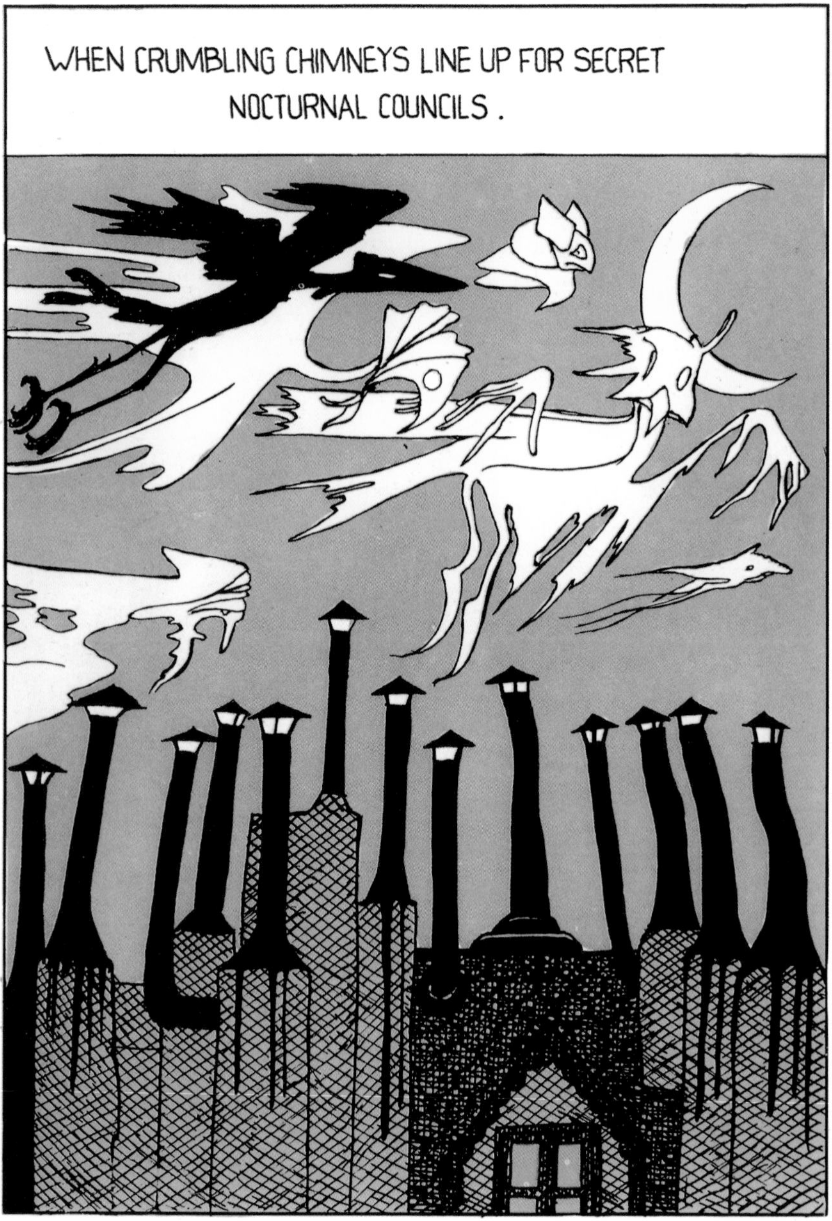
WHEN CRUMBLING CHIMNEYS LINE UP FOR SECRET NOCTURNAL COUNCILS .

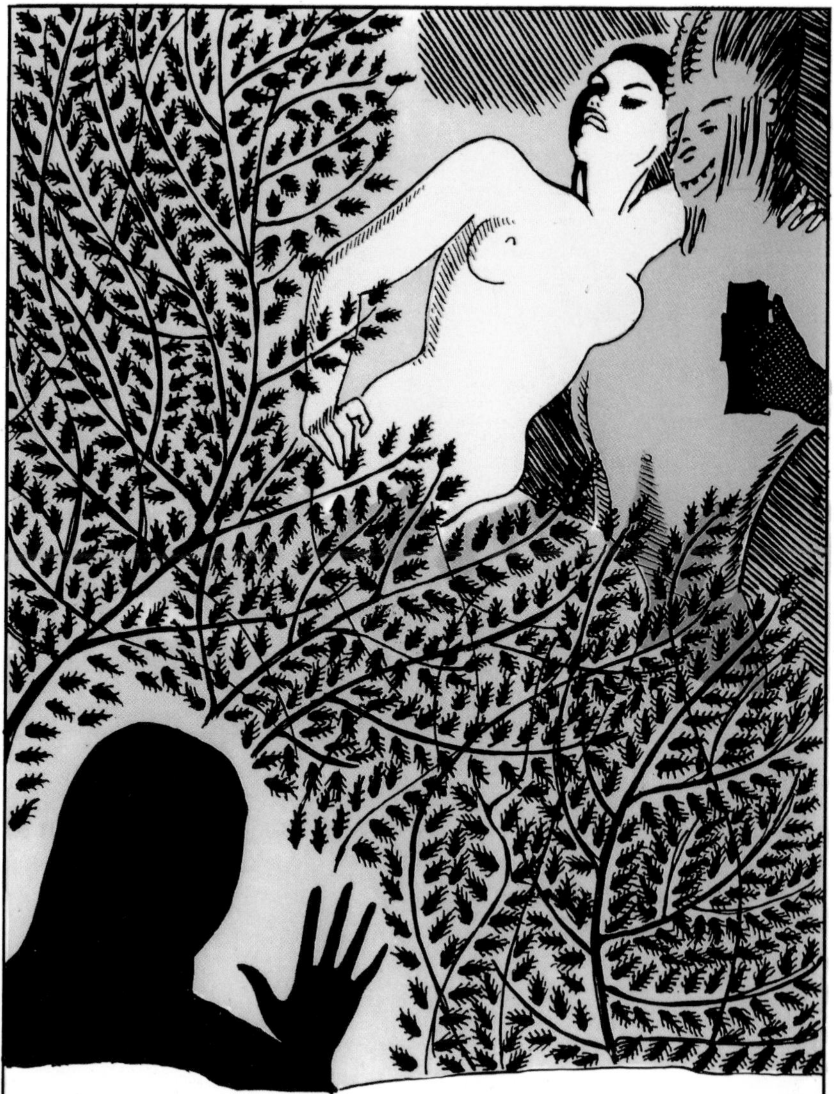

WHEN THE NUN ON A PILGRIMAGE GLIMPSES A BLACK SABBATH IN THE FOREST.

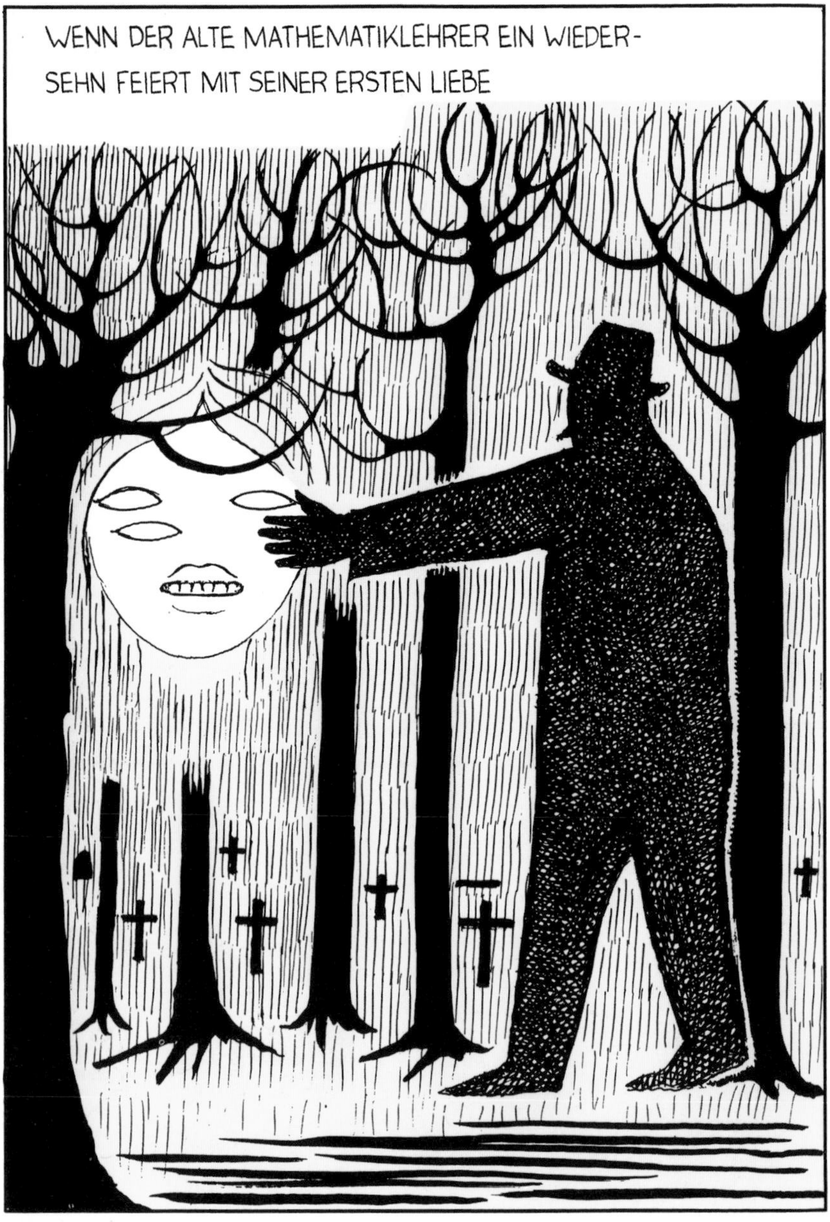
WENN DER ALTE MATHEMATIKLEHRER EIN WIEDER-
SEHN FEIERT MIT SEINER ERSTEN LIEBE

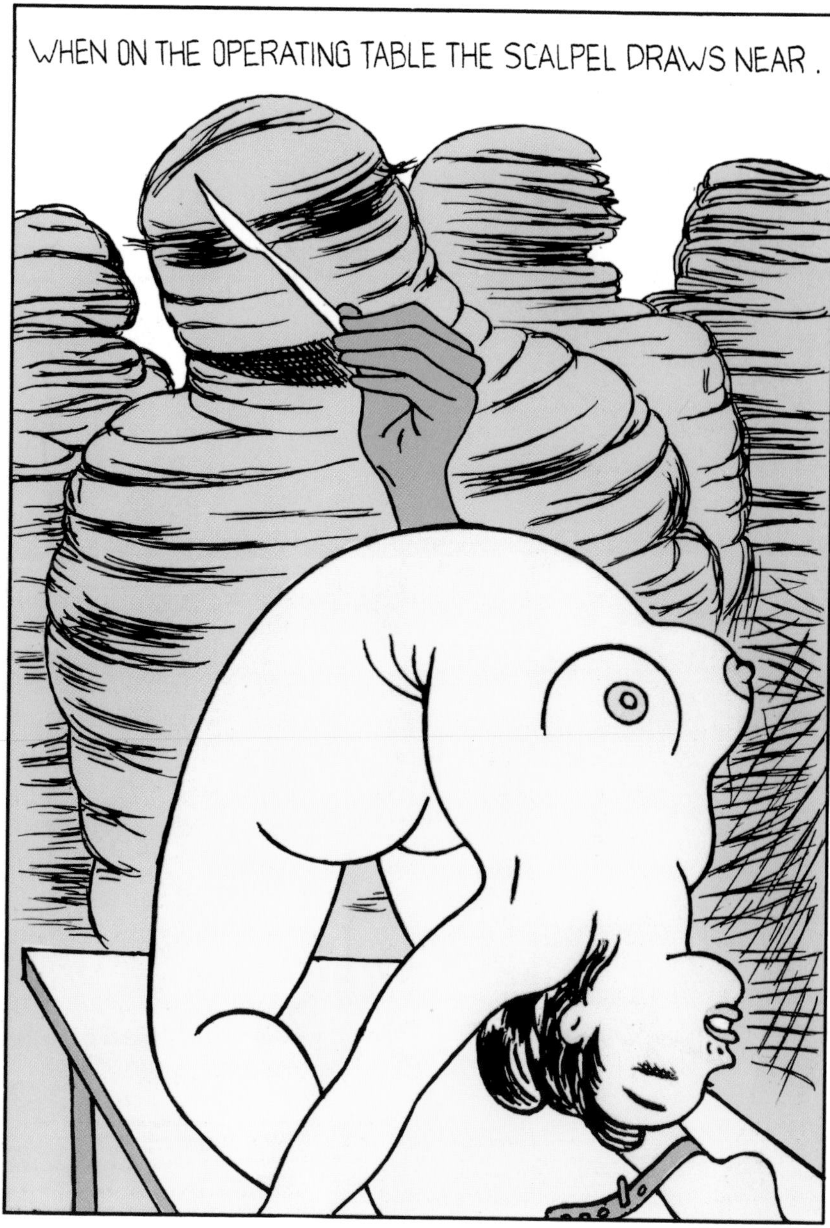
WHEN ON THE OPERATING TABLE THE SCALPEL DRAWS NEAR.

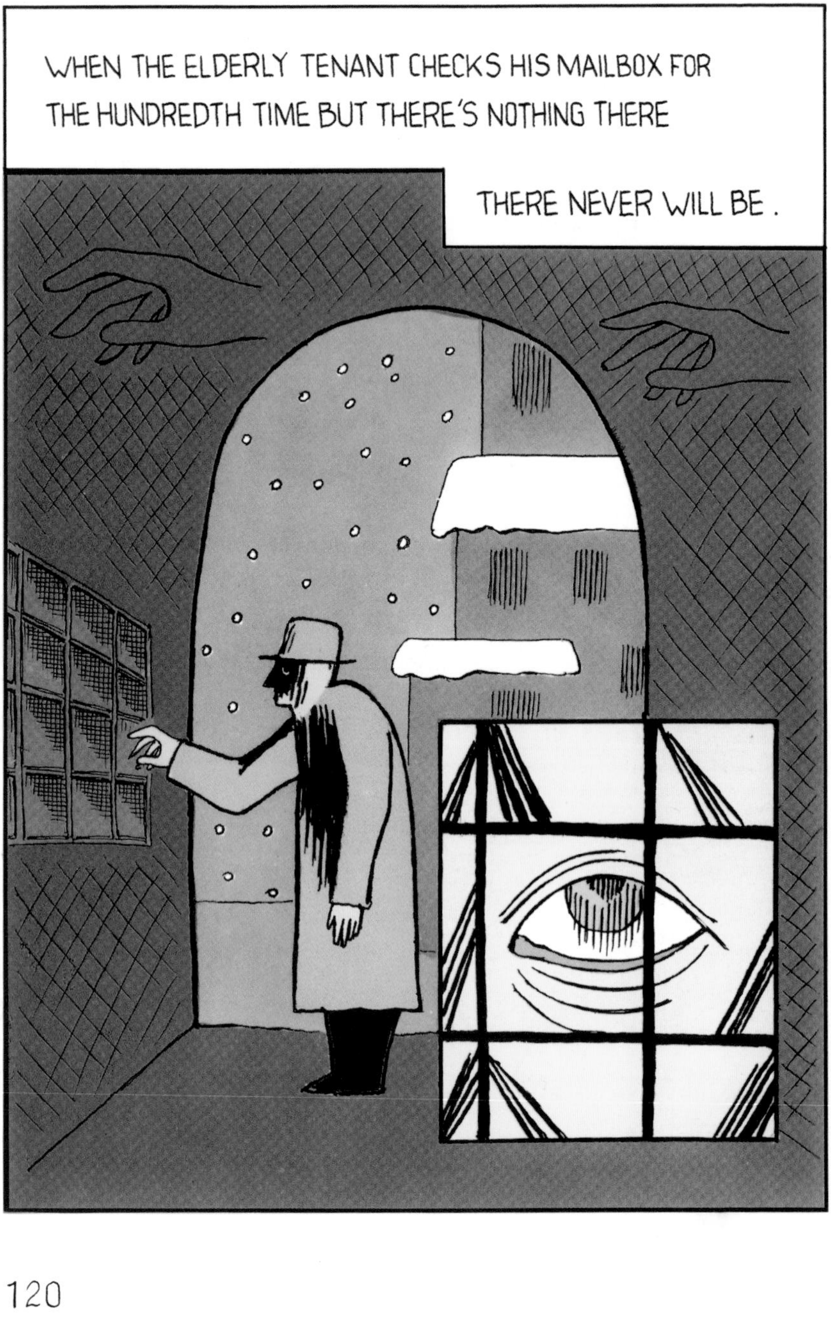
WHEN THE ELDERLY TENANT CHECKS HIS MAILBOX FOR THE HUNDREDTH TIME BUT THERE'S NOTHING THERE
THERE NEVER WILL BE .

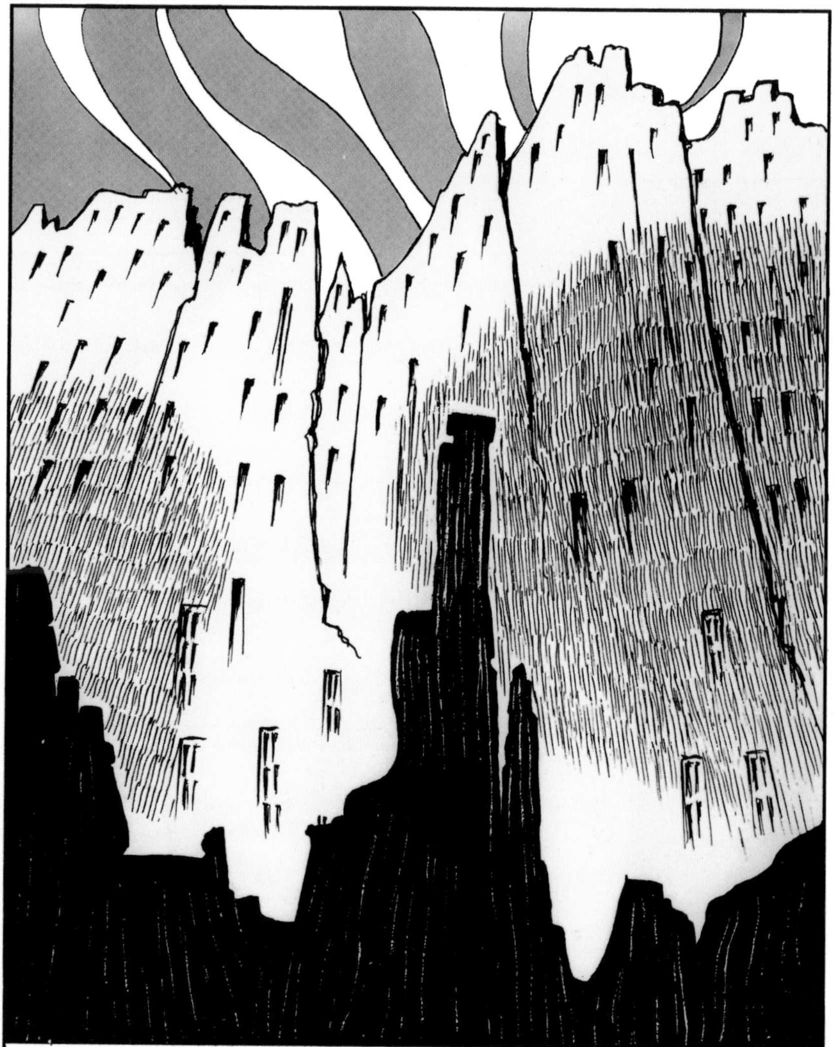

WHEN SUDDENLY THE LOOMING MOUNTAIN BECOMES OUR LIFE, OUR CITY, OUR OLD HOME, OUR ANCIENT TOMB.

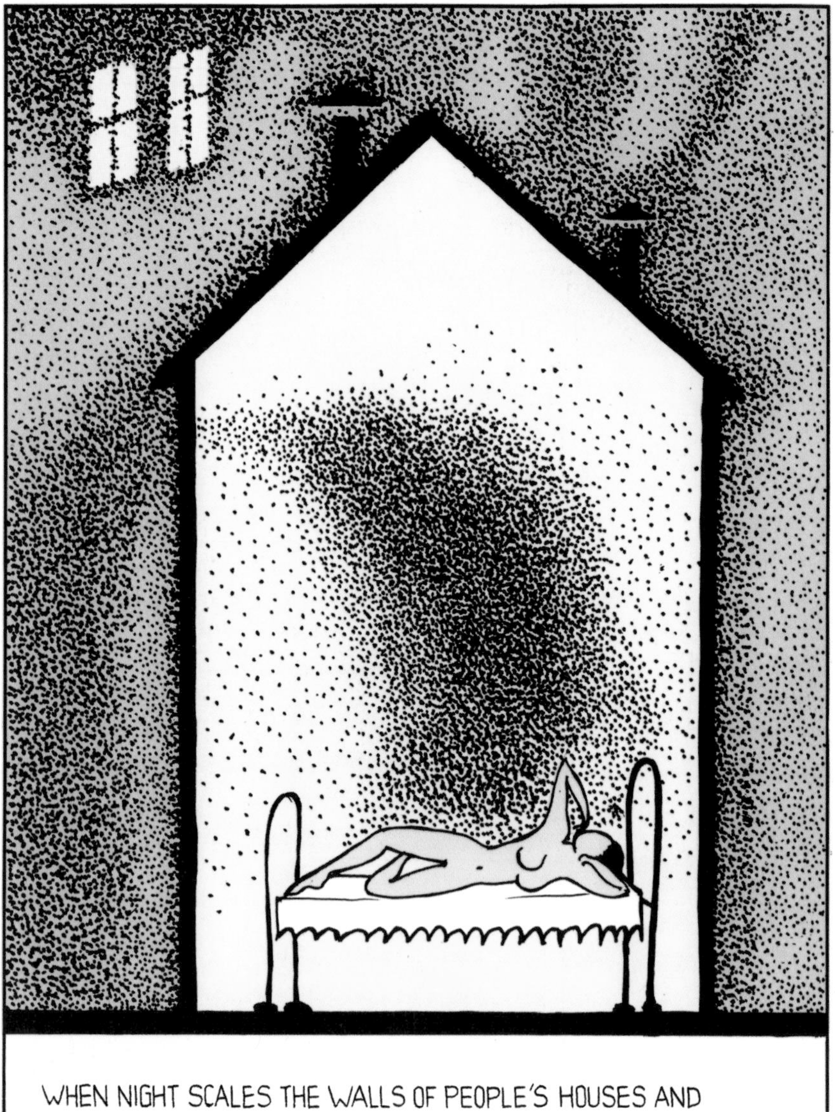
WHEN NIGHT SCALES THE WALLS OF PEOPLE'S HOUSES AND ENTERS THEIR ROOMS.

WHEN AT NIGHT
IN A SHELTER
THE FORBIDDING ROAR
OF A LANDSLIDE
IS HEARD.

BUT OUTSIDE
THERE IS NOTHING—
ONLY
THE SILENCE OF
THE MOUNTAINS
LIT BY
THE MOON.

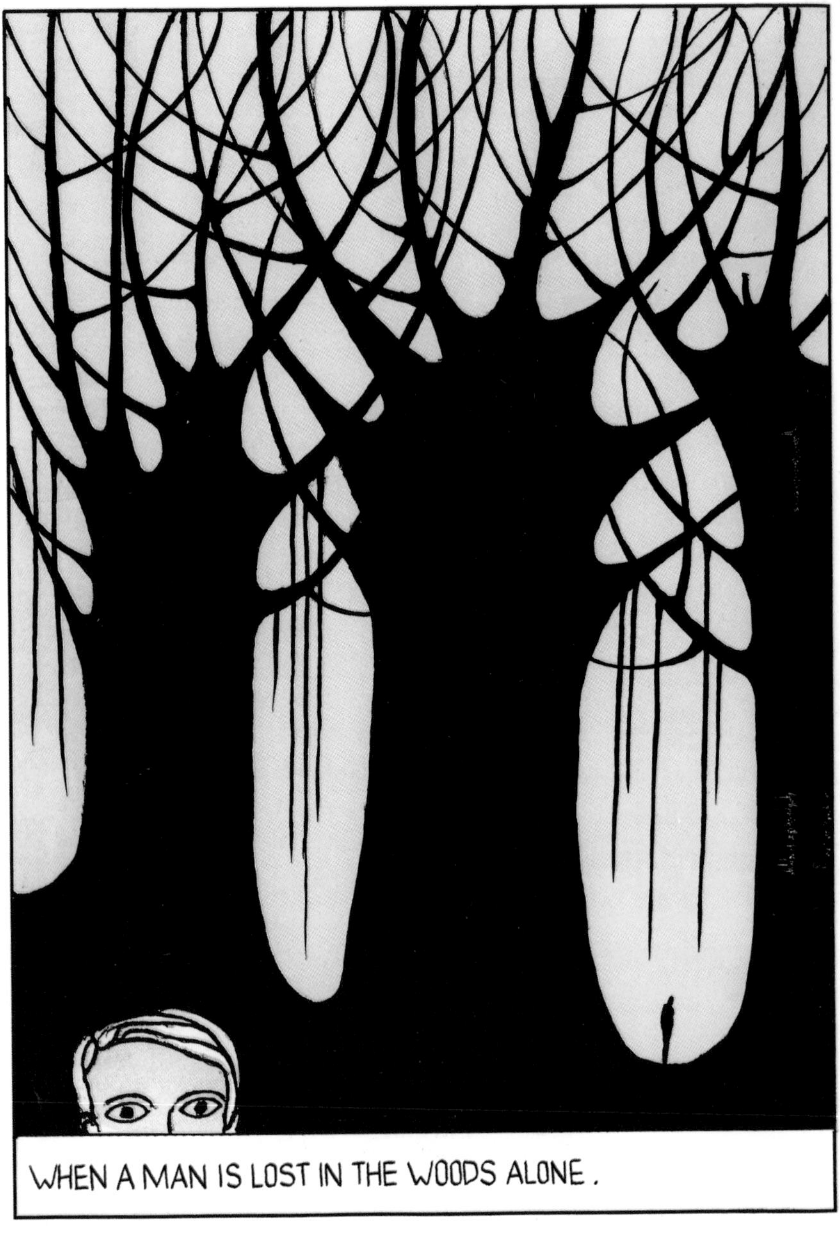
WHEN A MAN IS LOST IN THE WOODS ALONE.

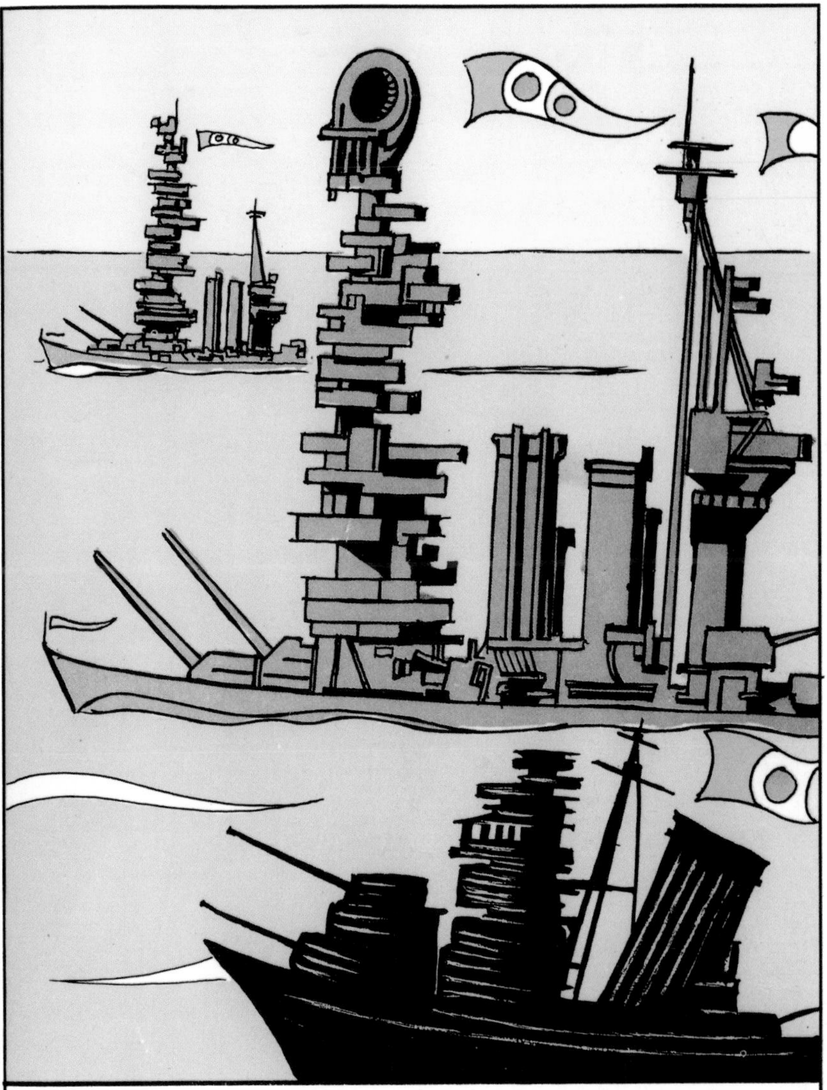

WHEN GREAT SHIPS SAIL FOR GLORY, BANNERS WAVING .

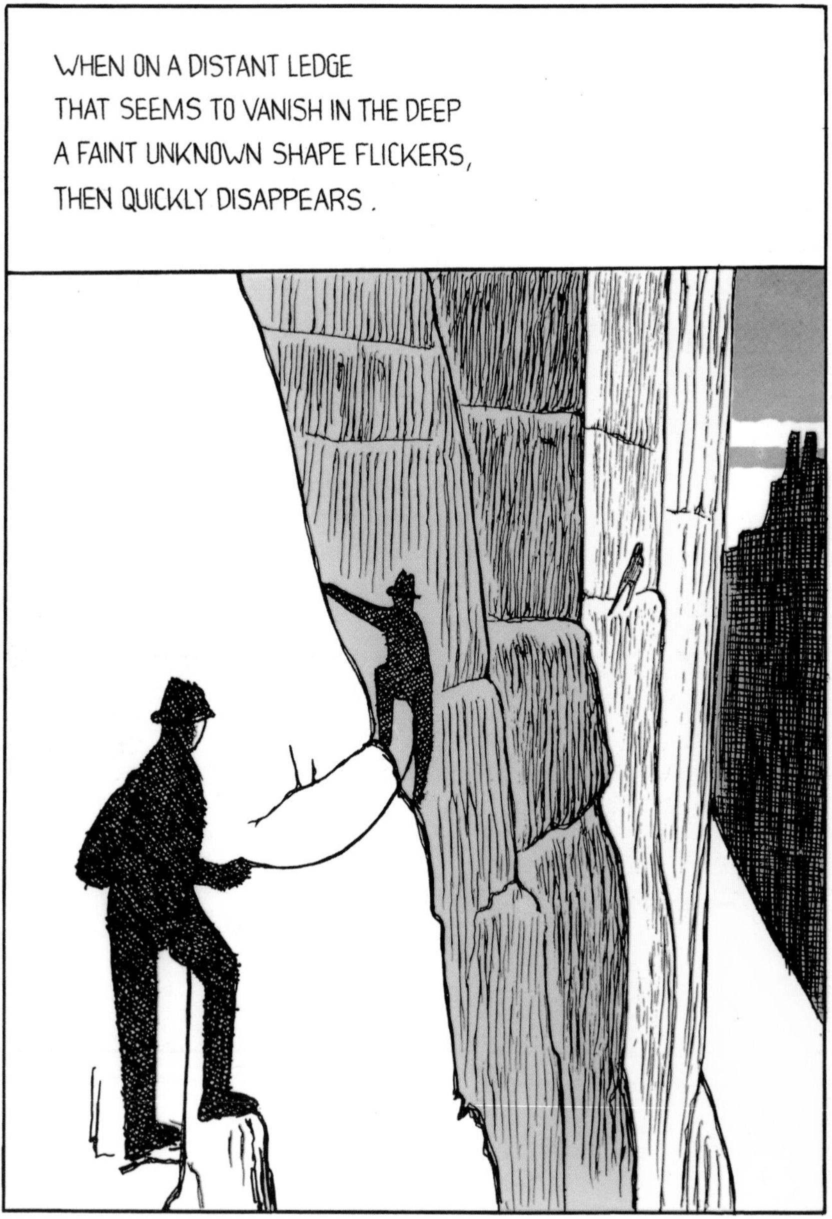
WHEN ON A DISTANT LEDGE
THAT SEEMS TO VANISH IN THE DEEP
A FAINT UNKNOWN SHAPE FLICKERS,
THEN QUICKLY DISAPPEARS .

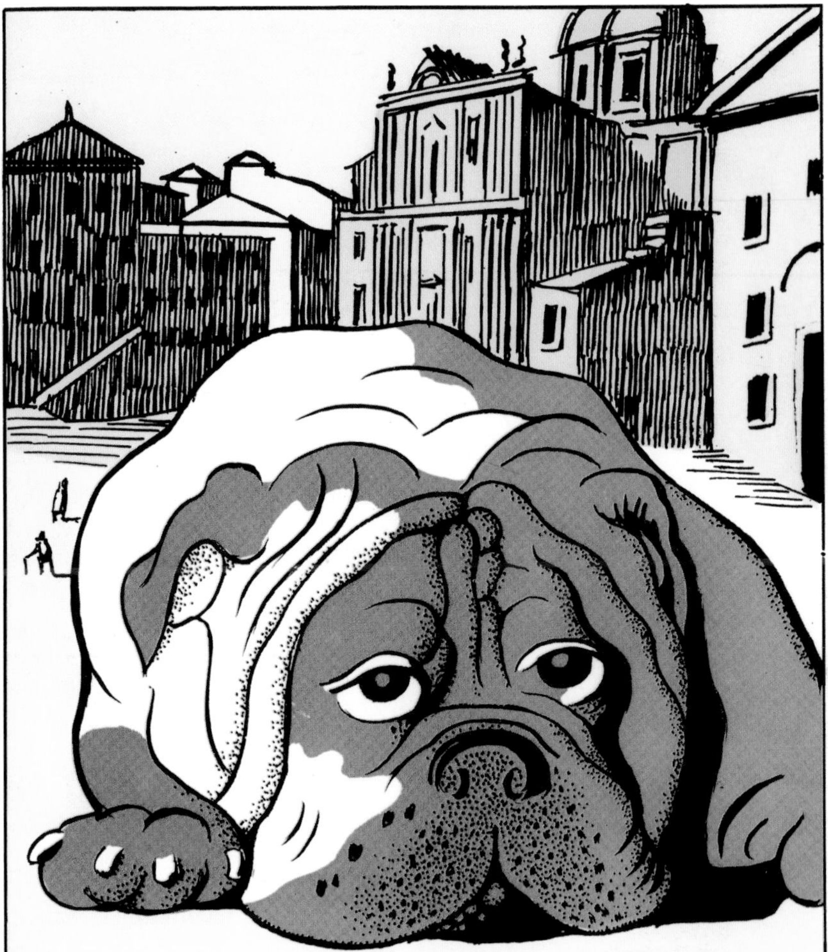

WHEN WE GET THE MESSAGE IN THE EYES
OF OUR SICK OLD DOG.

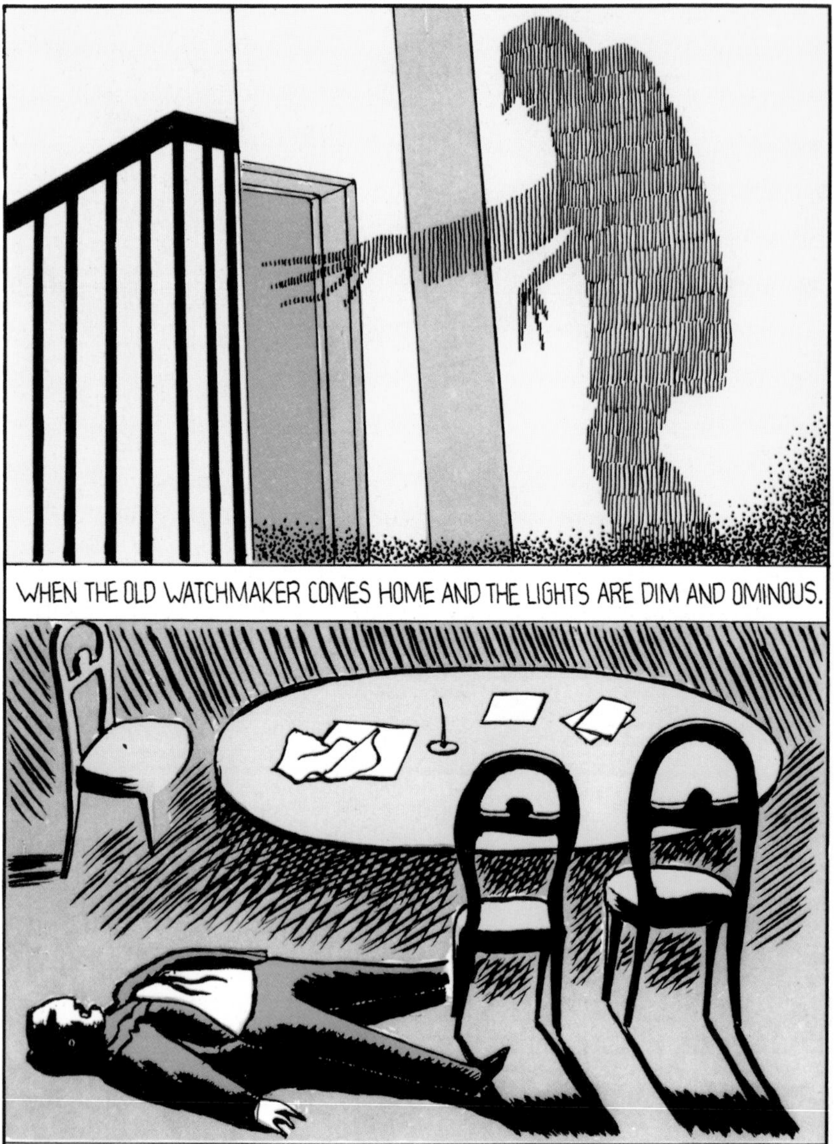
WHEN THE OLD WATCHMAKER COMES HOME AND THE LIGHTS ARE DIM AND OMINOUS.
WHEN THE COMBATIVE BOARD MEETING ENDS.

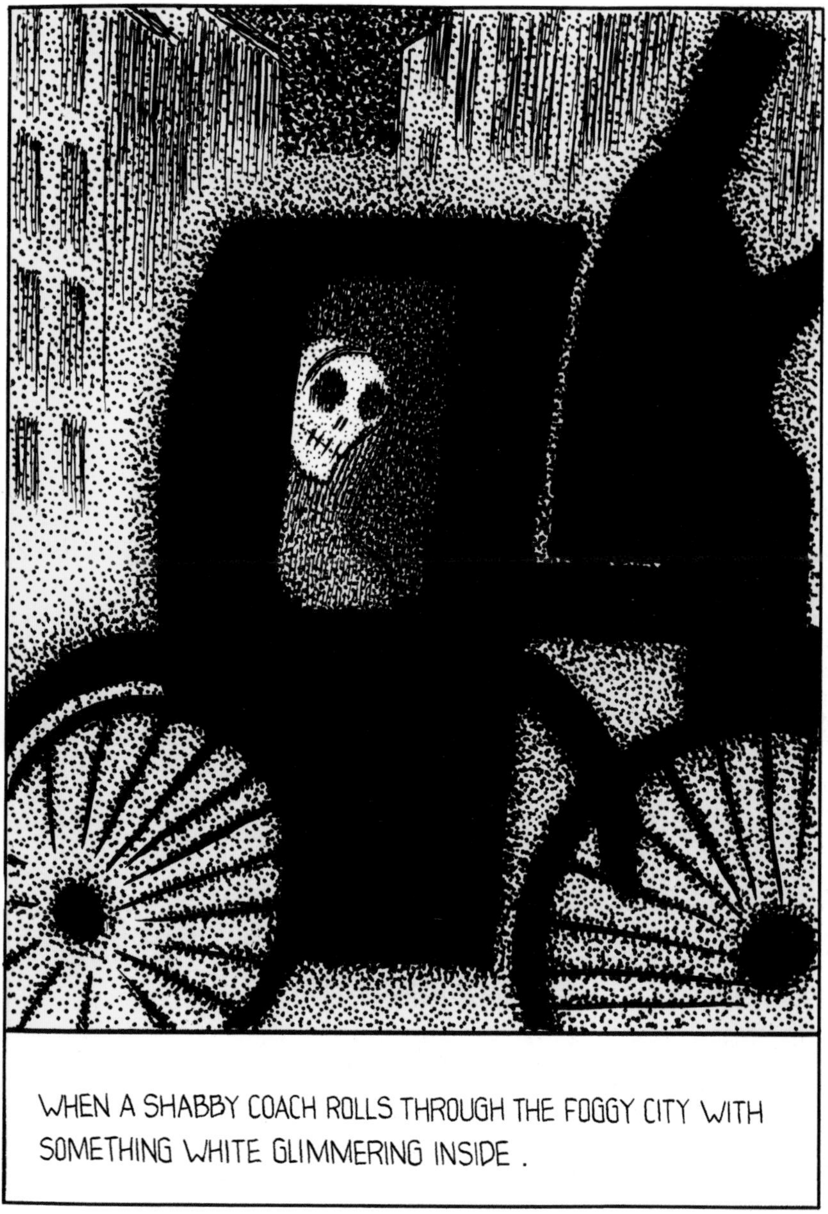

WHEN A SHABBY COACH ROLLS THROUGH THE FOGGY CITY WITH SOMETHING WHITE GLIMMERING INSIDE .

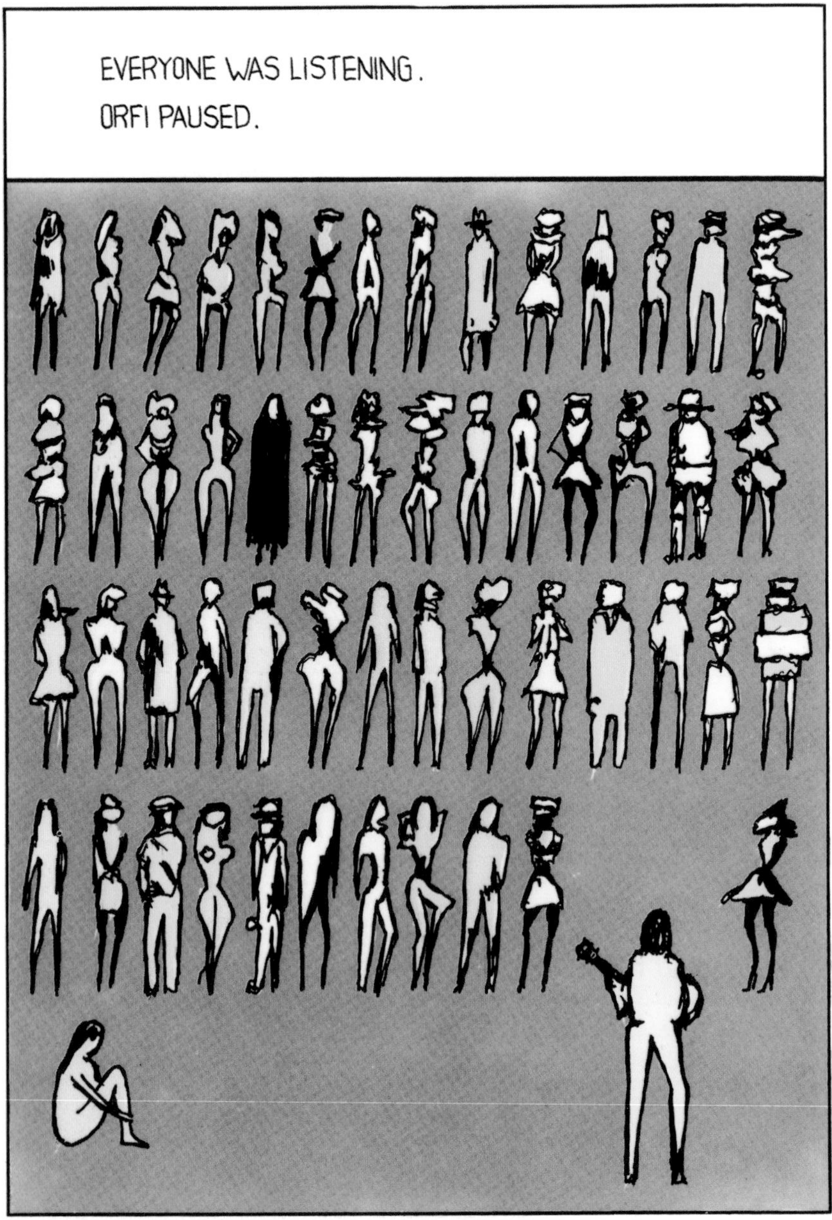
EVERYONE WAS LISTENING.
ORFI PAUSED.

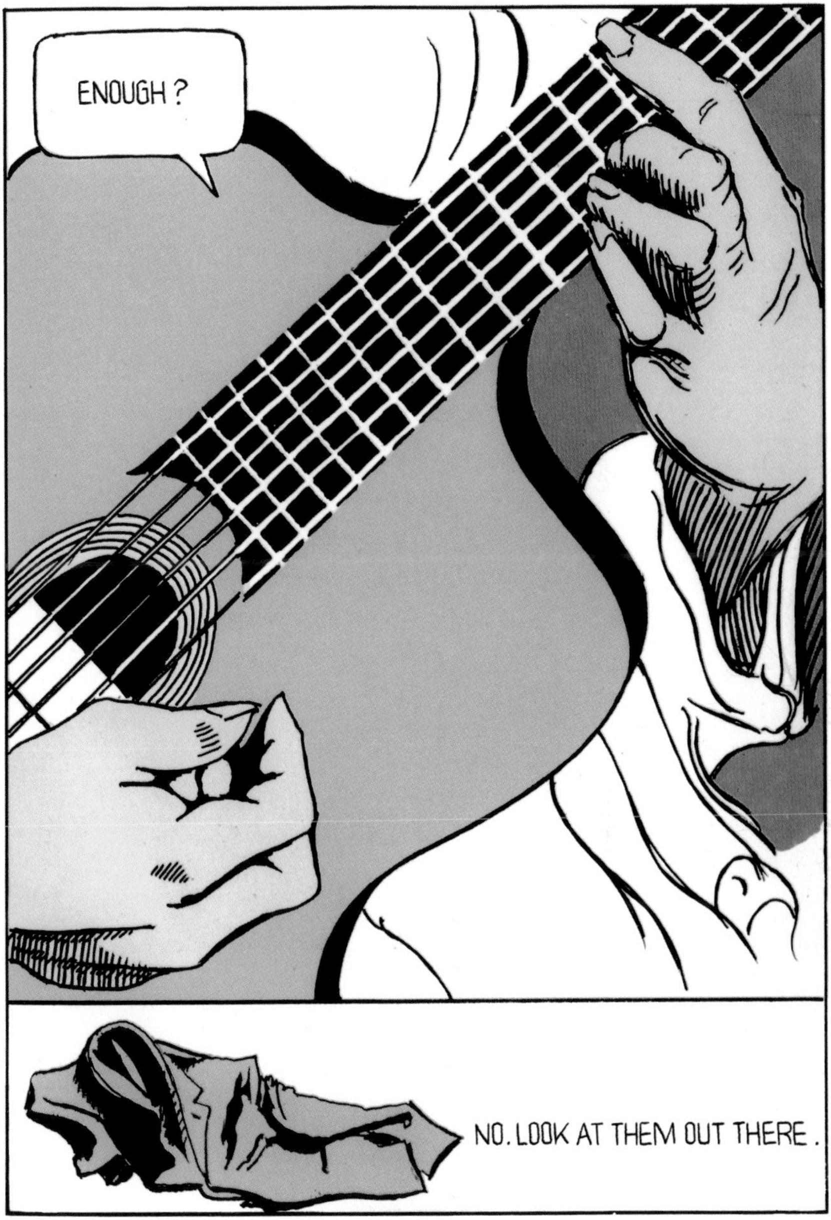
ENOUGH?
NO. LOOK AT THEM OUT THERE.

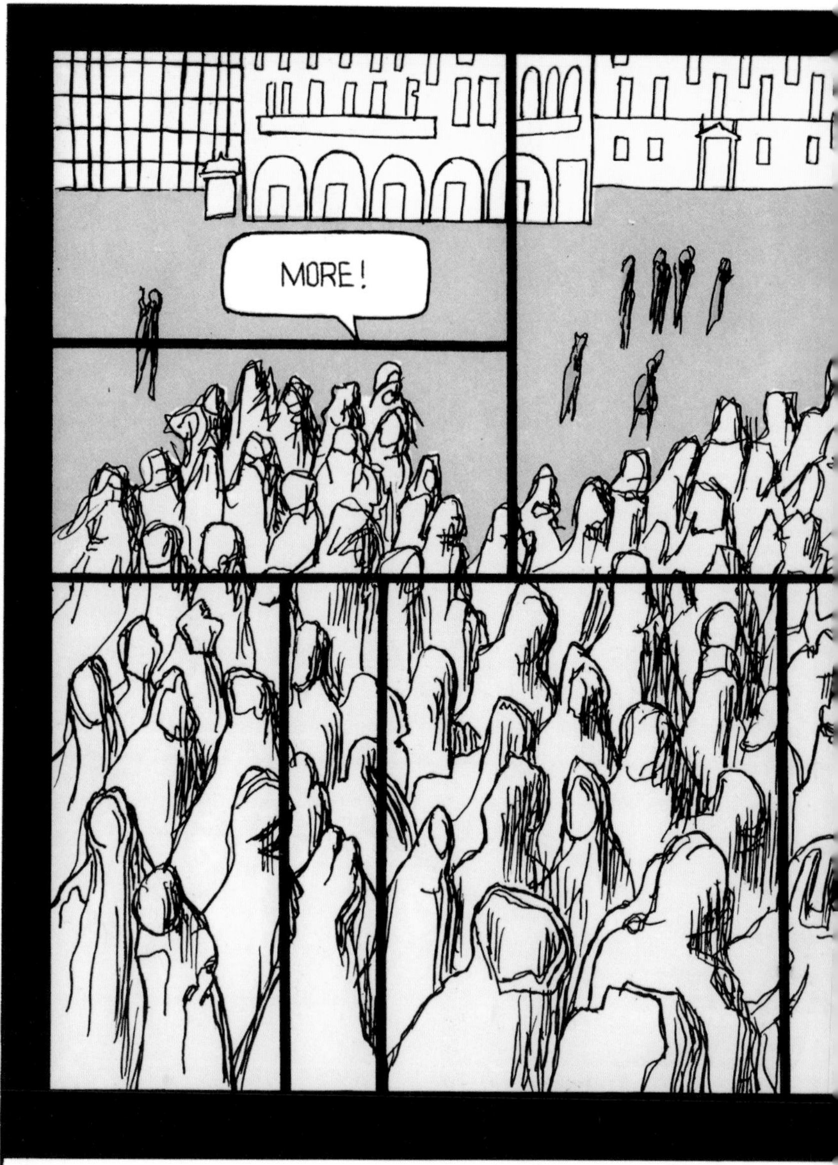
MORE!

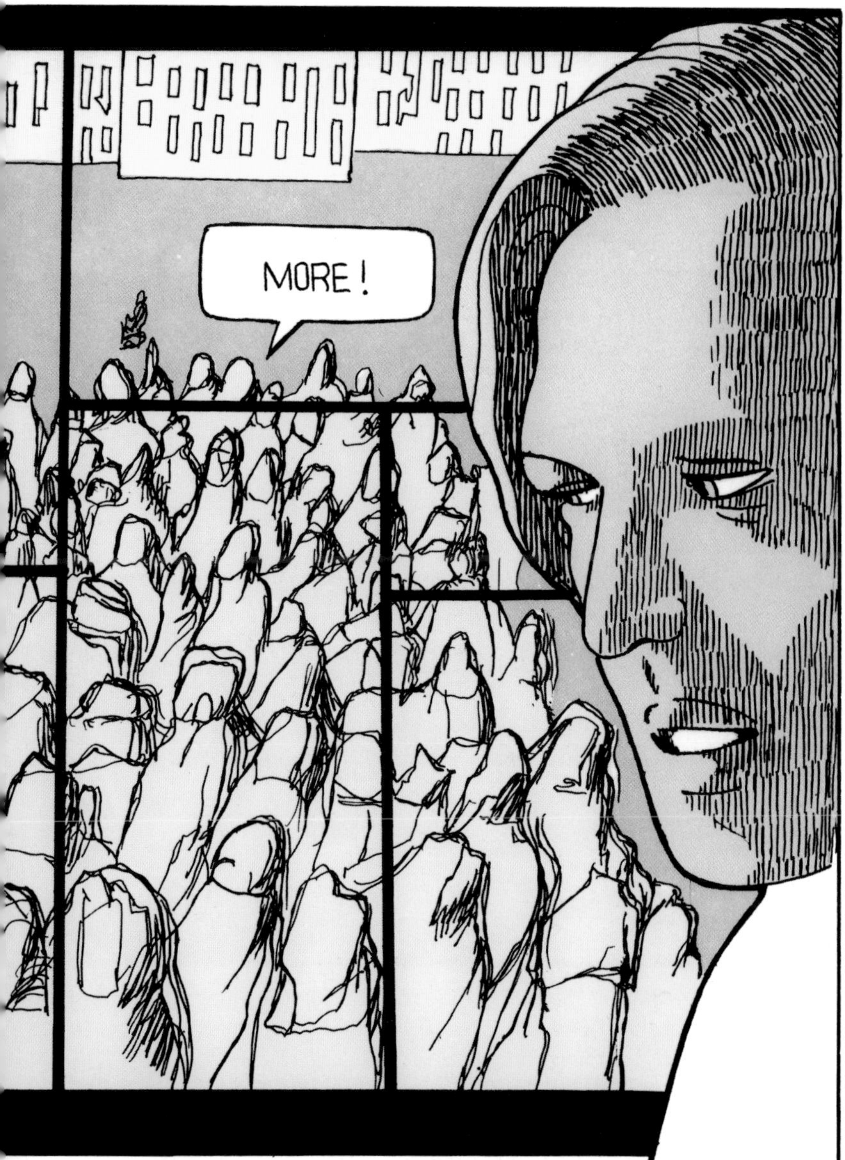
MORE!

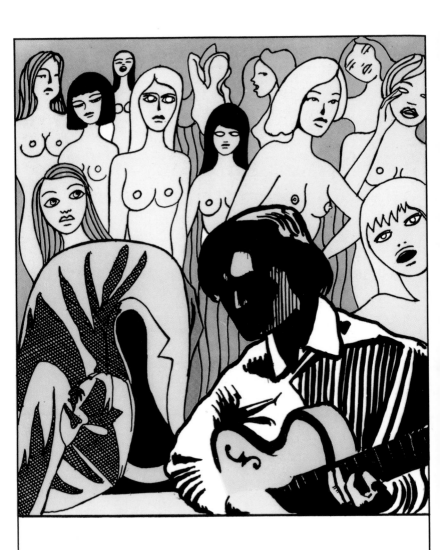

SO ORFI BEGAN AGAIN: I'LL SING AND I'LL TELL YOU SOME STORIES ABOUT

THE GREAT MYSTERY THAT DOES NOT EXIST HERE. LIKE WHEN

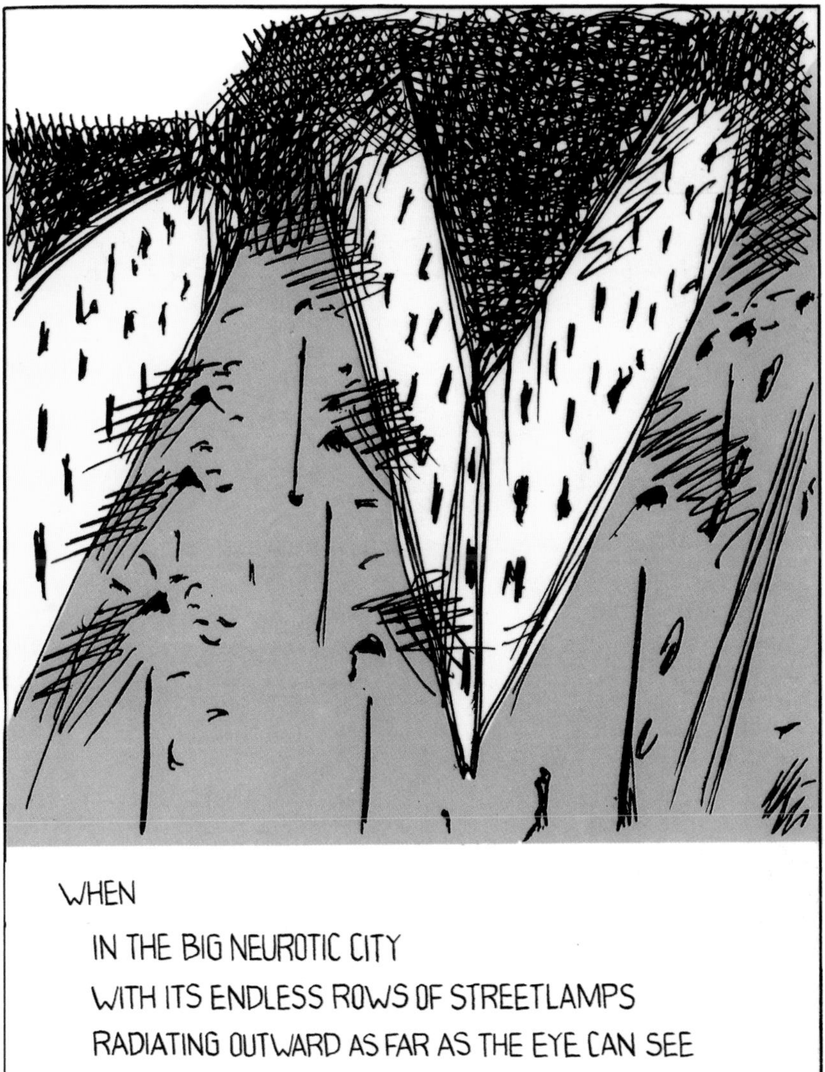
WHEN
IN THE BIG NEUROTIC CITY
WITH ITS ENDLESS ROWS OF STREETLAMPS
RADIATING OUTWARD AS FAR AS THE EYE CAN SEE
TOWARD ALL TWENTY-FOUR POINTS OF THE COMPASS
TOWARD THE COUNTRYSIDE AND POVERTY AND DARKNESS.

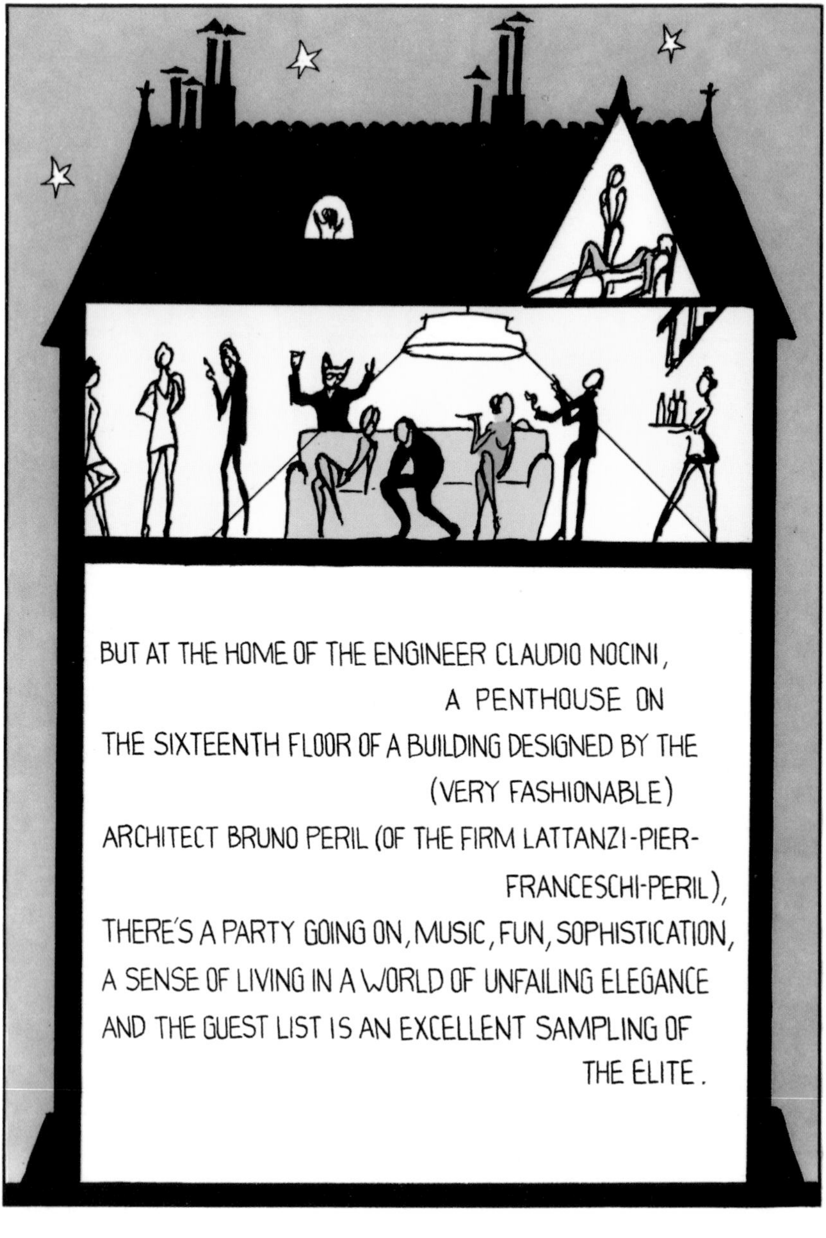
BUT AT THE HOME OF THE ENGINEER CLAUDIO NOCINI, A PENTHOUSE ON THE SIXTEENTH FLOOR OF A BUILDING DESIGNED BY THE (VERY FASHIONABLE) ARCHITECT BRUNO PERIL (OF THE FIRM LATTANZI-PIER-FRANCESCHI-PERIL), THERE'S A PARTY GOING ON, MUSIC, FUN, SOPHISTICATION, A SENSE OF LIVING IN A WORLD OF UNFAILING ELEGANCE AND THE GUEST LIST IS AN EXCELLENT SAMPLING OF THE ELITE.

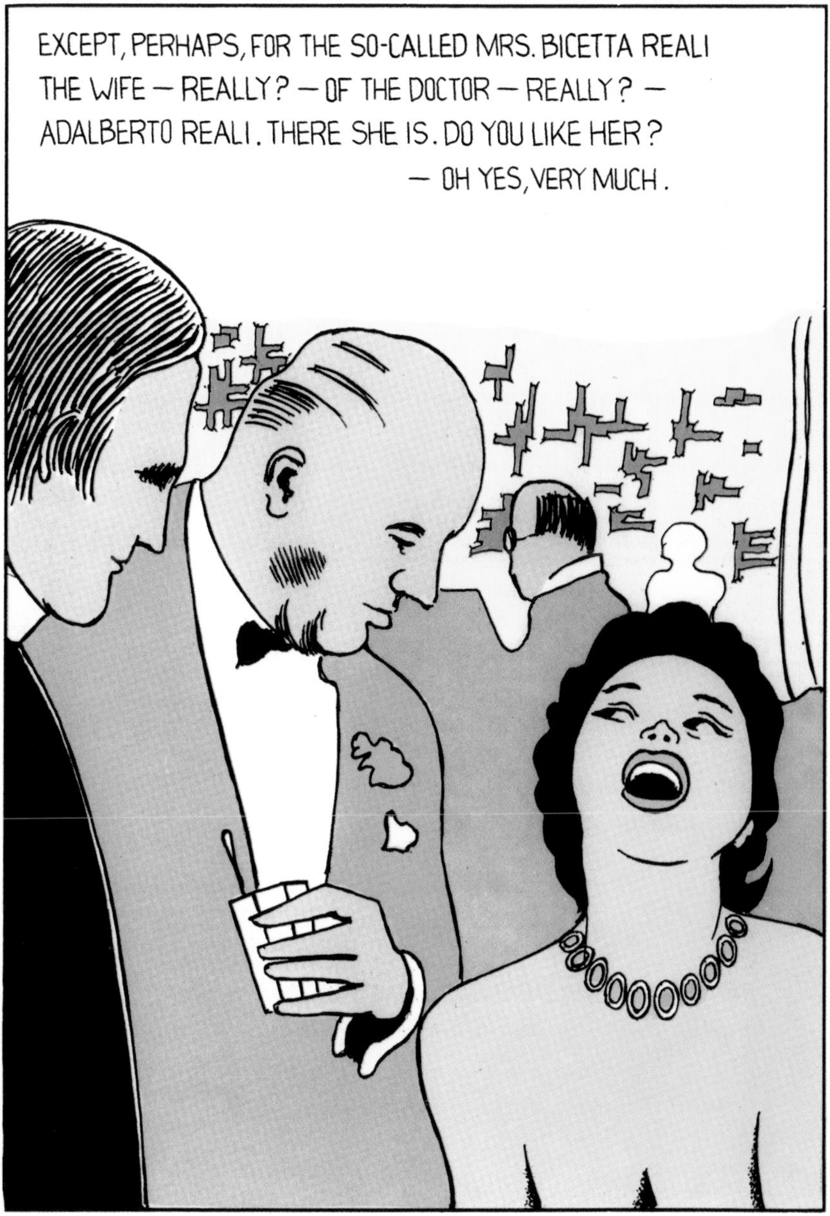
EXCEPT, PERHAPS, FOR THE SO-CALLED MRS. BICETTA REALI THE WIFE — REALLY? — OF THE DOCTOR — REALLY? — ADALBERTO REALI. THERE SHE IS. DO YOU LIKE HER?
— OH YES, VERY MUCH.

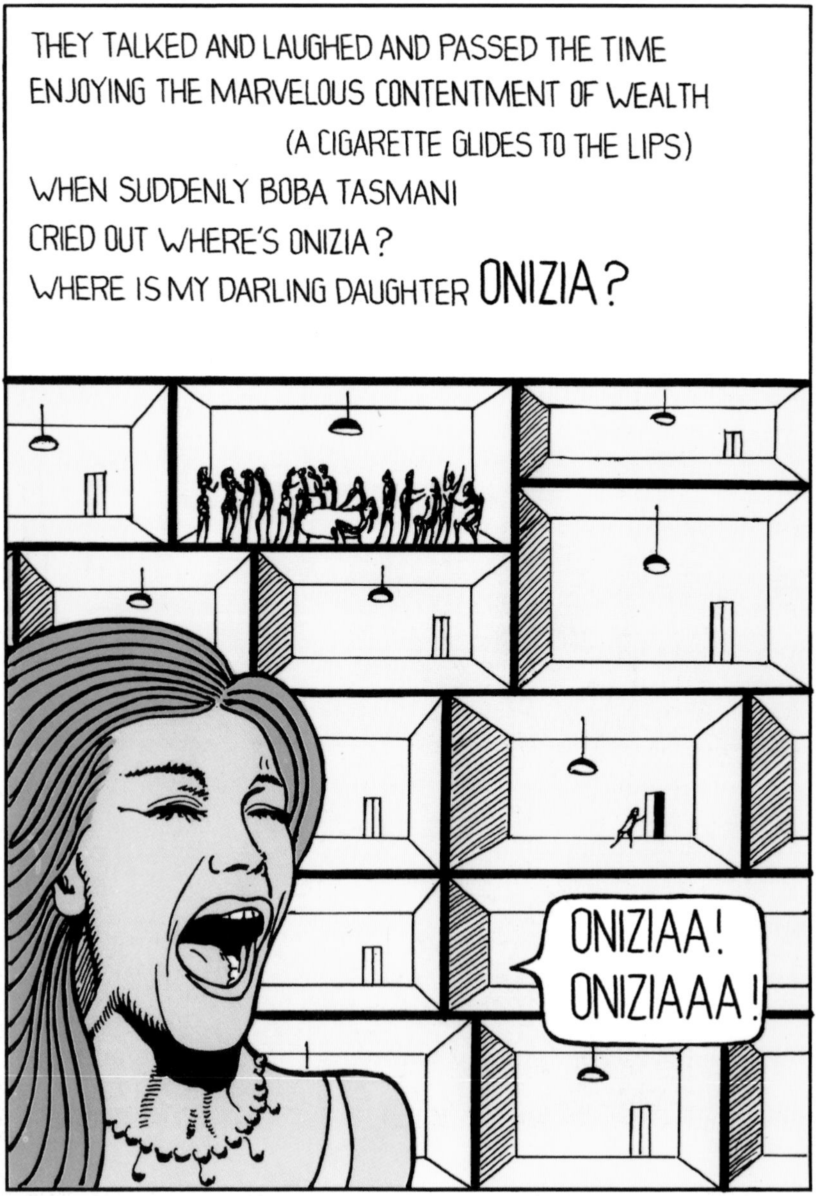
THEY TALKED AND LAUGHED AND PASSED THE TIME
ENJOYING THE MARVELOUS CONTENTMENT OF WEALTH
(A CIGARETTE GLIDES TO THE LIPS)
WHEN SUDDENLY BOBA TASMANI
CRIED OUT WHERE'S ONIZIA?
WHERE IS MY DARLING DAUGHTER ONIZIA?
ONIZIAA! ONIZIAAA!

SILENCE, A STRANGE SILENCE
        (THE COZY SOFA, EMPTY)
THEN THEY RAISE THE ALARM. THEY SEARCH, SEARCH.
UNTIL THEY FIND HER STANDING BY THE LAST MANSARD WINDOW
        (AN ELEGANT WINDOW)
PRESSED TO THE WINDOWPANE .
AND ON THE OTHER SIDE OF THE WINDOW THERE'S A FACE,
        A COUNTENANCE, A LITTLE MUG
IT DISAPPEARS IN THE FOG .

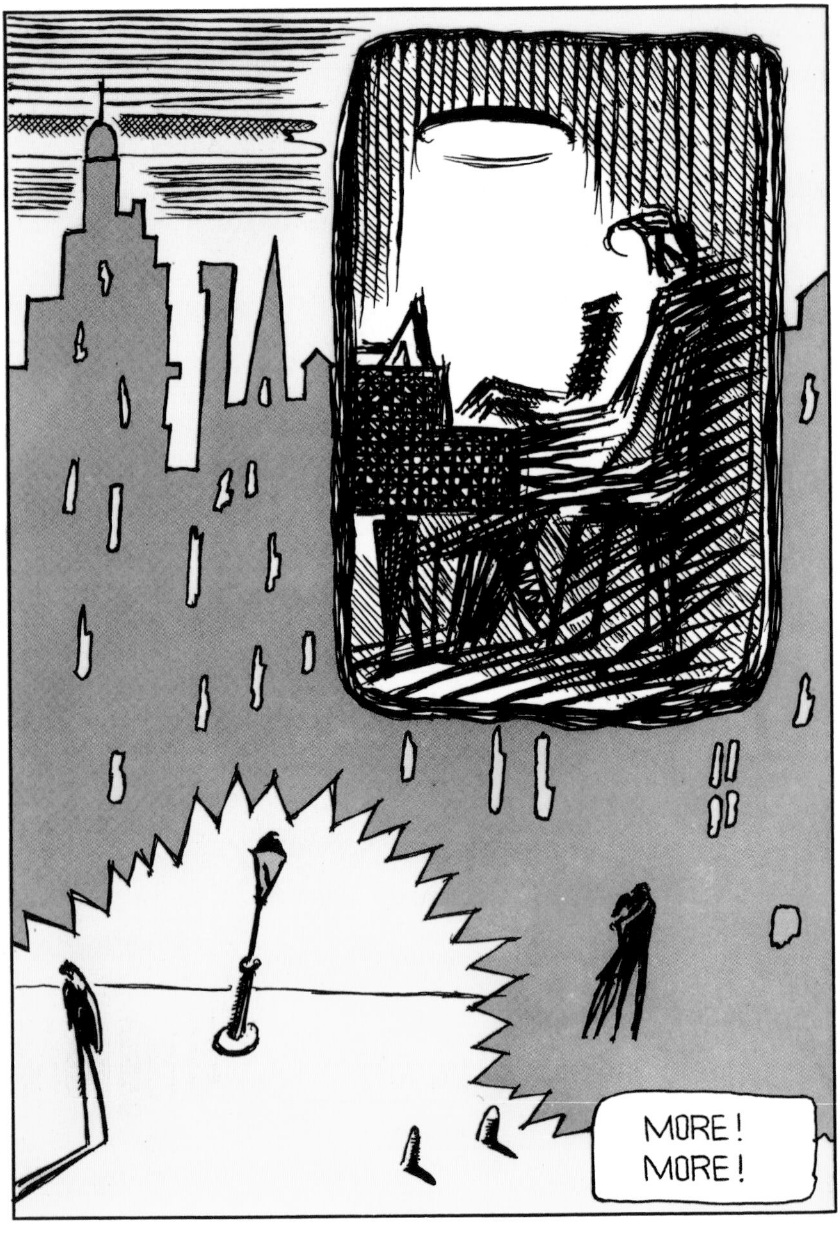
MORE! MORE!

DO YOU REMEMBER
                THE NIGHT
THE TWO OF THEM KISSED
AND YOU WERE ALONE? CHOPIN DESCENDED
FROM GOD'S GARRET
AND IT WAS A PERMANENT BLOW
SUDDENLY YOU WERE GROWN UP AND UNHAPPY

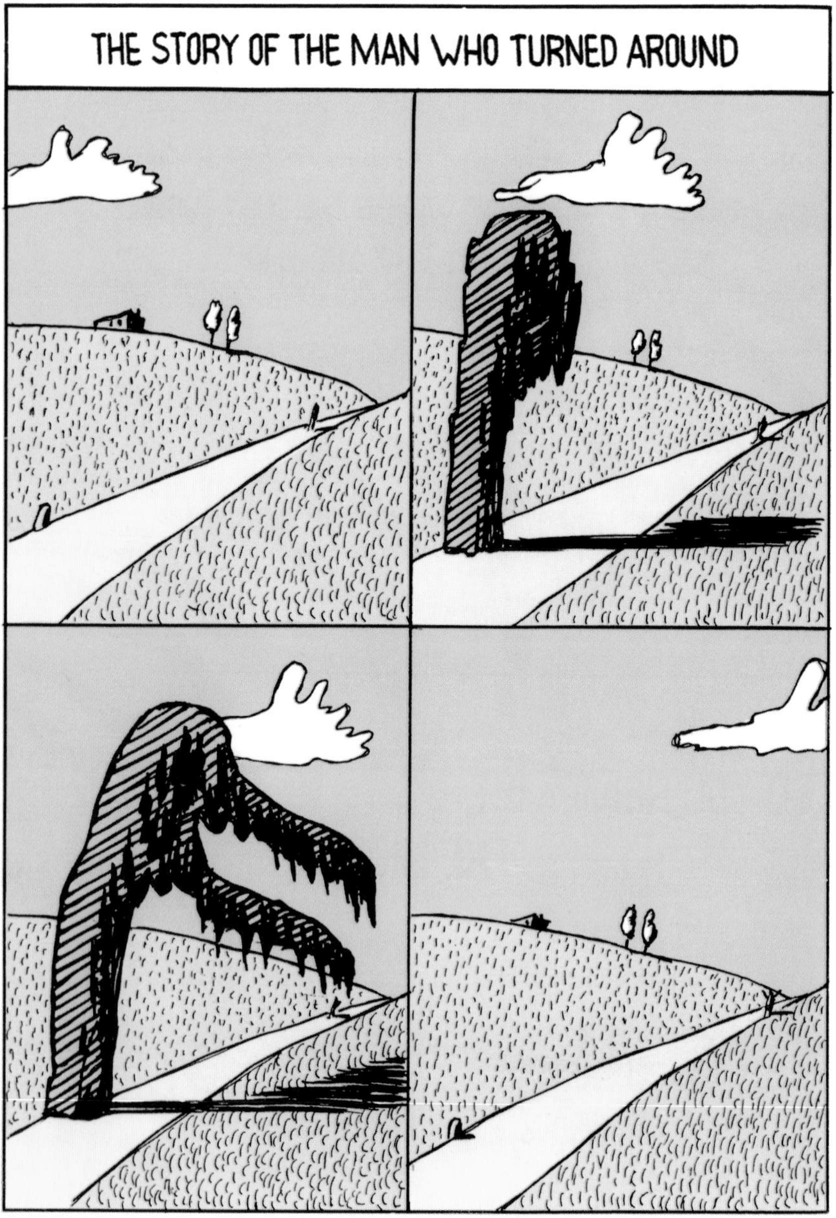
THE STORY OF THE MAN WHO TURNED AROUND

I WAS THE WAYFARER THE PILGRIM THE NOMAD OF
BYGONE HOURS

ON THE MOON-WHITE ROAD WHERE THE DUST TURNED
WHITE AS SNOW. SUDDENLY FROM BEHIND
AT THE SIDE OF THE ROAD THE THING ROSE UP
AND HELD OUT ITS TERRIFYING ARMS,
OH AND HOW MANY YEARS IT'S BEEN SINCE THEN.
I REMEMBER I TURNED AROUND STARTLED
BY SOMETHING SENSED AT THE CORNER OF MY EYE.
A LITTLE AFRAID, I TURNED AROUND. THERE WAS NOTHING
EXCEPT THE RESIGNED SLOW INTENSE PEACE
OF THE ANCIENT ROAD CLIMBING UP THE HILL.
AND BEYOND, WHERE DID IT GO?

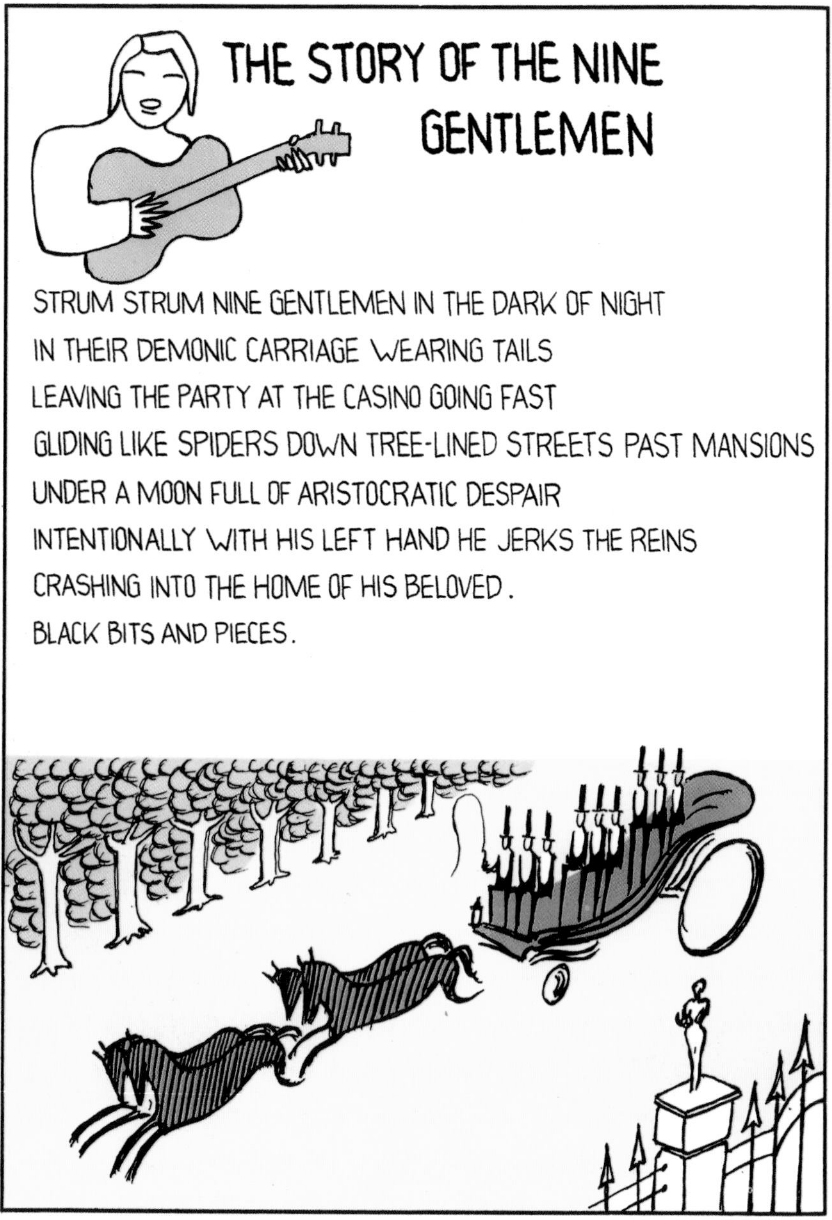
THE STORY OF THE NINE GENTLEMEN
STRUM STRUM NINE GENTLEMEN IN THE DARK OF NIGHT
IN THEIR DEMONIC CARRIAGE WEARING TAILS
LEAVING THE PARTY AT THE CASINO GOING FAST
GLIDING LIKE SPIDERS DOWN TREE-LINED STREETS PAST MANSIONS
UNDER A MOON FULL OF ARISTOCRATIC DESPAIR
INTENTIONALLY WITH HIS LEFT HAND HE JERKS THE REINS
CRASHING INTO THE HOME OF HIS BELOVED.
BLACK BITS AND PIECES.

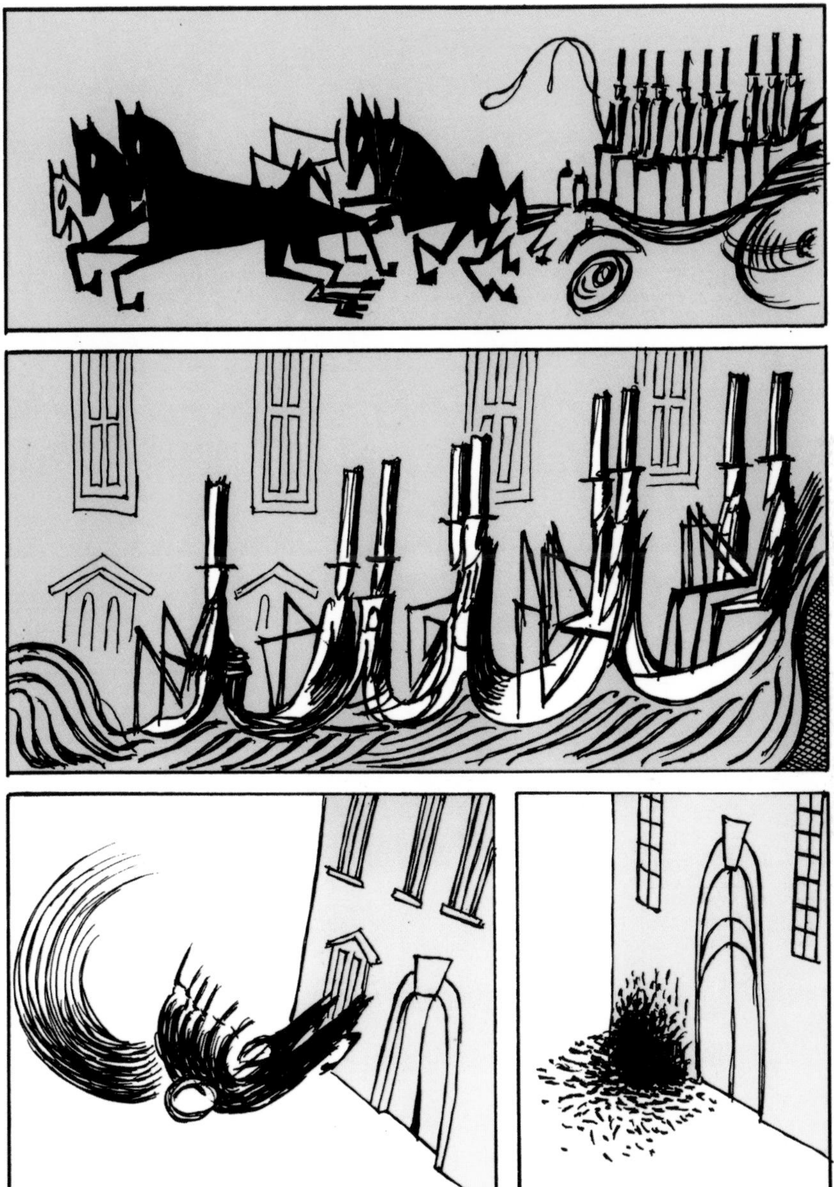

THE STORY OF THE LINE INSPECTOR

WHEN THE LIGHT STILL SHINES
IN THE WINDOWS OF THE LINE INSPECTOR'S HUT
NEAR THE OLD ABANDONED TRACK
ON A WINDY AUTUMN NIGHT,
HE WAITS. WHO WILL RIDE BY TONIGHT
ON THE PHANTOM EXPRESS
LIT BY A BLUE GLOW
FROM BEYOND THE GRAVE ?

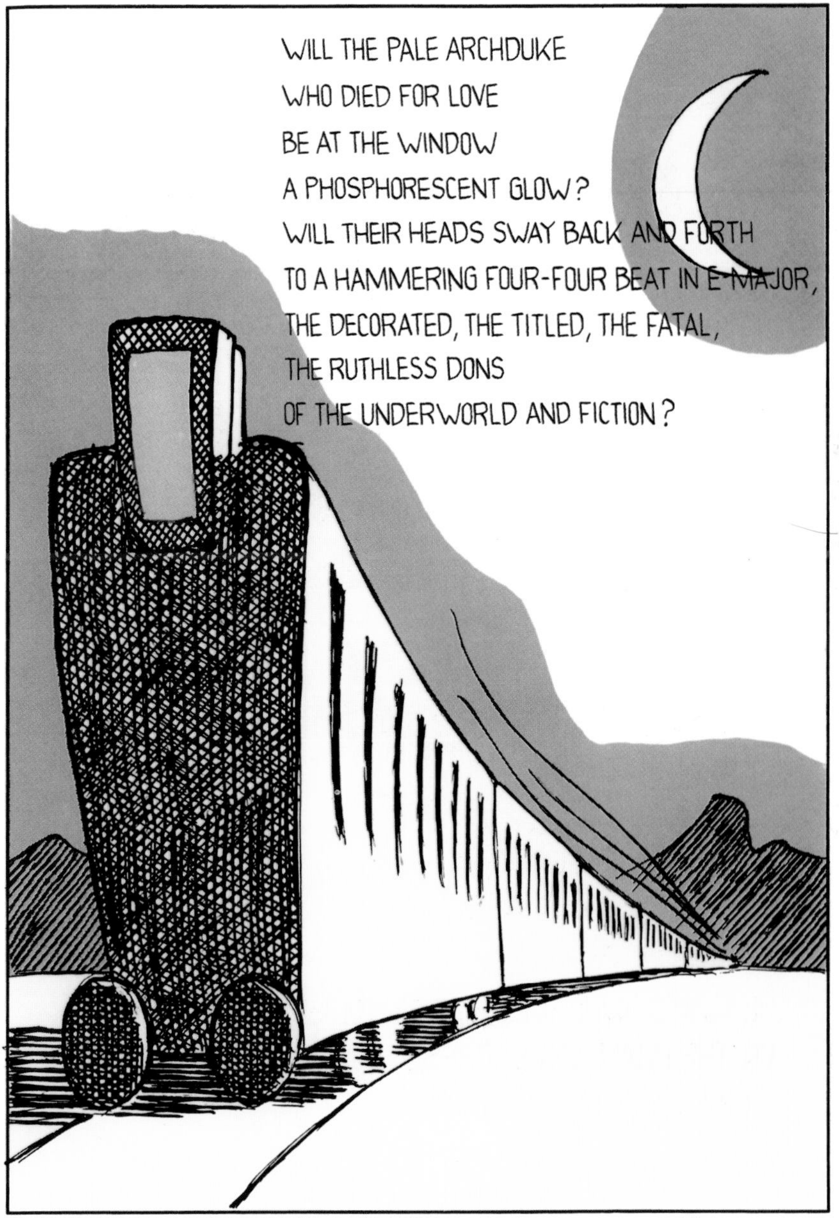
WILL THE PALE ARCHDUKE
WHO DIED FOR LOVE
BE AT THE WINDOW
A PHOSPHORESCENT GLOW?
WILL THEIR HEADS SWAY BACK AND FORTH
TO A HAMMERING FOUR-FOUR BEAT IN E-MAJOR,
THE DECORATED, THE TITLED, THE FATAL,
THE RUTHLESS DONS
OF THE UNDERWORLD AND FICTION?

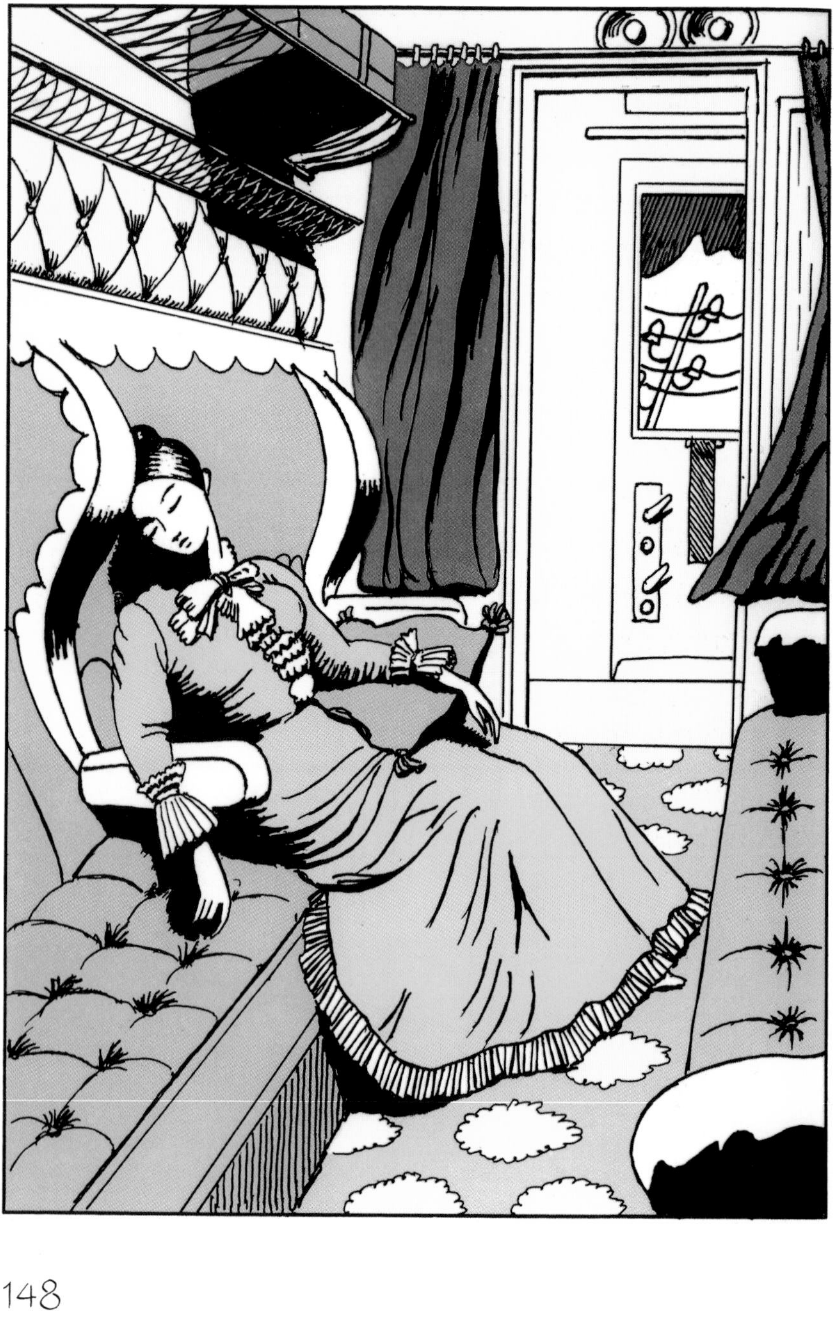

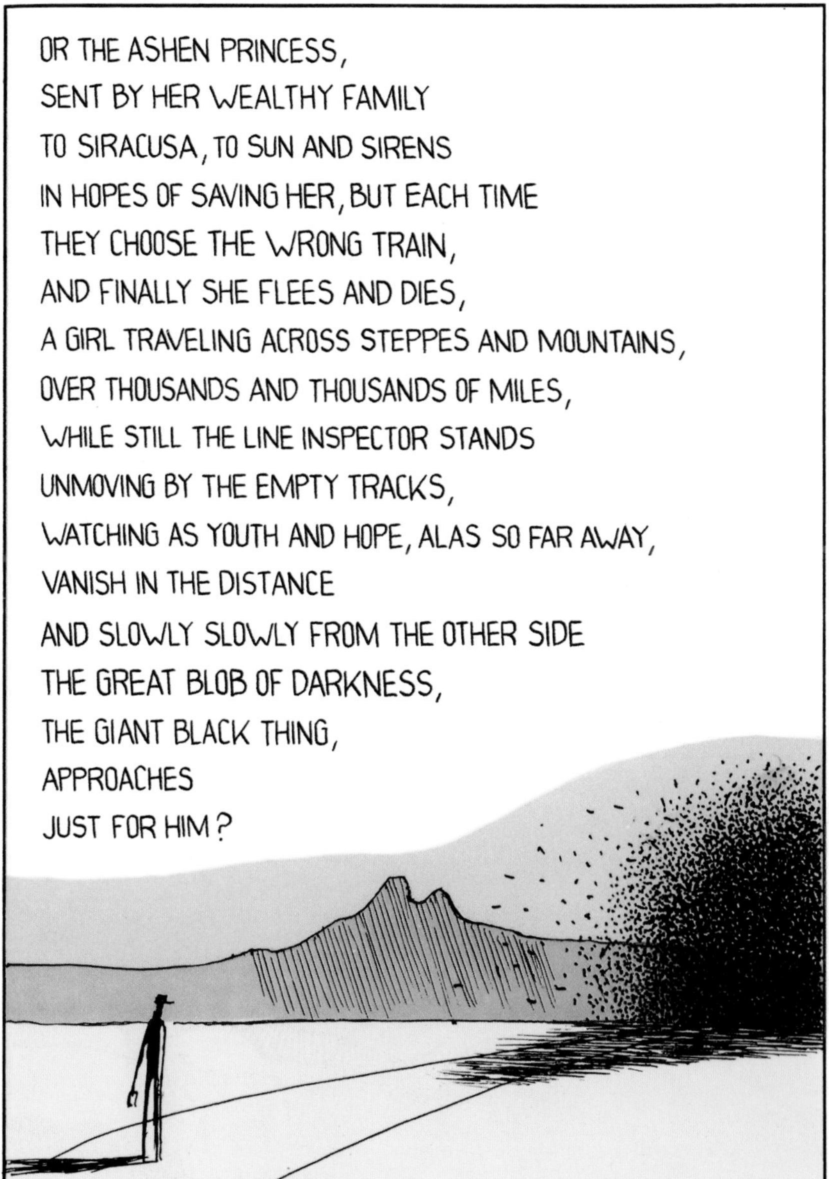
OR THE ASHEN PRINCESS,
SENT BY HER WEALTHY FAMILY
TO SIRACUSA, TO SUN AND SIRENS
IN HOPES OF SAVING HER, BUT EACH TIME
THEY CHOOSE THE WRONG TRAIN,
AND FINALLY SHE FLEES AND DIES,
A GIRL TRAVELING ACROSS STEPPES AND MOUNTAINS,
OVER THOUSANDS AND THOUSANDS OF MILES,
WHILE STILL THE LINE INSPECTOR STANDS
UNMOVING BY THE EMPTY TRACKS,
WATCHING AS YOUTH AND HOPE, ALAS SO FAR AWAY,
VANISH IN THE DISTANCE
AND SLOWLY SLOWLY FROM THE OTHER SIDE
THE GREAT BLOB OF DARKNESS,
THE GIANT BLACK THING,
APPROACHES
JUST FOR HIM?

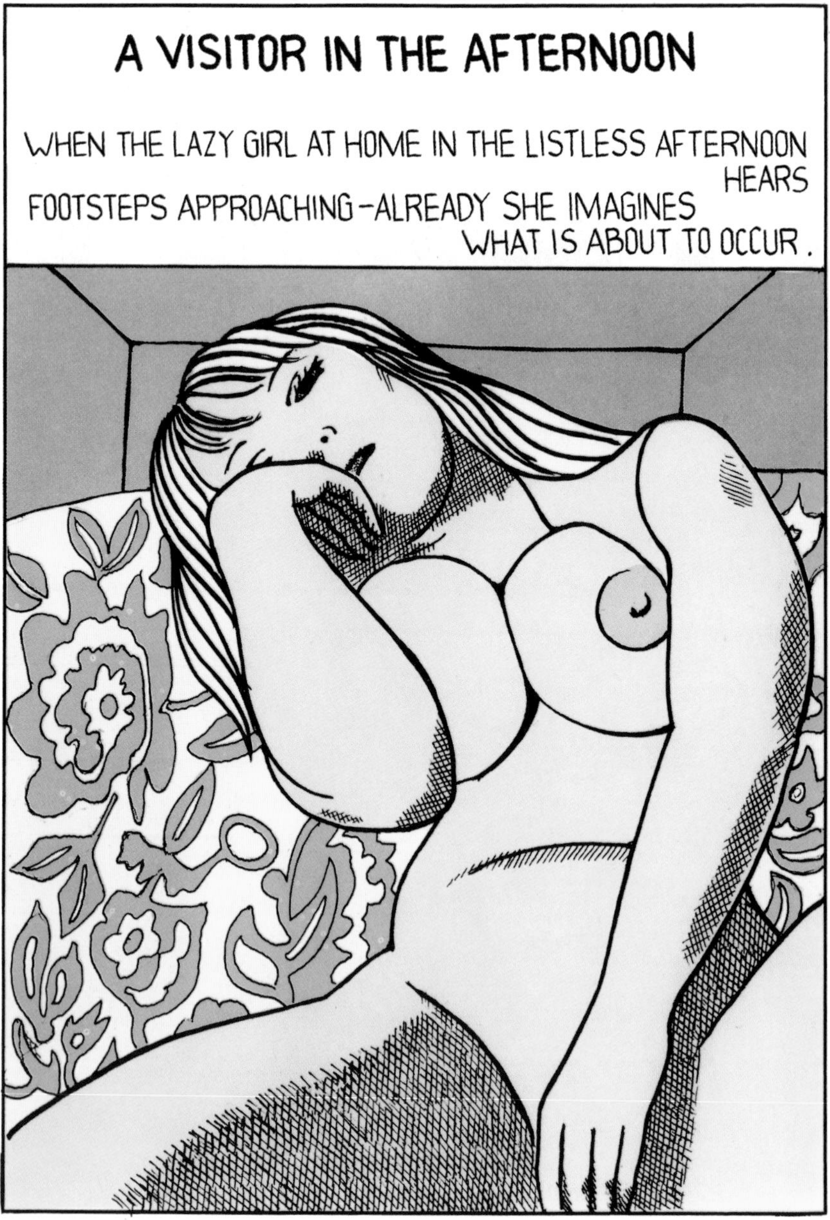
A VISITOR IN THE AFTERNOON
WHEN THE LAZY GIRL AT HOME IN THE LISTLESS AFTERNOON HEARS FOOTSTEPS APPROACHING – ALREADY SHE IMAGINES WHAT IS ABOUT TO OCCUR.

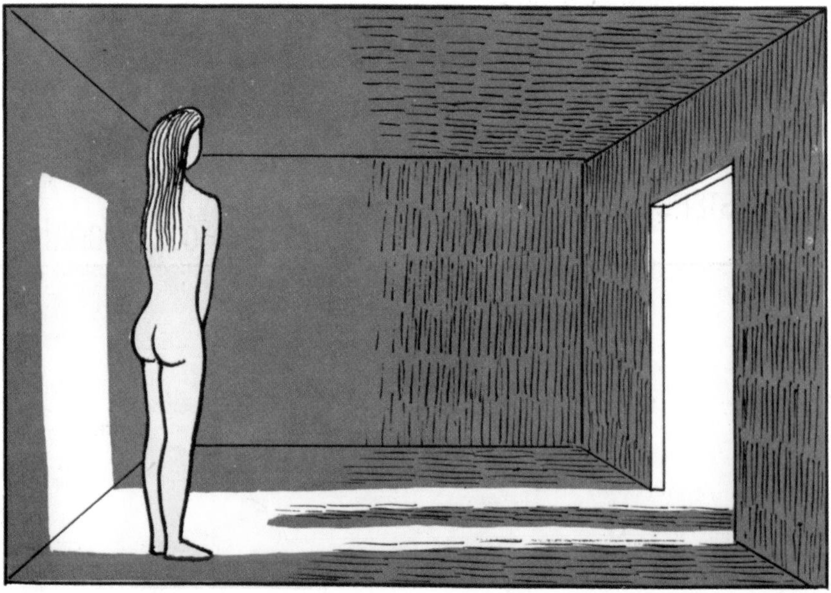

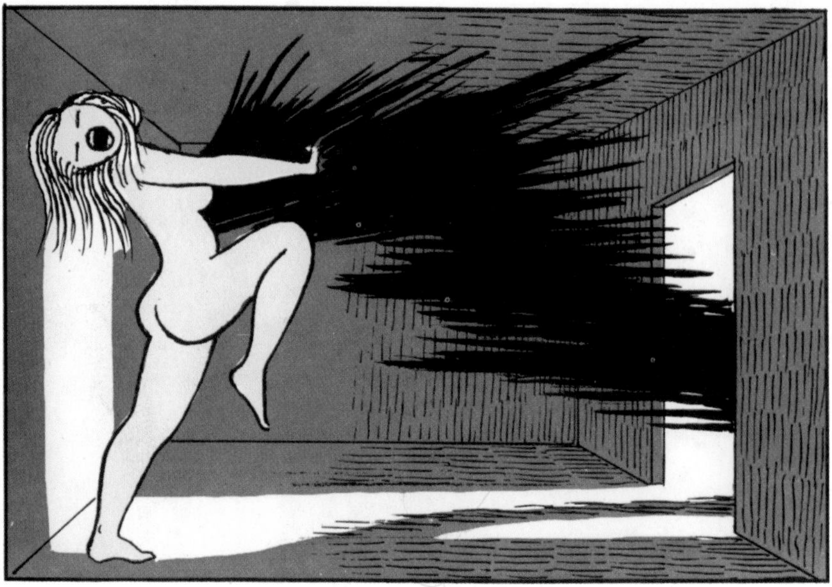

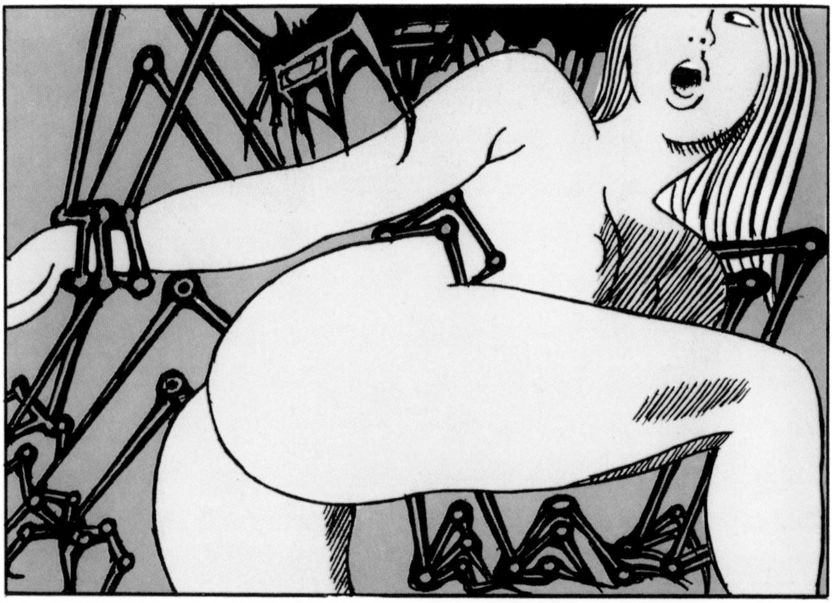

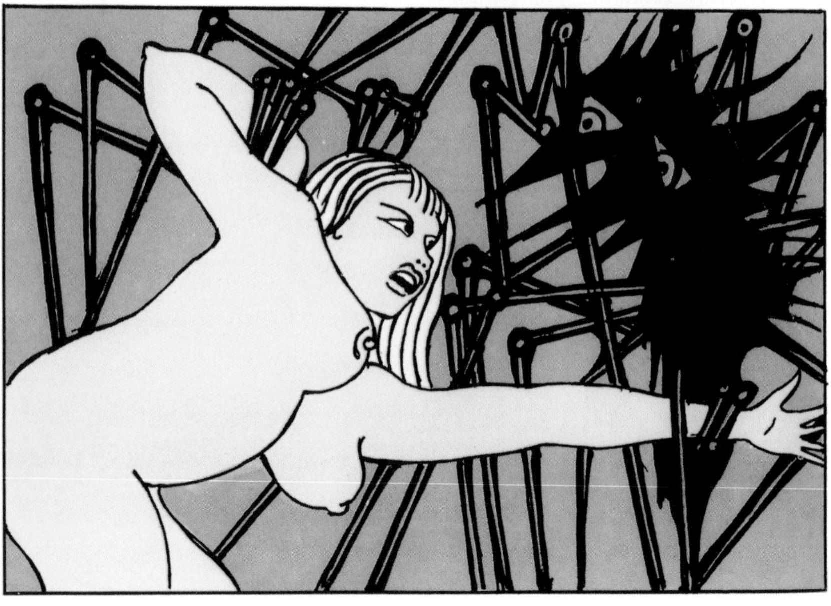

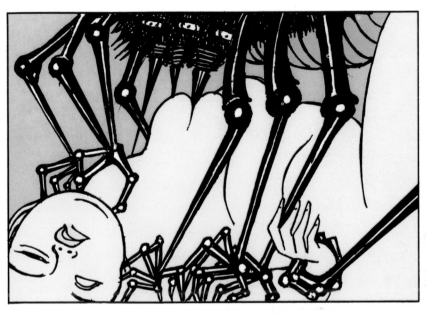

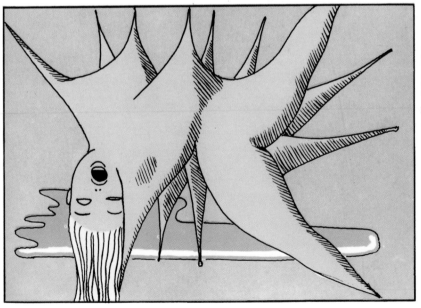

THE STORY OF THE NYMPHS

WHERE DO YOU THINK THEY COME FROM
THE NYMPHS OF THE FIELDS OF THE FORESTS OF THE VALLEY?
THE NYMPHS OF THE ANCIENT MOUNTAINS?
SWEET INTANGIBLE PLUMES LIKE FLYING SEED
THEY ESCORT POOR WEAK MEN
TO THE END OF THE LINE THE BORDER STATIONS
THEY MAY BE OPEN OR NOT, IT DEPENDS .

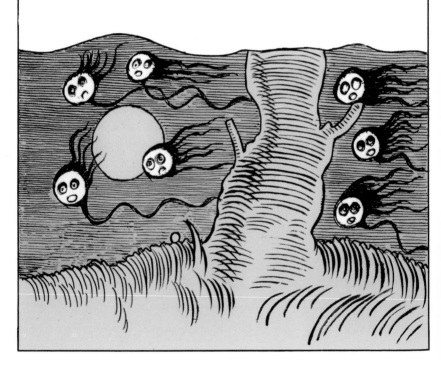

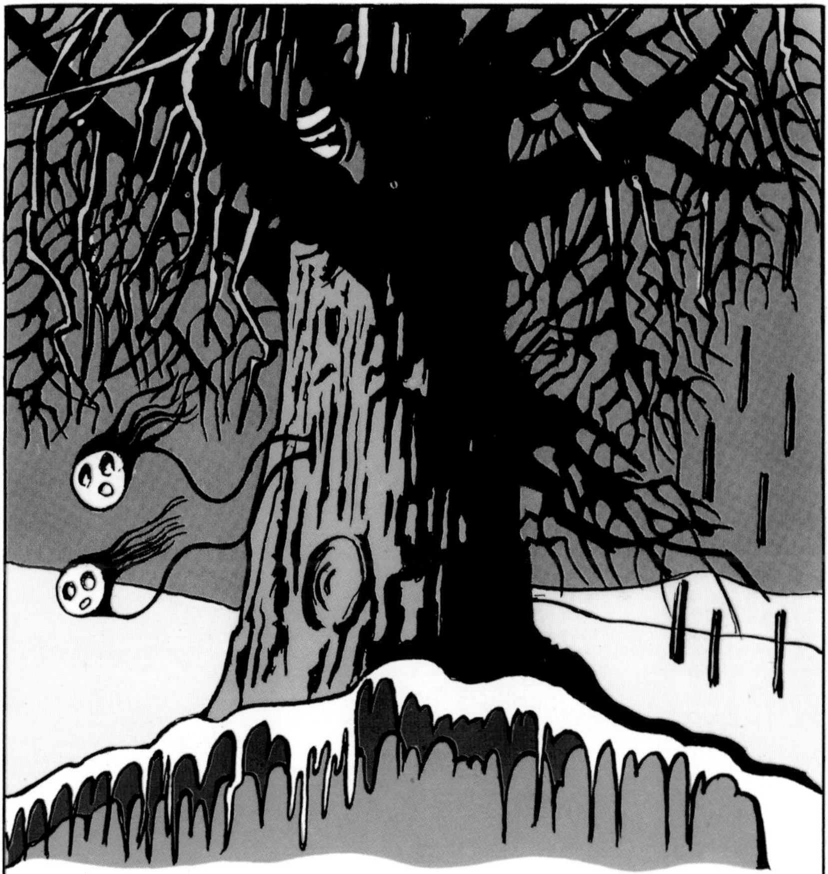

THEY RISE OUT OF TINY BLACK CRACKS
IN THE DRIED-OUT PREHISTORIC TREE TRUNK
EXPLORED BY COUNTLESS ANTS,
THE WELL-KNOWN, SKEPTICAL, WEARY, ROMANTIC TREE
LONGED-FOR REFUGE FROM OUR TROUBLES AND YOURS, REMEMBER?
ITS ROOTS HANG DOWN OVER HELL.

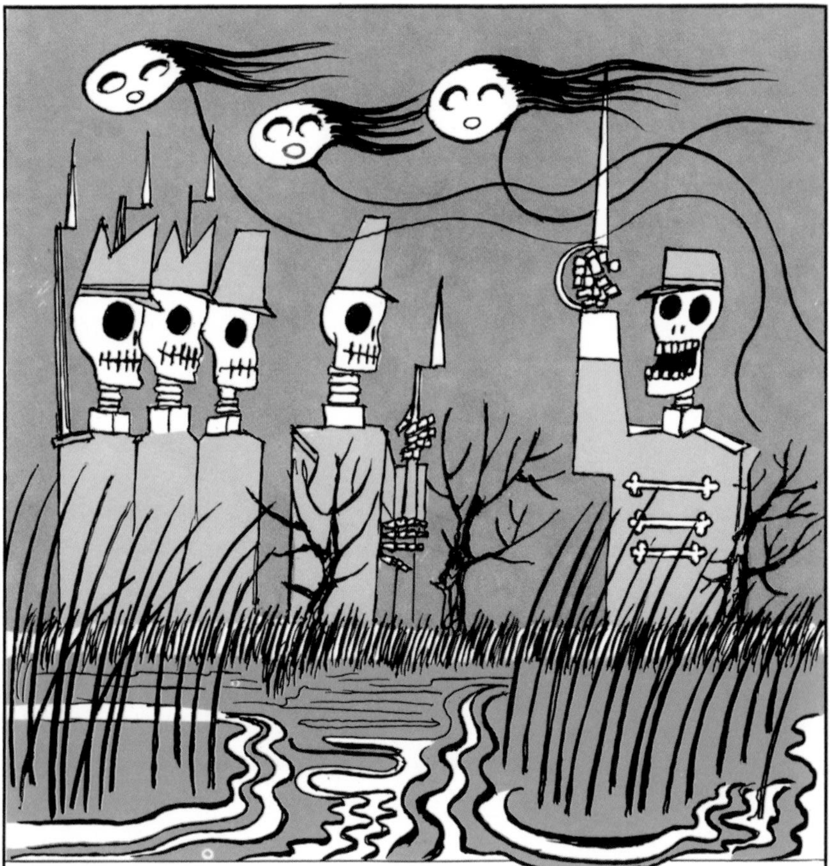

TERRIFYING INSECTS FROM THE BOG OF HISTORY
FILLED TO THE BRIM WITH HISTORIC SUICIDES,
WITH HISTORIC BATTLES LOST.
WHAT FINE HANDSOME BOYS STAND TO ATTENTION
ON THE MURKY SHORES. ONWARD, ONWARD, HURRY,
LONG IS THE ROAD HOME.

OR IF NIGHT FALLS OVER THE COUNTRYSIDE,

AND THE BEECHES HORNBEAMS OAKS

ANCIENT TIRED TWISTED TREES

HUDDLE TOGETHER DARKLY IN CLUMPS AND CLUSTERS

AND THE FIELDS ARE TOO BARE,

THEN THE NYMPHS RISE UP FROM THE ROOTS AND HOLLOWS.

SUDDENLY LITTLE ANDREINA REMEMBERS

SHE LEFT HER RAG DOLL

OUTSIDE ON THE LOW WALL.

SHE RUNS OUT, TAKING THEM BY SURPRISE.

ANDREINA, ANDREINA, WILL YOU REMEMBER WHAT YOU SAW?

AND NOW THE STORY THAT HURTS THE MOST, OF LOVE —
WHICH IS DENIED YOU. THE DIVINE ABANDON,
THE DARKNESS AT ITS CORE.

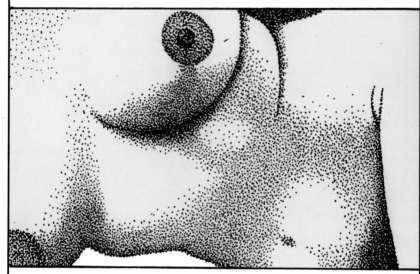

HALF ASLEEP WITH HER LYING CLOSE BY
SHE BECAME AN UNKNOWN LANDSCAPE,
TENDER, CARNAL, PROFOUND, PERISHABLE,
A FLOWER.
IN HER FLOWERLIKE BEING ALREADY A FAREWELL.
LOVE, I'M TELLING YOU, THE SECRET TYRANT OF THE WORLD ABOVE
WILL YOU LISTEN
ONE MORE TIME?

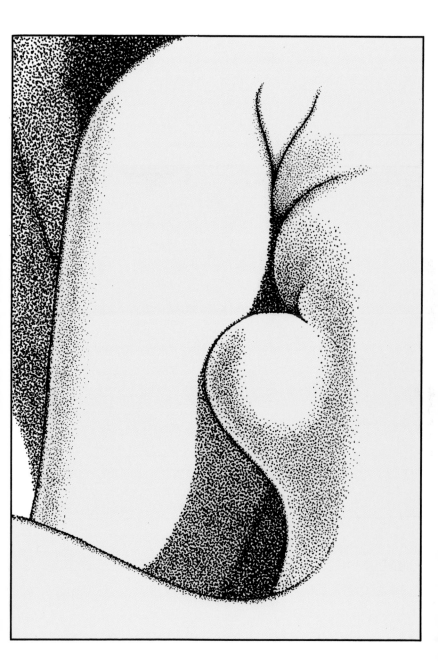

DO YOU REMEMBER, FRIENDS?
THE ULTIMATE BLISS
BUT NEVER JOYFUL, NEVER.
FOR IT WOULD BE NOTHING
WITHOUT THE KNOWLEDGE DEEP DOWN
THAT ONE DAY ALL THIS WOULD END.
YES, NATURE URGED US ON,
ENCOURAGING EVEN THE MOST TWISTED VICE
TO PROPAGATE THE SPECIES, REMINDING US
OF OUR COMMON DESTINY.
THAT FLESH IS PARADISE BUT ONLY
SO THAT EACH WILL LEAVE ANOTHER IN HIS PLACE
AND SO AFTER THIS DIVINE UNION
HE SAW ALL AROUND HIM AN ENDLESS MARSH
BENEATH A STEADY RAIN, AND NOT A SOUL
EXCEPT TWO LEPERS IN THE DISTANCE.
AND THE CURSED BELLS RANG OUT.

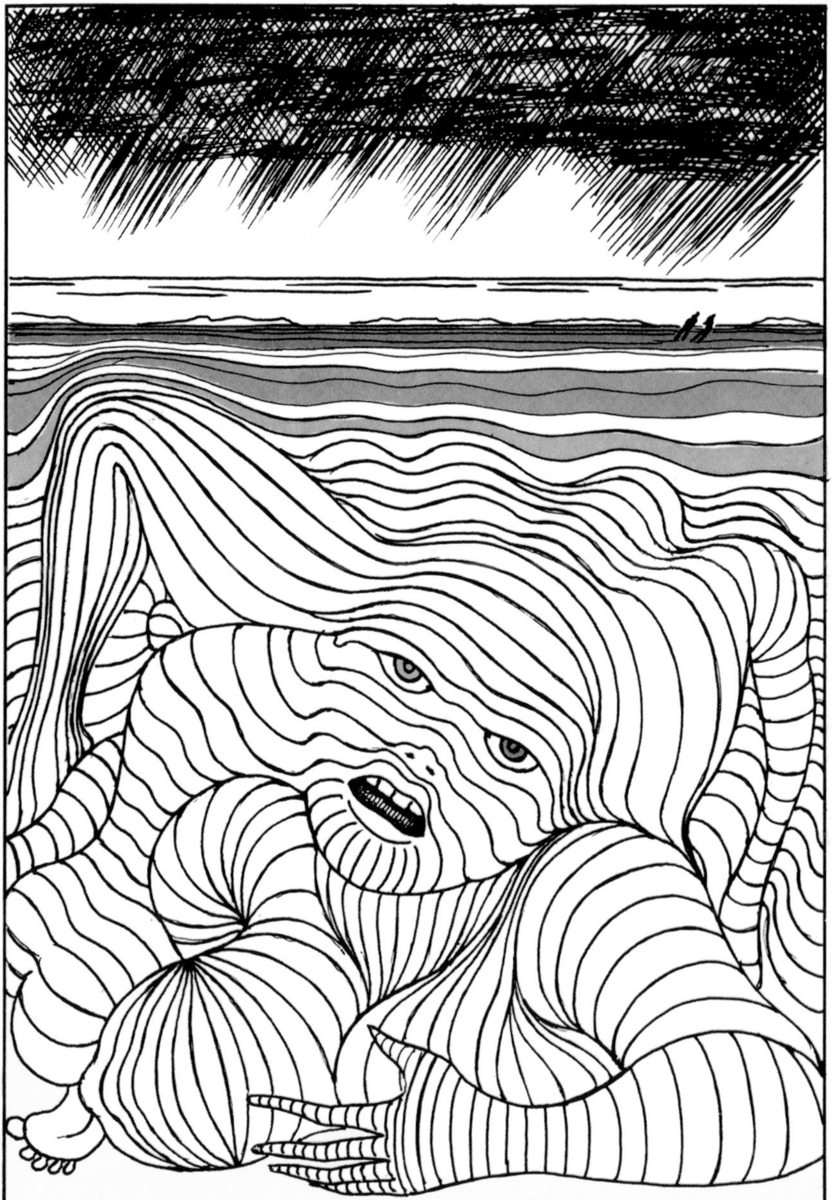

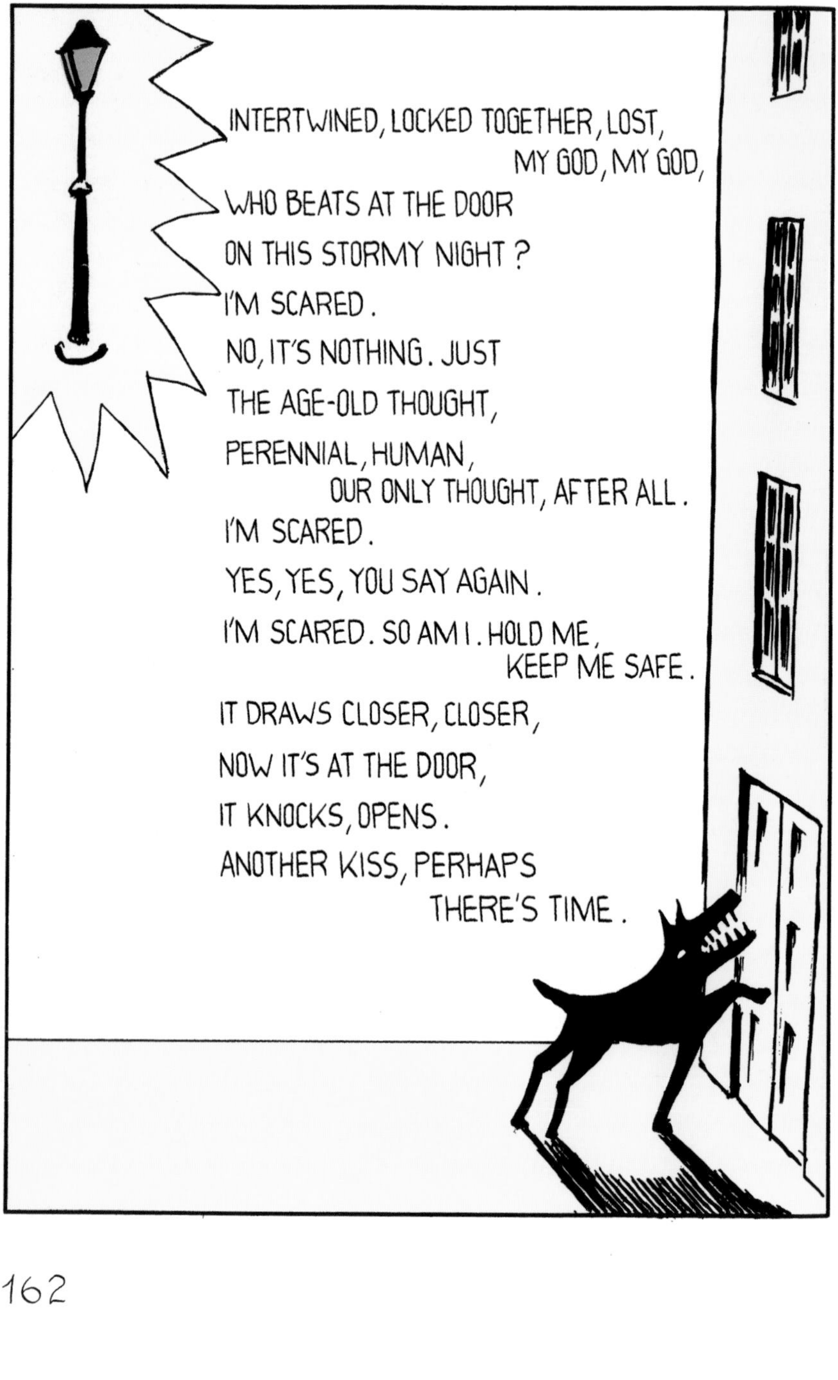
INTERTWINED, LOCKED TOGETHER, LOST,
MY GOD, MY GOD,
WHO BEATS AT THE DOOR
ON THIS STORMY NIGHT?
I'M SCARED.
NO, IT'S NOTHING. JUST
THE AGE-OLD THOUGHT,
PERENNIAL, HUMAN,
OUR ONLY THOUGHT, AFTER ALL.
I'M SCARED.
YES, YES, YOU SAY AGAIN.
I'M SCARED. SO AM I. HOLD ME,
KEEP ME SAFE.
IT DRAWS CLOSER, CLOSER,
NOW IT'S AT THE DOOR,
IT KNOCKS, OPENS.
ANOTHER KISS, PERHAPS
THERE'S TIME.

AGAIN . ANOTHER KNOCK . DID YOU HEAR ?
WHO CAN IT BE SO LATE ? I'M SCARED.
WHAT ARE YOU AFRAID OF ? ON A NIGHT LIKE THIS
ONLY THE WOLVES ARE ABOUT,
BUT WOLVES DON'T KNOCK,
UNLESS ...

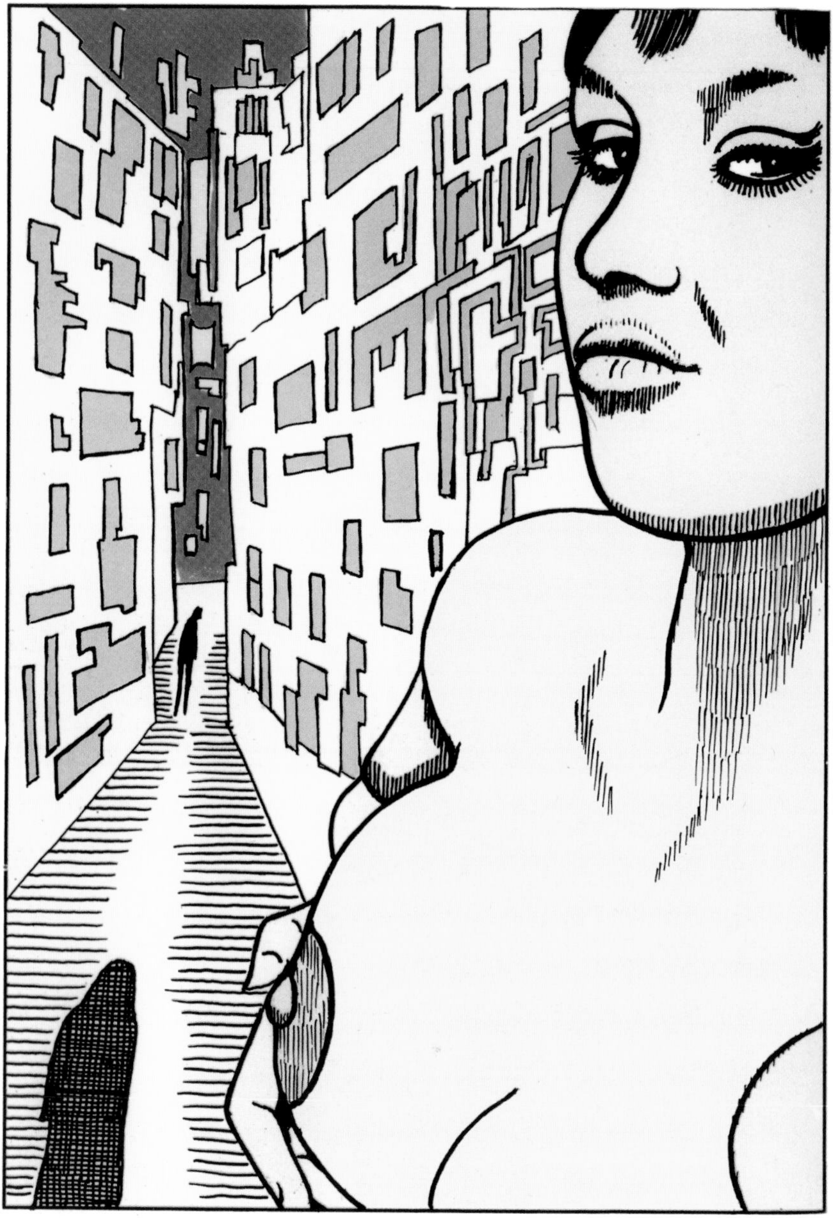

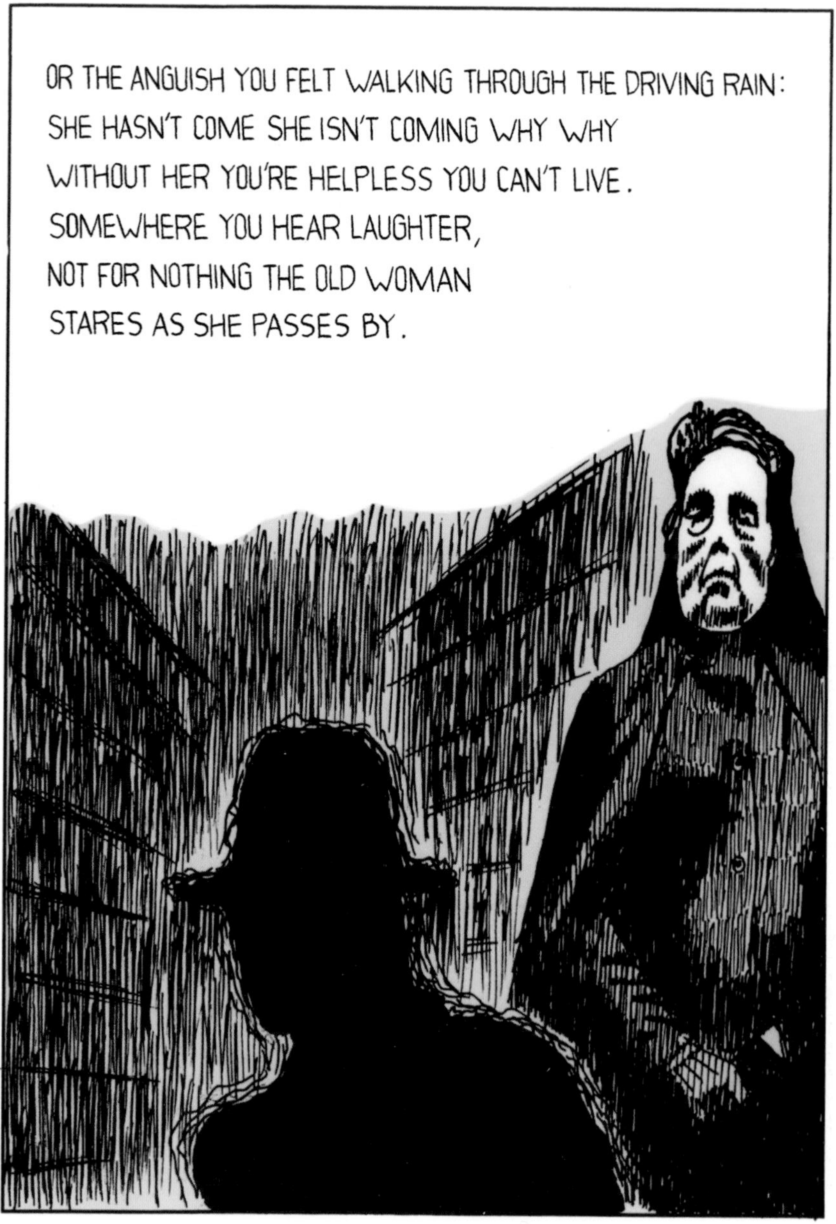
OR THE ANGUISH YOU FELT WALKING THROUGH THE DRIVING RAIN:
SHE HASN'T COME SHE ISN'T COMING WHY WHY
WITHOUT HER YOU'RE HELPLESS YOU CAN'T LIVE.
SOMEWHERE YOU HEAR LAUGHTER,
NOT FOR NOTHING THE OLD WOMAN
STARES AS SHE PASSES BY.

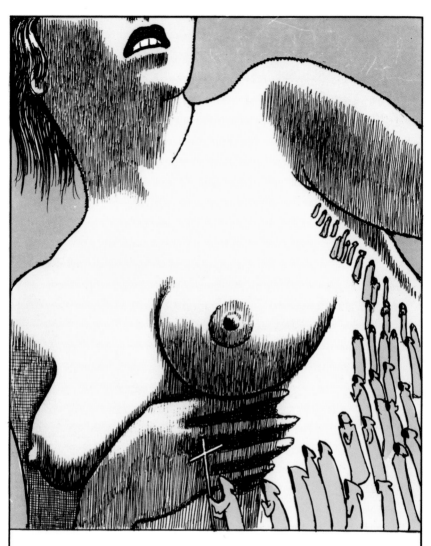

WHEN AFTER LOVE THE FLESH IS TIRED AND PROCESSIONS
OF HOODED MONKS DESCEND

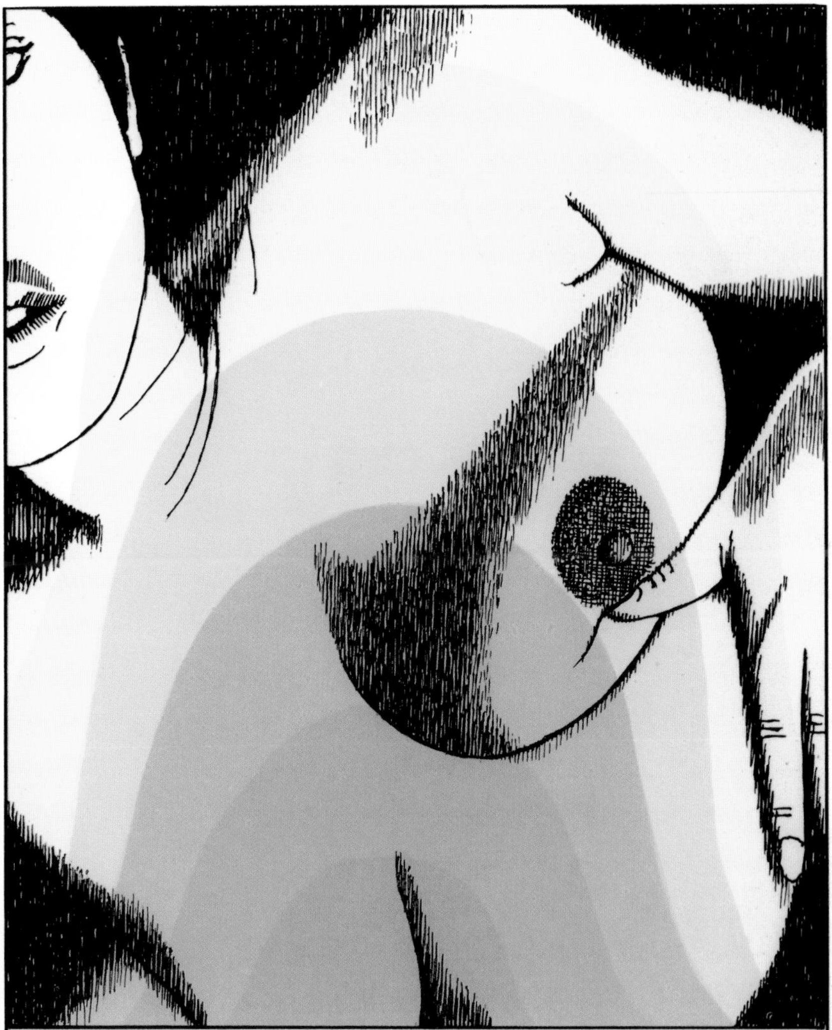

WHEN AFTER LOVE THE FLESH IS TIRED AND YOU HEAR THE
ROAR OF FARAWAY WATERFALLS COMING DOWN

OR SOMETHING THAT CLIMBS, FLOATING HIGHER,
THE SAVAGE THROB OF DESIRE,
OF JOY AND AGONY,
TIGHTENING SWELLING TOWARD THE BRIM
OF THE ABYSS, WAIT I BEG YOU,
A MOMENT LONGER,
MAKE ME, HURT ME.

HOVERING AT THE TRANSLUCENT CREST
OF THE GENITAL WAVE
THAT UNEXPECTEDLY OVERFLOWS,
BREAKS, DISSOLVES, *DON'T*
CRY, MY LOVE, DRAWS
THE MIND DOWN TO THE GROIN,
VOLCANO, FLAG, TORMENT,
RELEASE, THE BURSTING DAM.

AND THEN A LANDSLIDE
A LIQUID BURNING GORGE,
ARTICULATED DELIRIUM BEATING TIME
DESCENDING EVER DEEPER,
FOR HOURS FOR DAYS FOR MONTHS,
TO END? IN DARKNESS, IN NOTHINGNESS.

TO LEAVE THE FLESH BEHIND, A HOLLOW MANTIS SHELL,
SPENT, NO LONGER OF USE ?
"PETITE MORT", AS THE FRENCH SAY.
AND DAWN LEAKS THROUGH THE BLINDS.

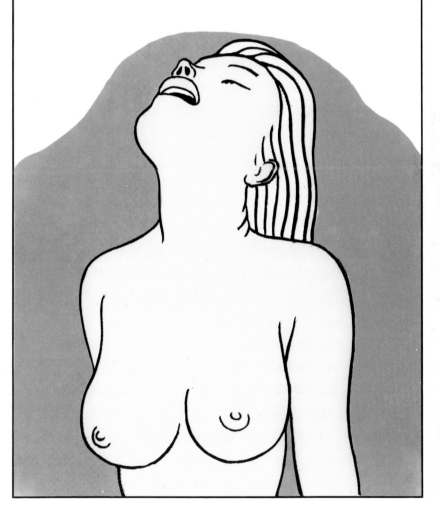

FINALLY, THE STORY OF GOD
THE GOD YOU NO LONGER HAVE,
SINCE FOR YOU, ALAS, HE IS SUPERFLUOUS.

THE GOD OF FIRST COMMUNIONS

THE GOD OF HELL AND DEVILS

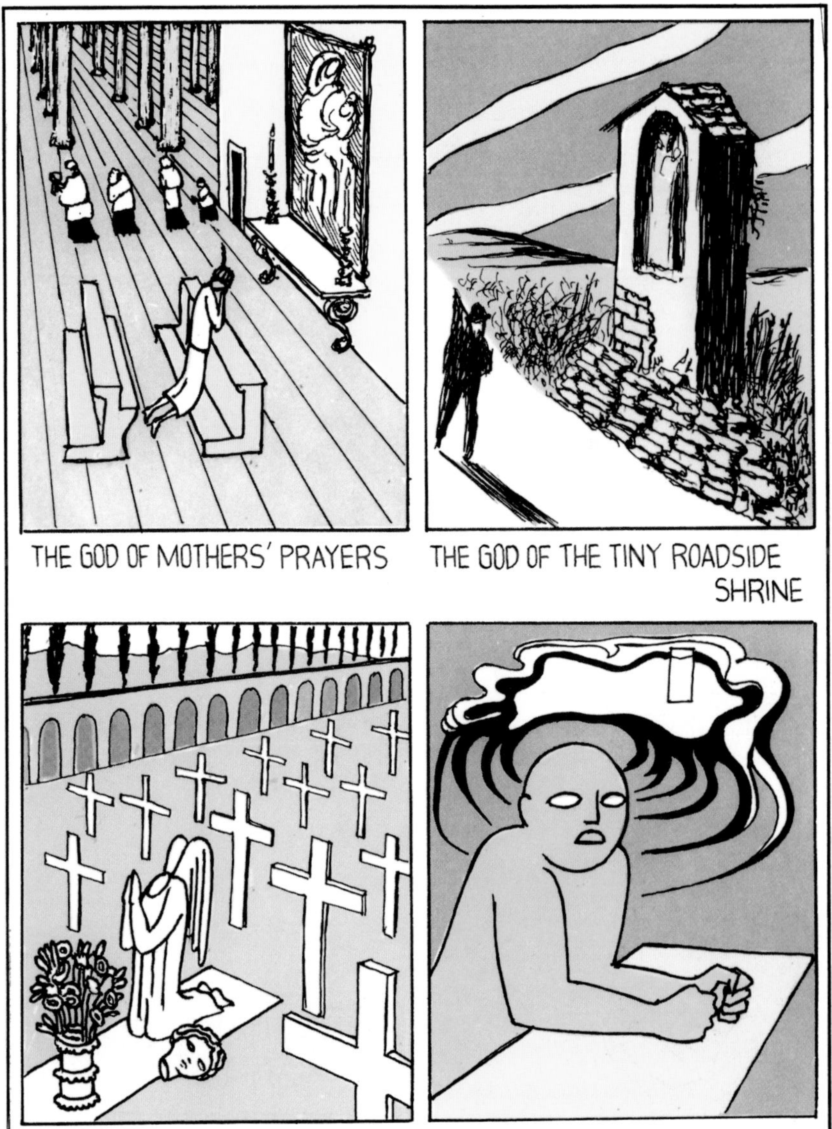
THE GOD OF MOTHERS' PRAYERS
THE GOD OF THE TINY ROADSIDE SHRINE
THE GOD OF CRYPTS AND CEMETERIES
THE GOD OF REMORSE AT THE END OF DAY

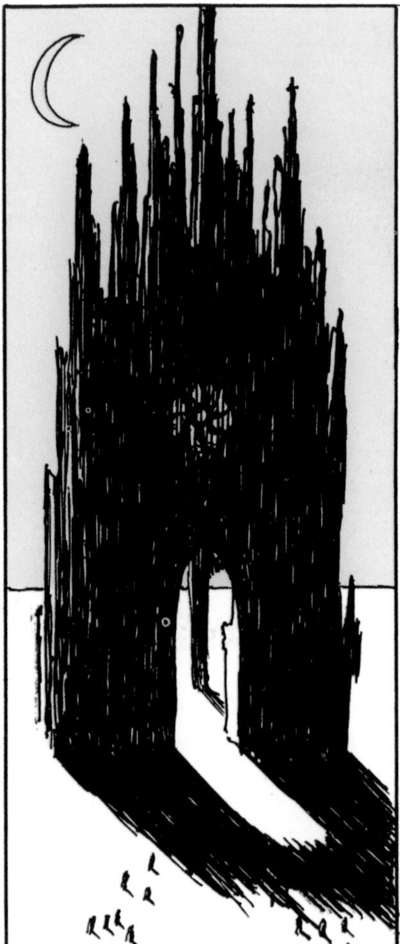

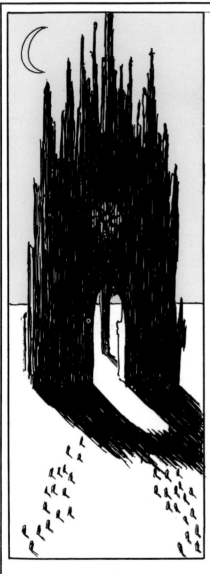

THE GOD OF CATHEDRALS

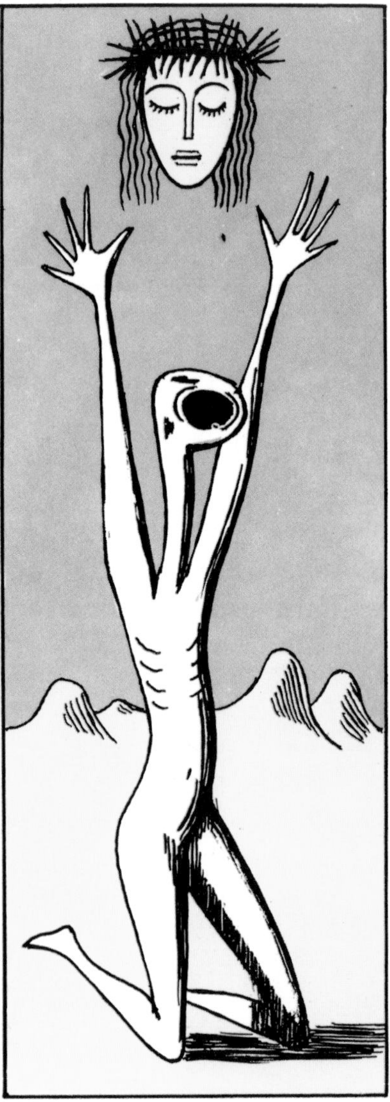

THE GOD OF DESPAIR

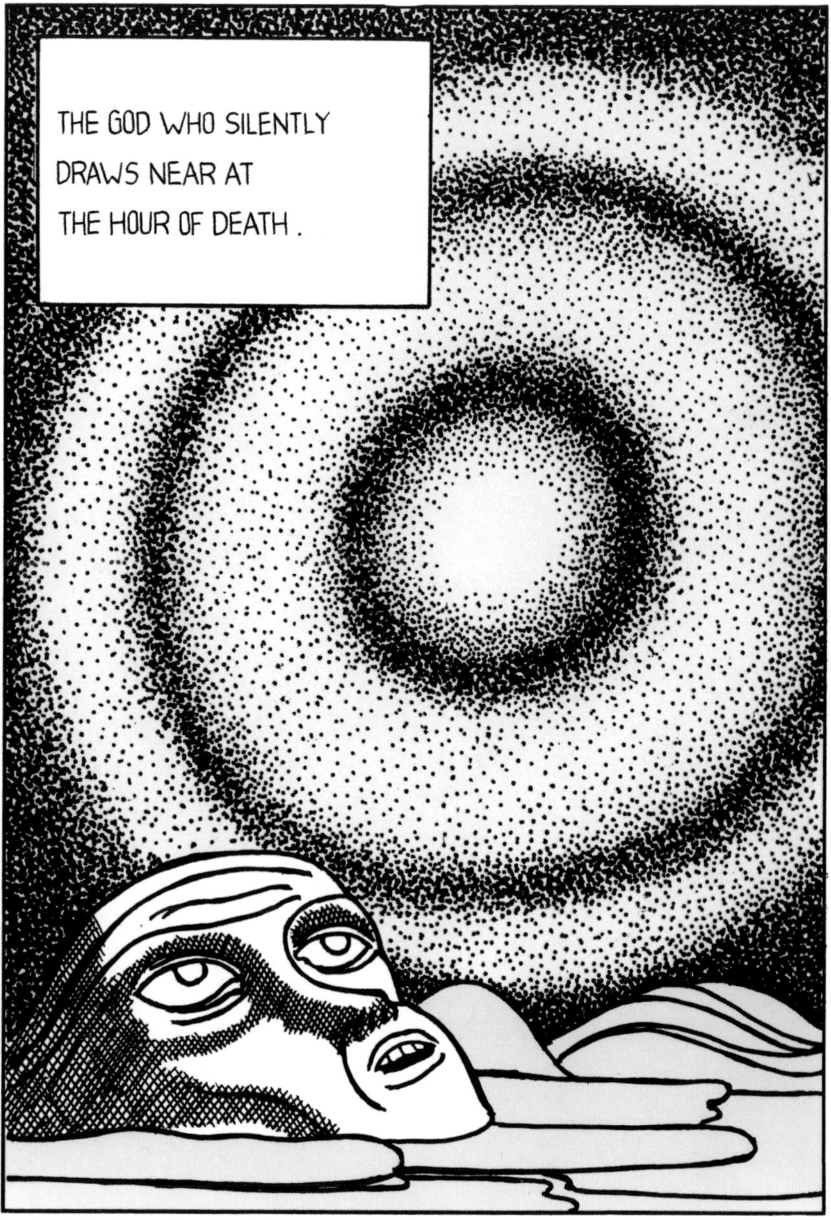
THE GOD WHO SILENTLY DRAWS NEAR AT THE HOUR OF DEATH .

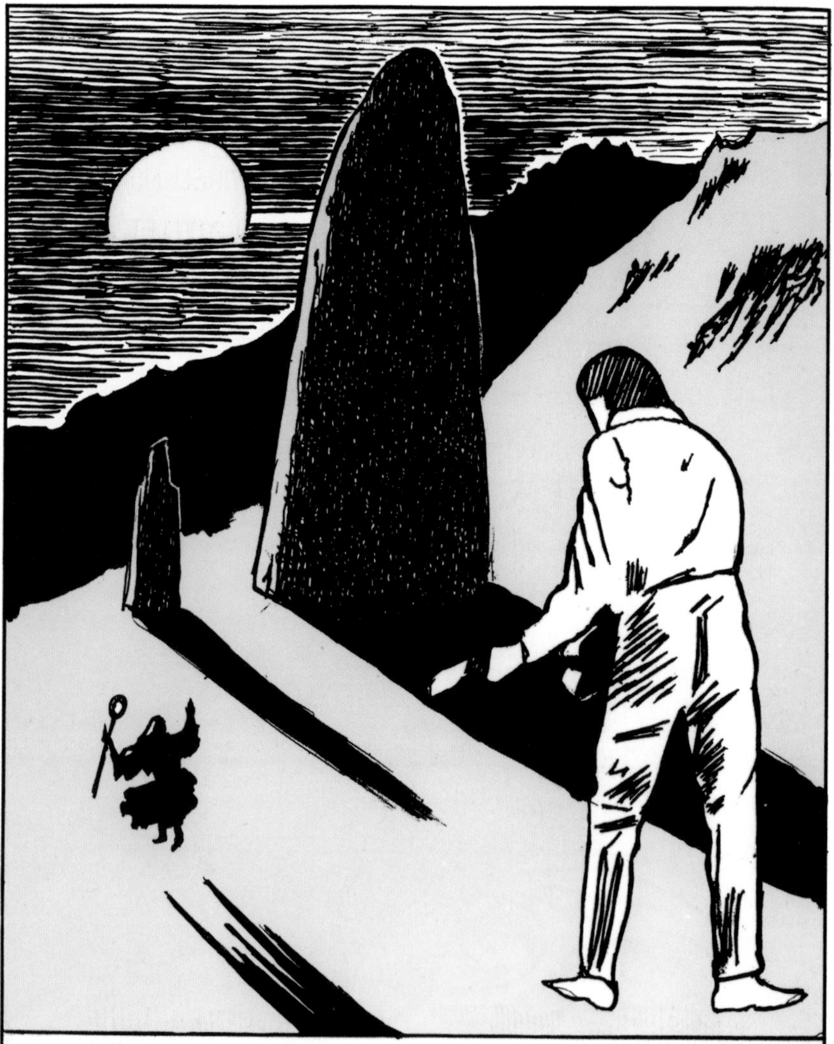

BUT AT THIS POINT, ON THE VERGE OF CONJURING YET ANOTHER MEMORY CONTAINING THE GREAT FATAL IDEA, ORFI PAUSED.

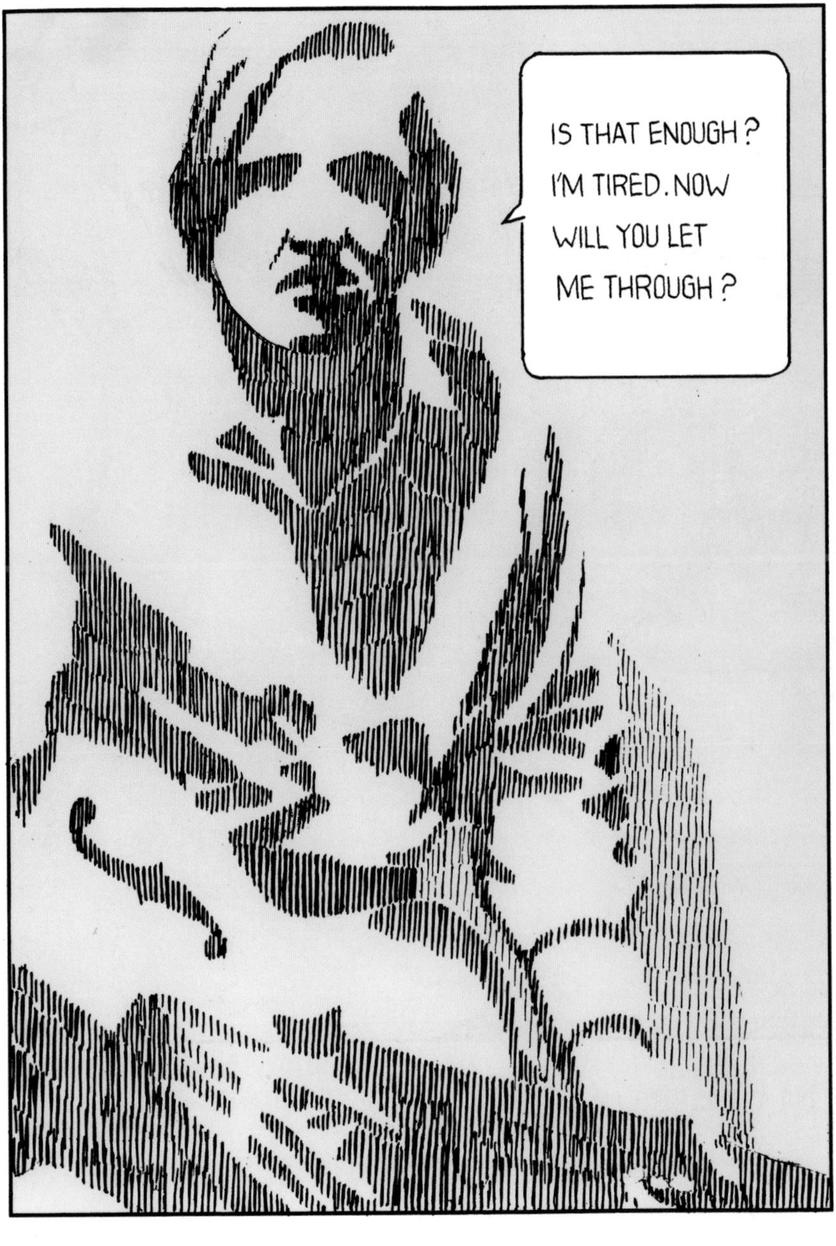
IS THAT ENOUGH? I'M TIRED. NOW WILL YOU LET ME THROUGH?

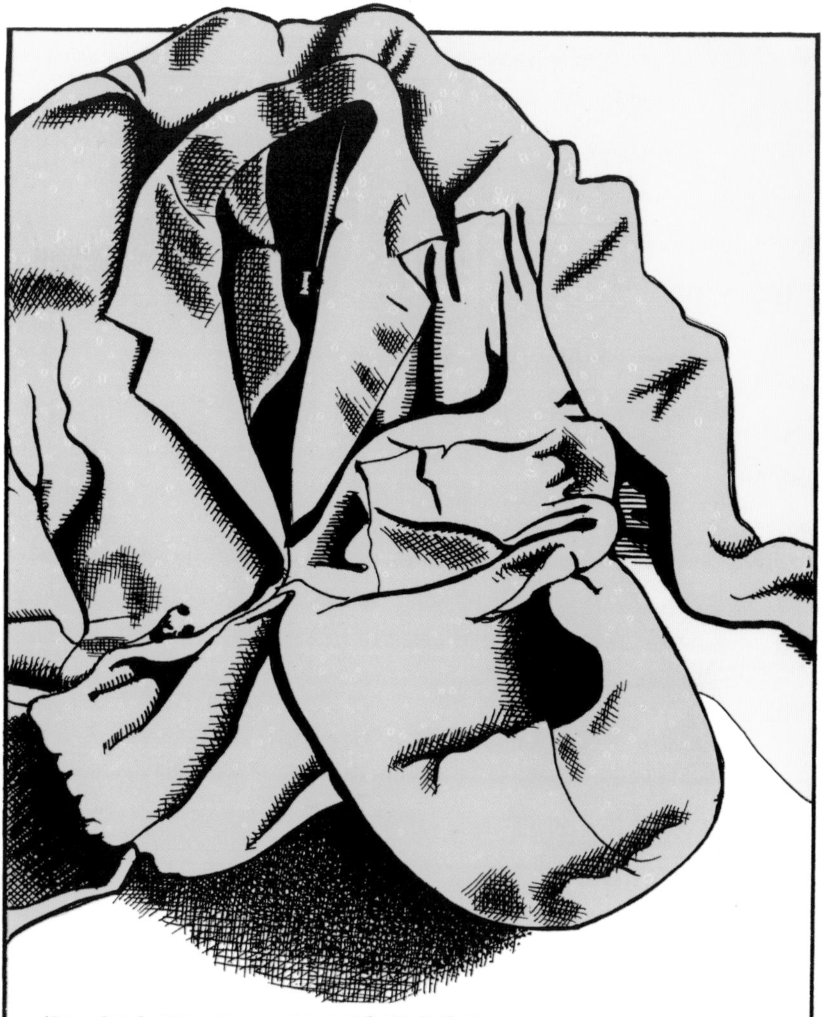

— YES, YOUNG ORFI, YOU HAVE MOVED US AND IT IS ENOUGH. YOU'RE YOUNG, BUT YOU UNDERSTAND MANY THINGS.

YOU MAY COME IN. YOU MAY ENTER.

YOU HAVE BEEN GRANTED TWENTY-FOUR HOURS.

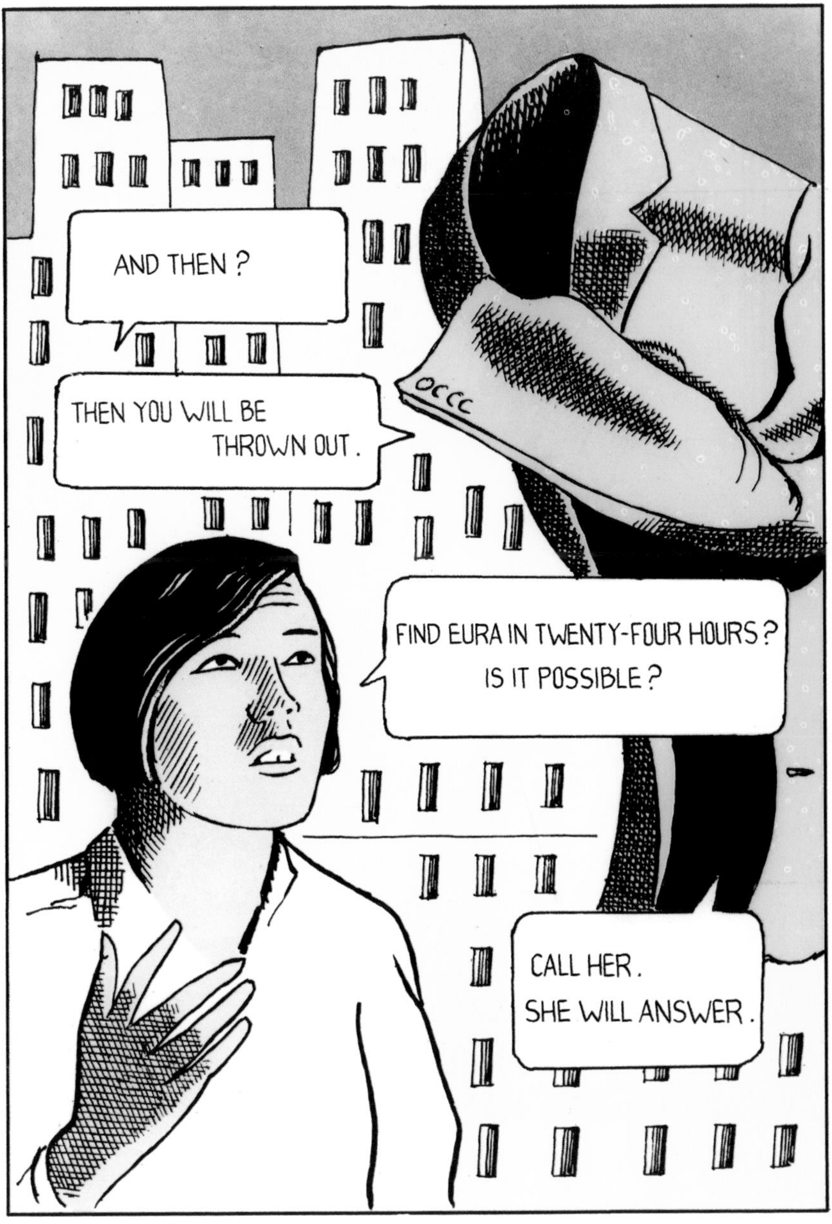
AND THEN ?
THEN YOU WILL BE THROWN OUT.
FIND EURA IN TWENTY-FOUR HOURS ? IS IT POSSIBLE ?
CALL HER. SHE WILL ANSWER.

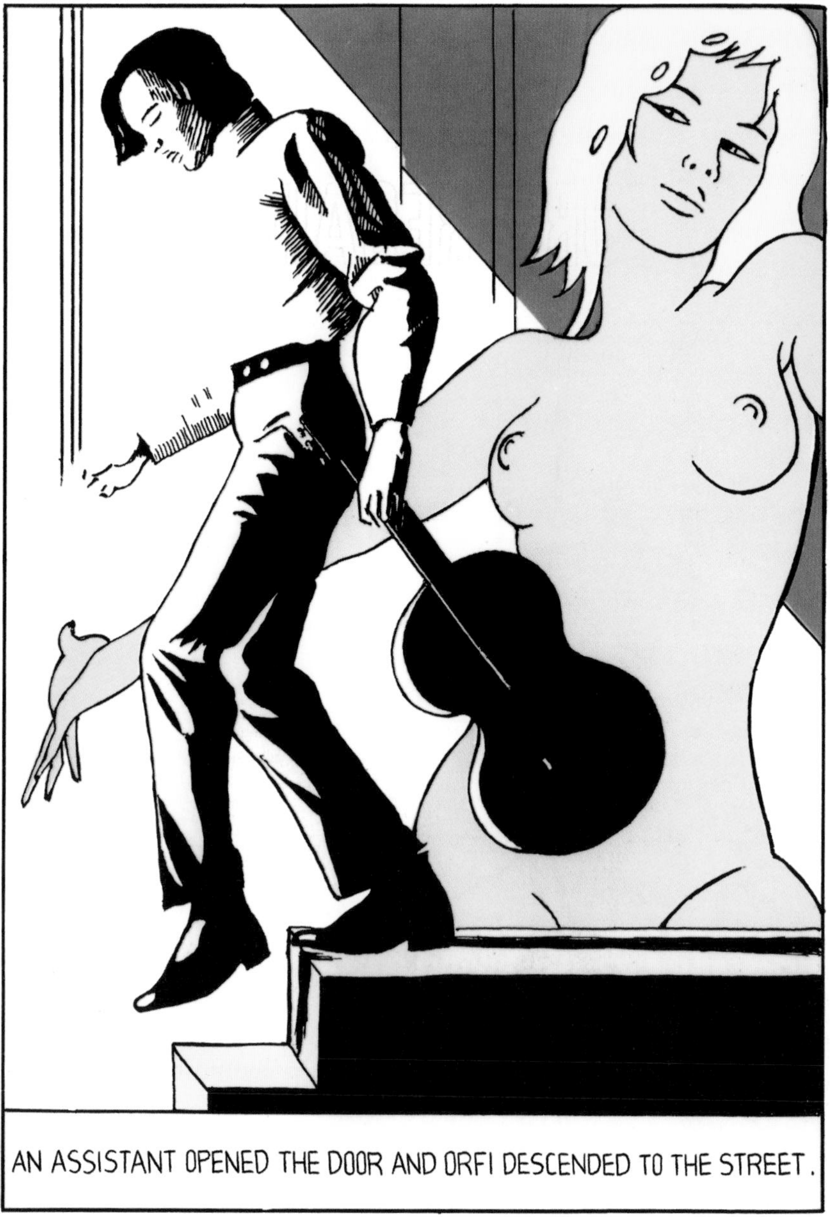
AN ASSISTANT OPENED THE DOOR AND ORFI DESCENDED TO THE STREET.

EURA REGAINED

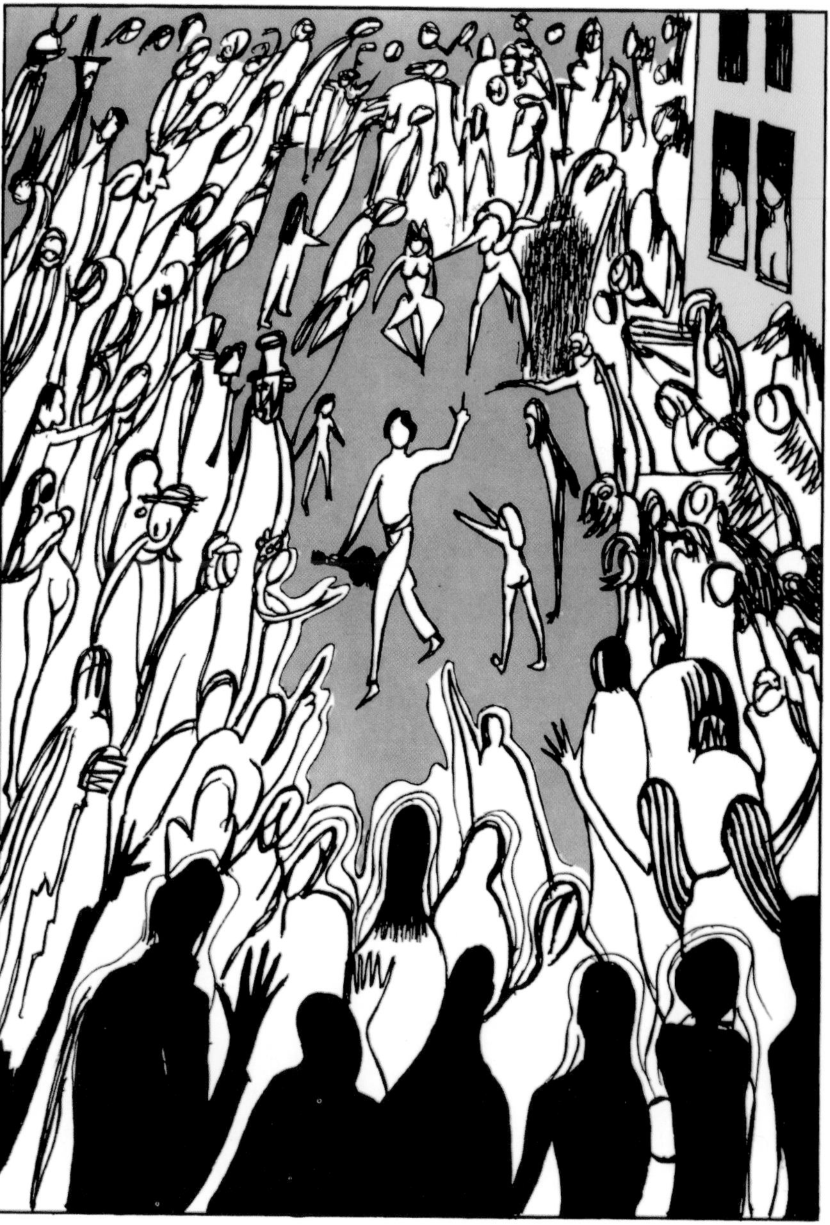

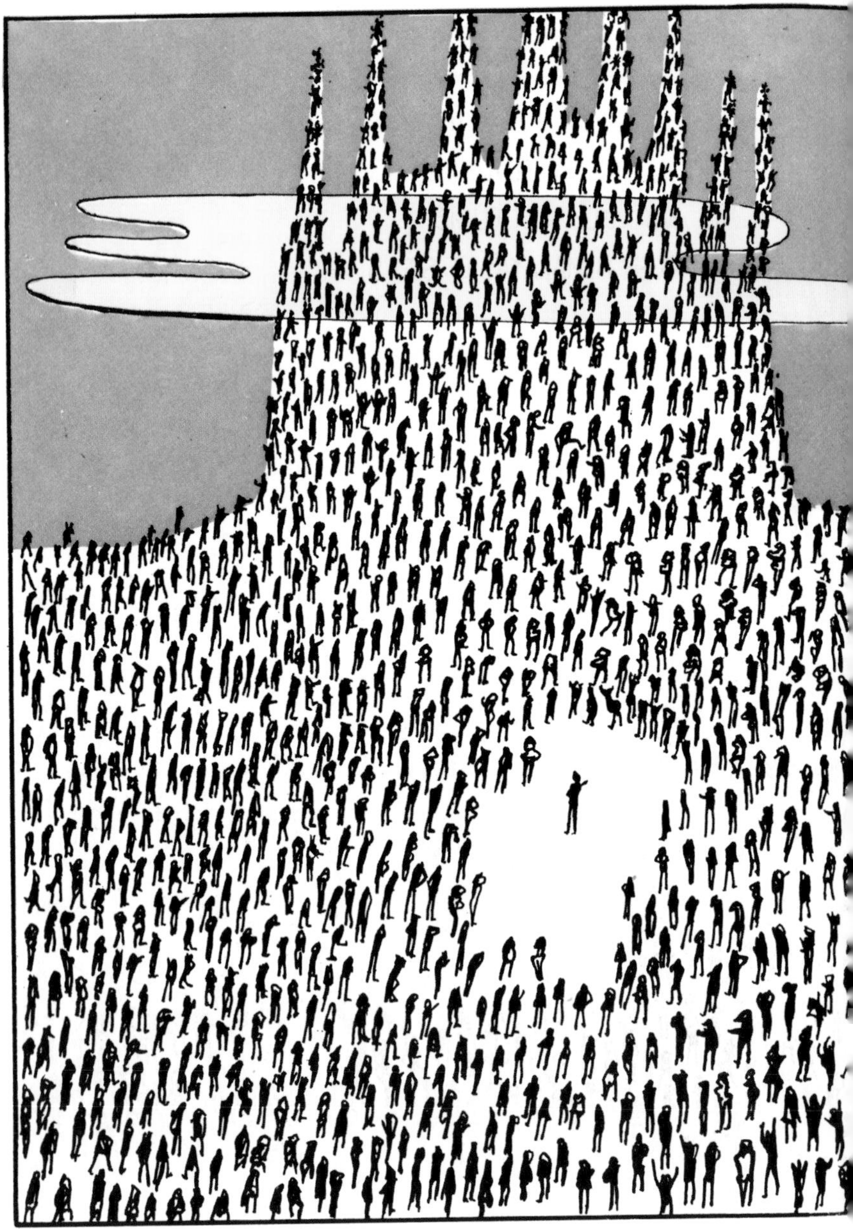

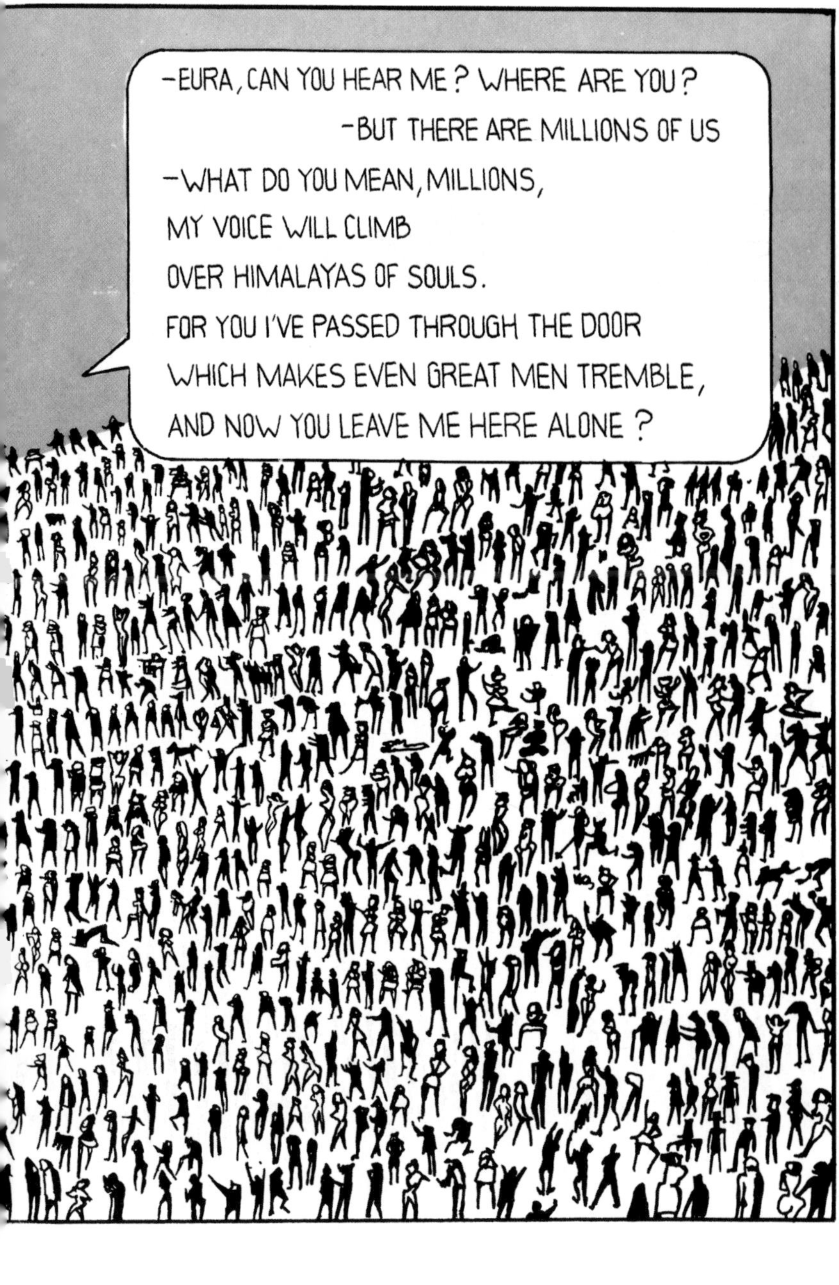
-EURA, CAN YOU HEAR ME? WHERE ARE YOU?
-BUT THERE ARE MILLIONS OF US
-WHAT DO YOU MEAN, MILLIONS,
MY VOICE WILL CLIMB
OVER HIMALAYAS OF SOULS.
FOR YOU I'VE PASSED THROUGH THE DOOR
WHICH MAKES EVEN GREAT MEN TREMBLE,
AND NOW YOU LEAVE ME HERE ALONE?

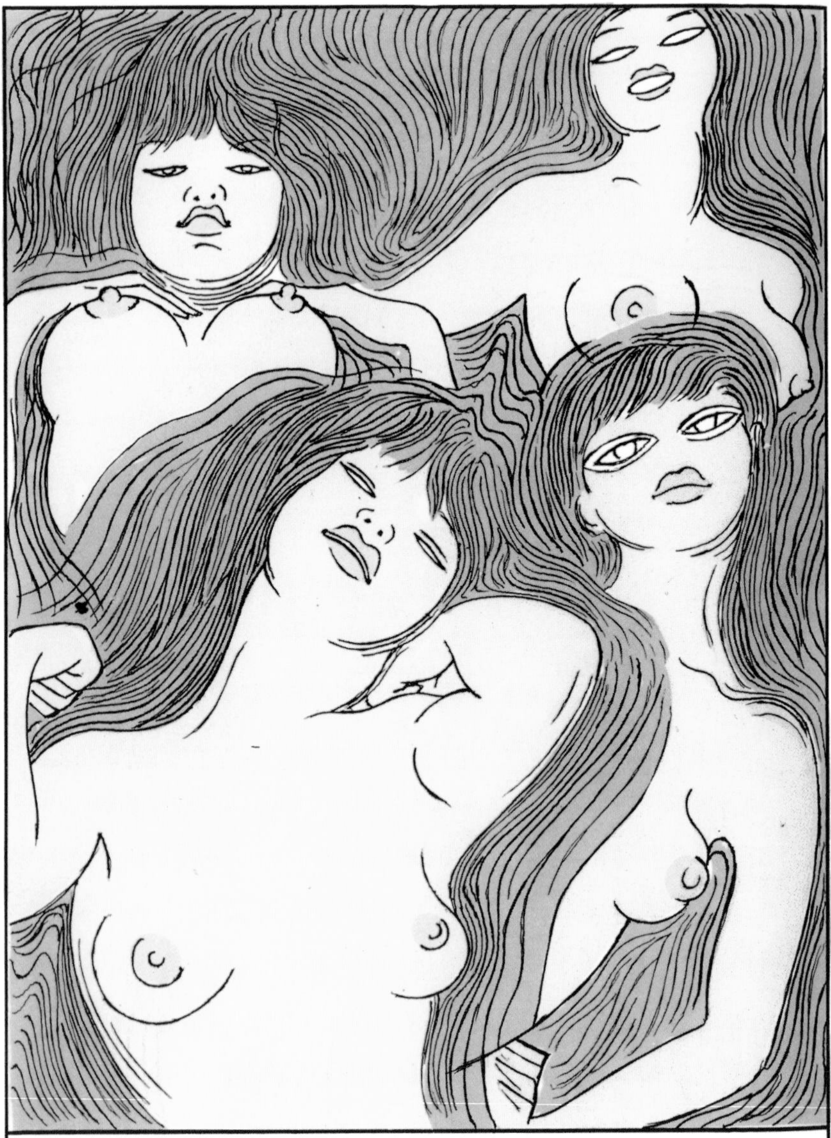

BRAZEN GIRLS DRAW NEAR, ENTICING HIM.

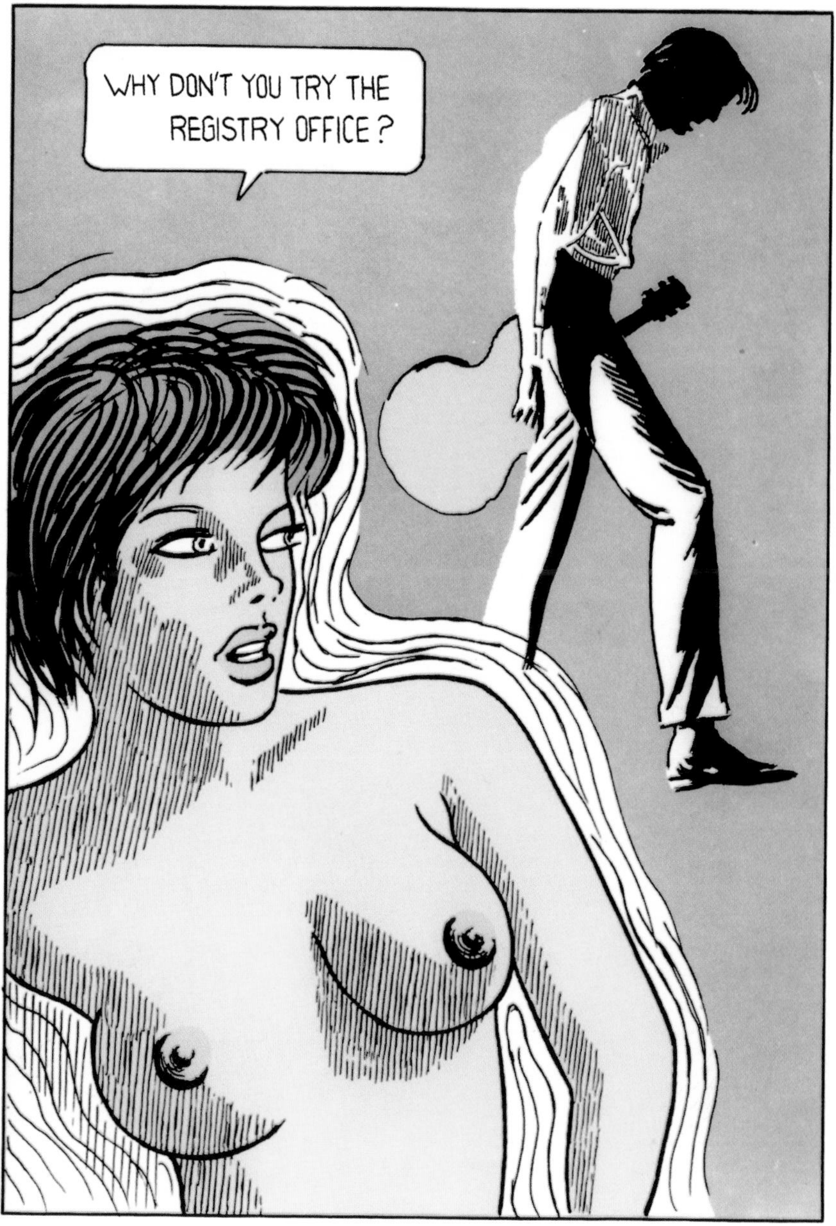
WHY DON'T YOU TRY THE REGISTRY OFFICE?

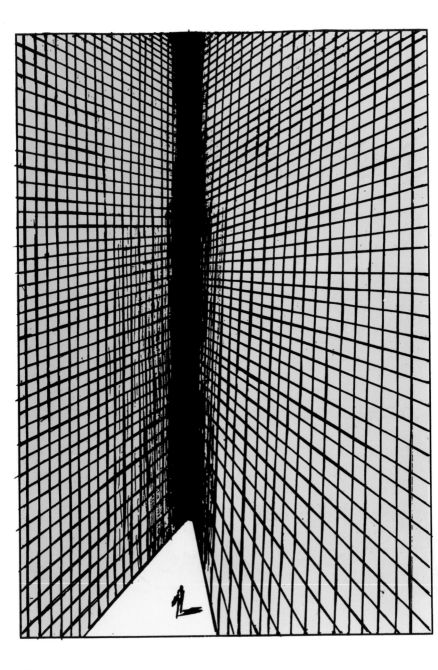

186

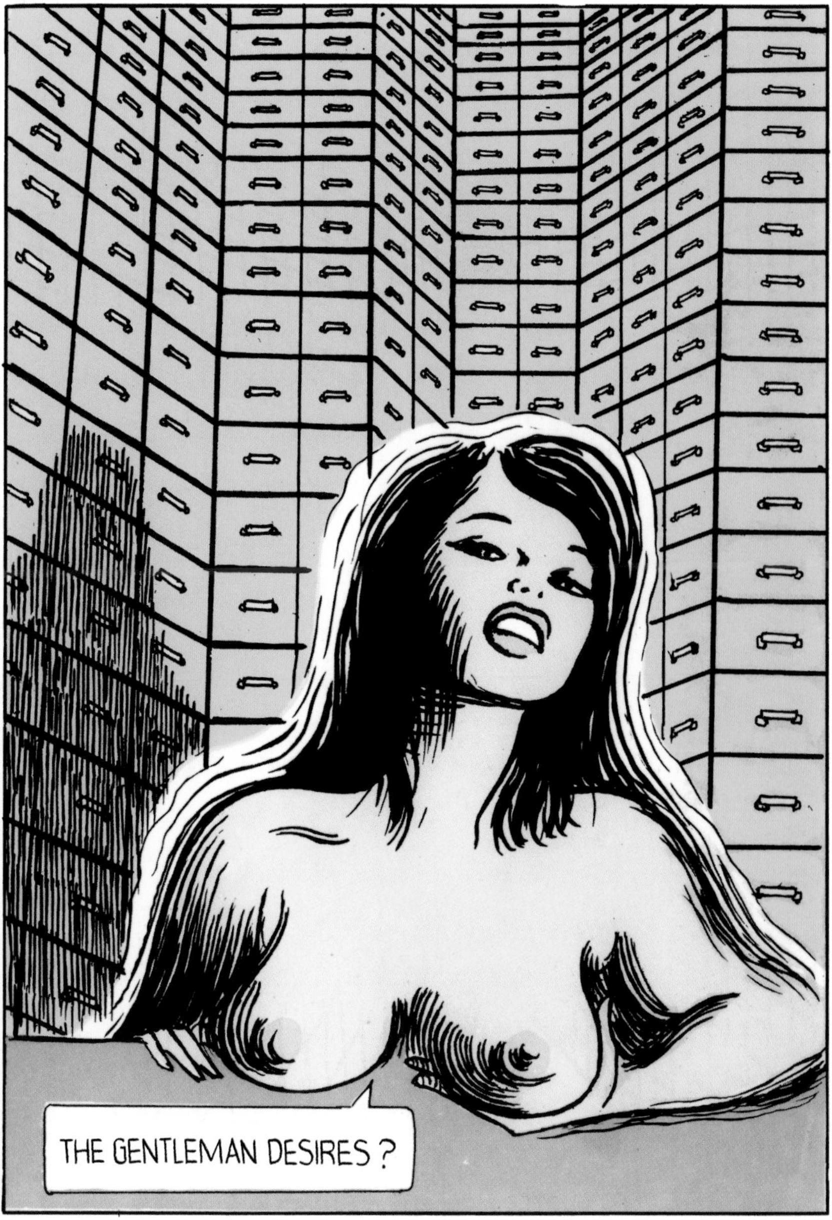
THE GENTLEMAN DESIRES ?

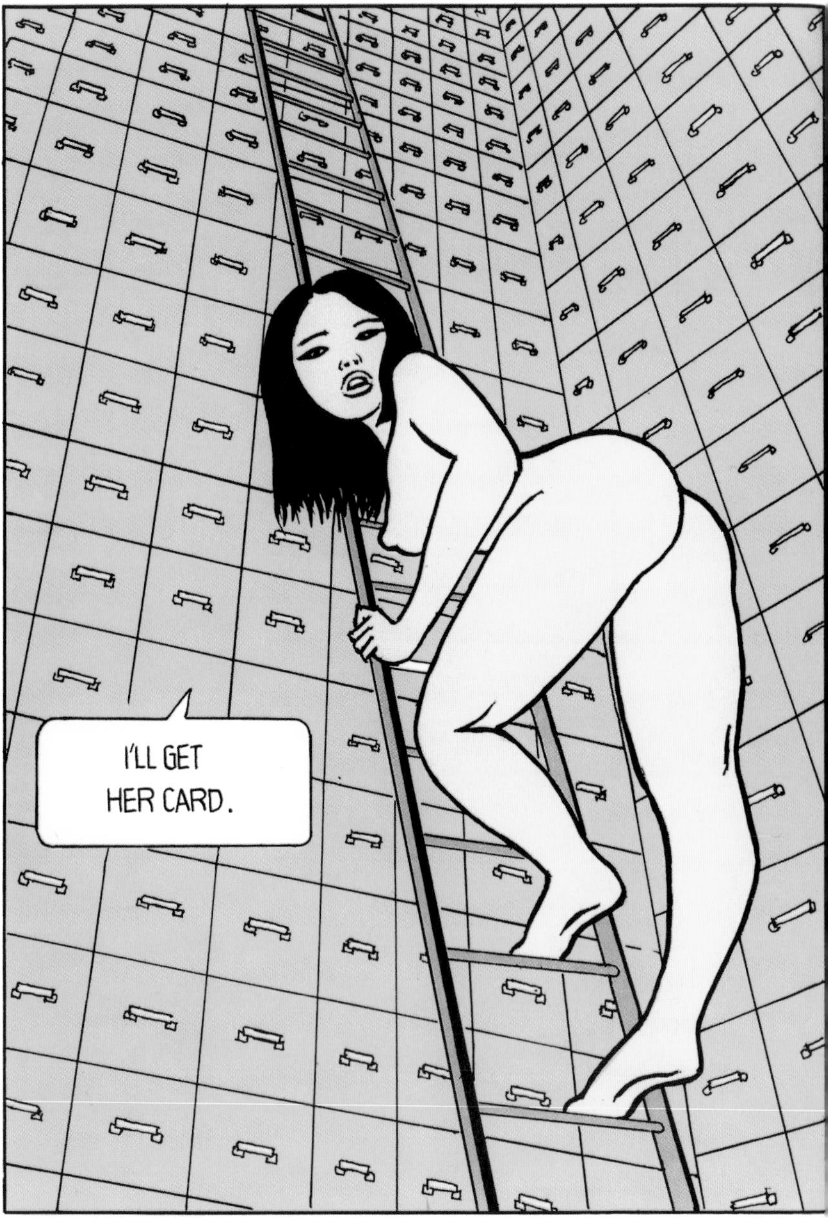
I'LL GET HER CARD.

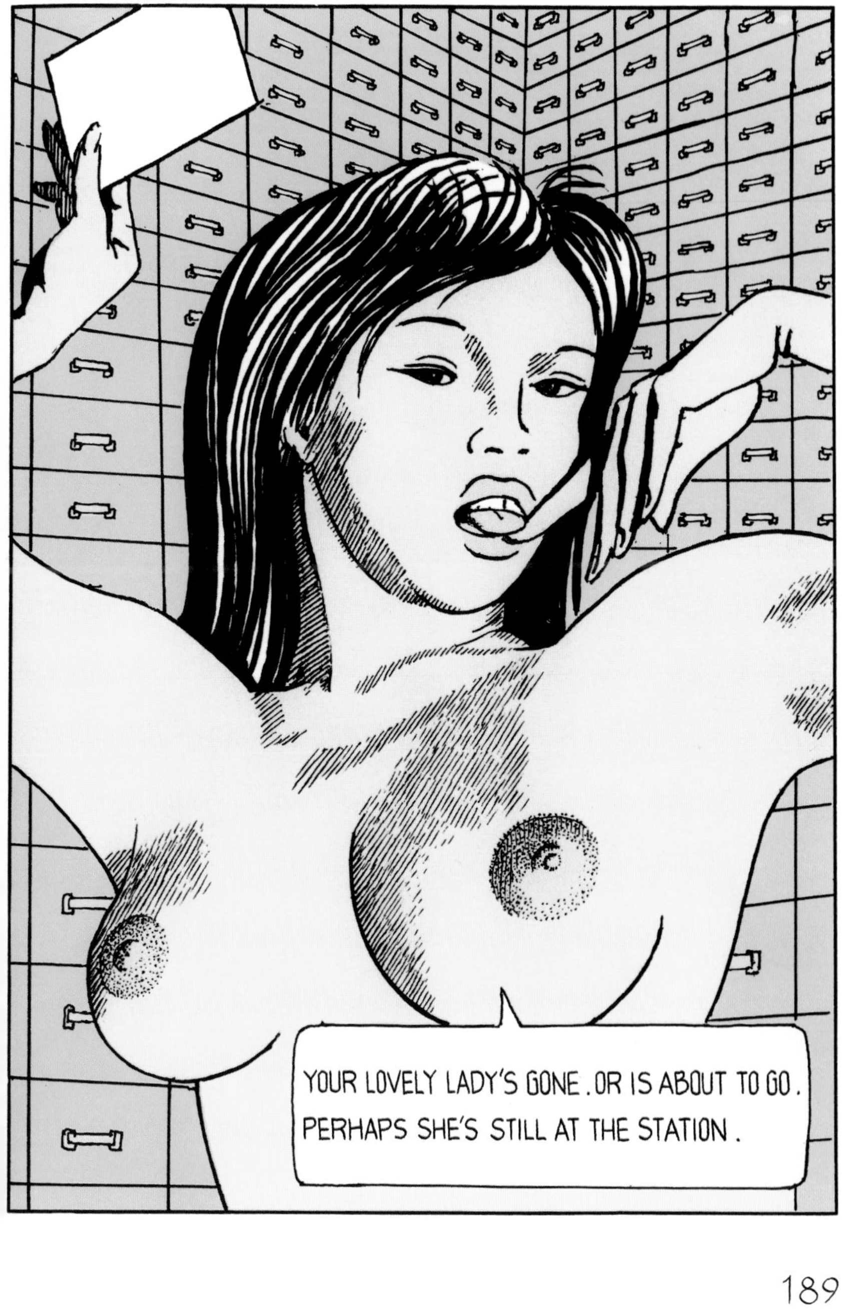
YOUR LOVELY LADY'S GONE . OR IS ABOUT TO GO .
PERHAPS SHE'S STILL AT THE STATION .

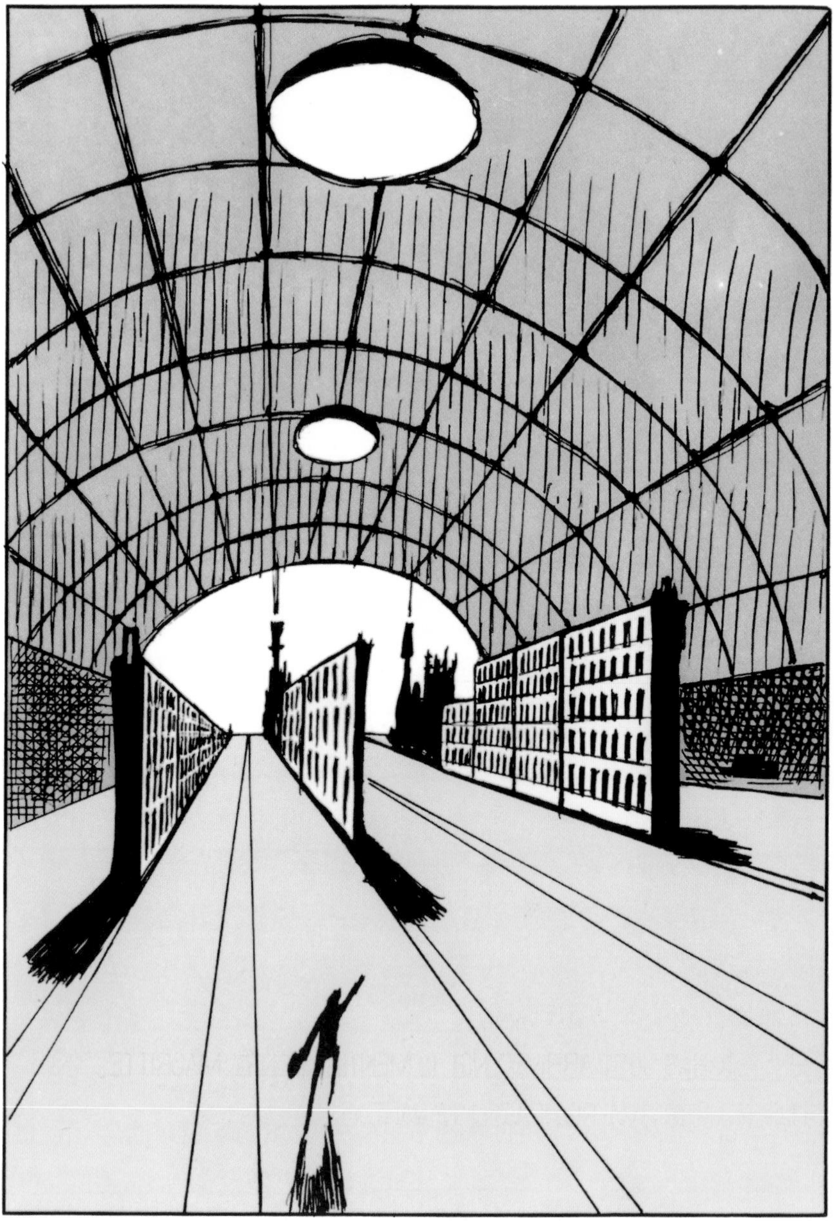

THE DIRECT TRAINS THE EXPRESS TRAINS THE TRAINS HEADED
FOR ETERNITY AND DEATH DEPART AT FIFTEEN PAST THE 199TH HOUR
AT TWO PAST THE ZERO HOUR, BUT WHERE DO THEY GO? THEY GO.
THE REST IS THE SECRET OF THE SECOND LIFE, IF THERE IS ONE, THERE
LIES THE MYSTERY, THE EVERLASTING QUESTION. THEY LEAVE FOR
REMOTE AND UNKNOWABLE DESTINATIONS. THE STATIONMASTER
SOUNDS THE BLESSED WHISTLE, THE LOCOMOTIVE STARTS UP AND PUFFS
SMOKE, THE WINDOWS ARE ILLUMINATED, THE CHEFS ON THE INTERNATIONAL
LINES RUSH TO AND FRO IN A FLURRY OF EXCITEMENT, TOSCANINI
IS HERE, MARILYN IS ON BOARD,
EINSTEIN HAS JUST ARRIVED, NOT TO MENTION HENRY MAGRITTE,
HURRY HURRY, WE'RE HEADED TOWARD

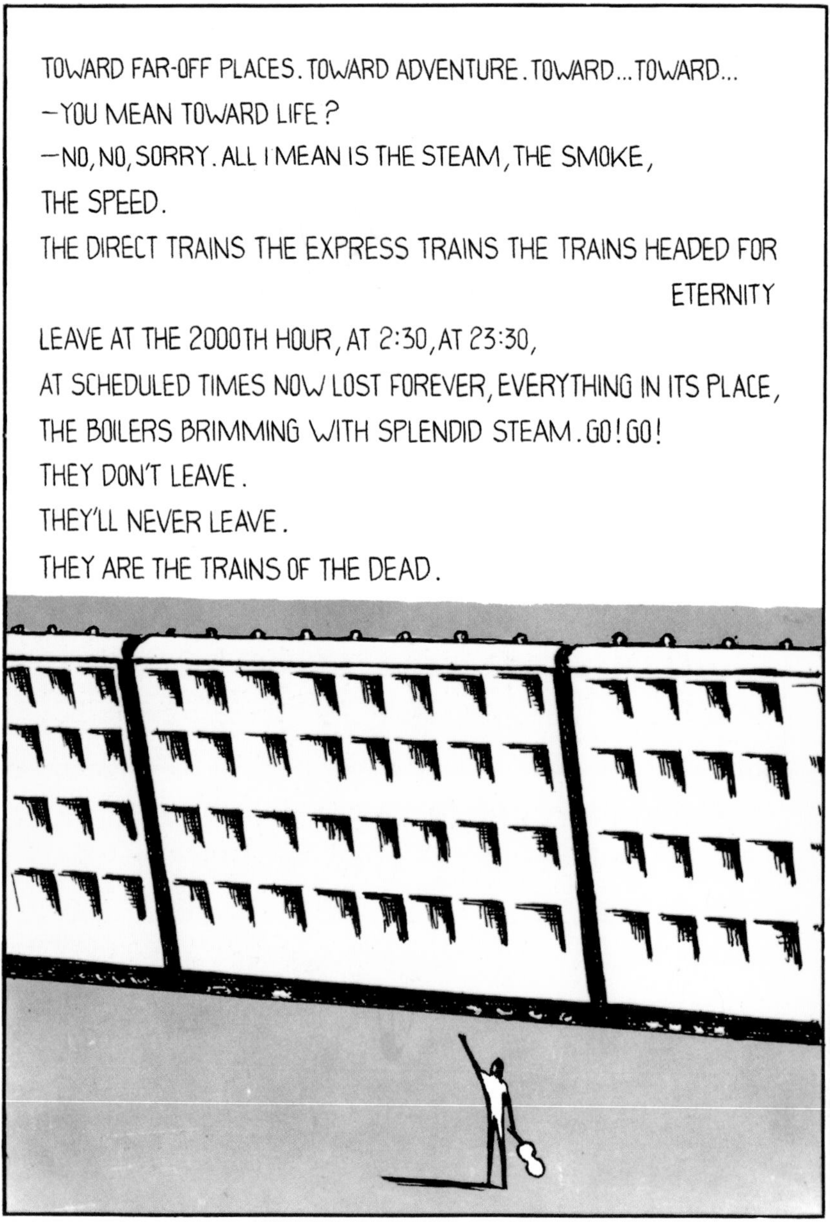
TOWARD FAR-OFF PLACES. TOWARD ADVENTURE. TOWARD... TOWARD...
—YOU MEAN TOWARD LIFE?
—NO, NO, SORRY. ALL I MEAN IS THE STEAM, THE SMOKE, THE SPEED.
THE DIRECT TRAINS THE EXPRESS TRAINS THE TRAINS HEADED FOR ETERNITY
LEAVE AT THE 2000TH HOUR, AT 2:30, AT 23:30,
AT SCHEDULED TIMES NOW LOST FOREVER, EVERYTHING IN ITS PLACE,
THE BOILERS BRIMMING WITH SPLENDID STEAM. GO! GO!
THEY DON'T LEAVE.
THEY'LL NEVER LEAVE.
THEY ARE THE TRAINS OF THE DEAD.

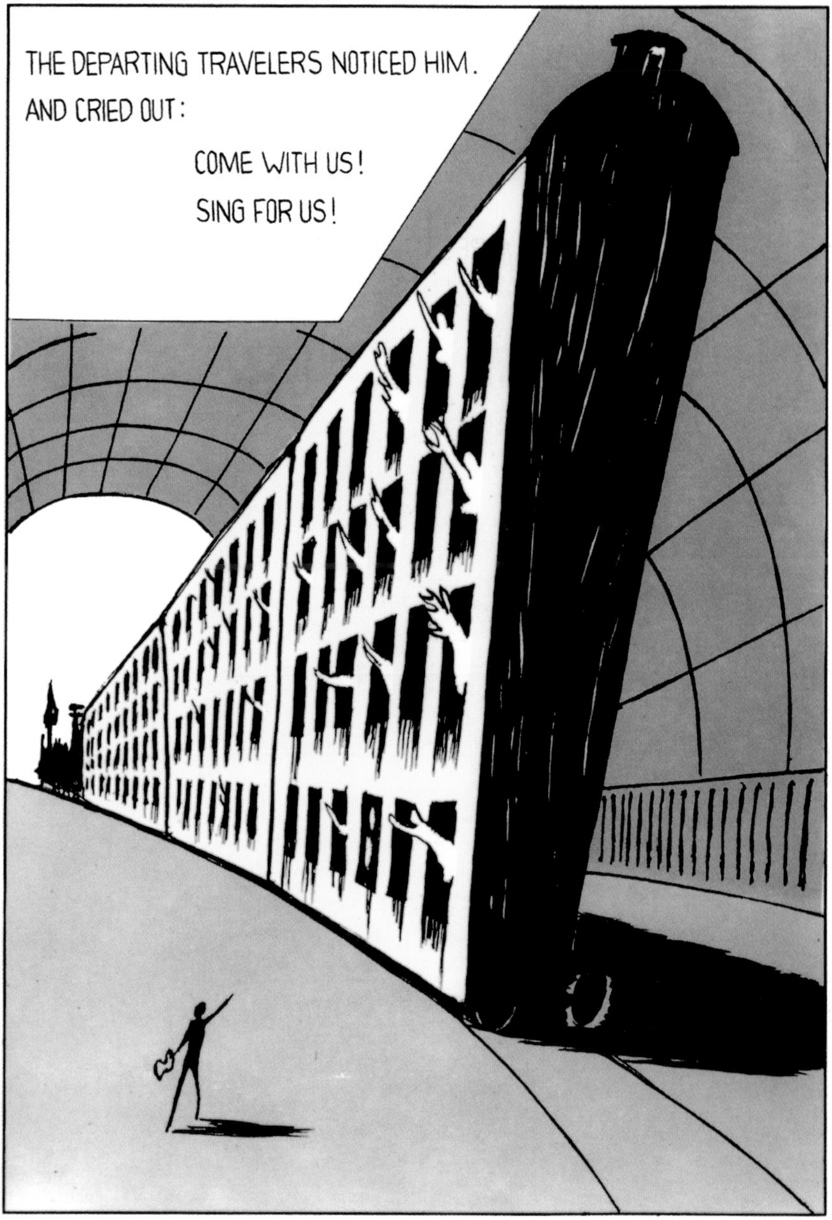
THE DEPARTING TRAVELERS NOTICED HIM.
AND CRIED OUT:
COME WITH US!
SING FOR US!

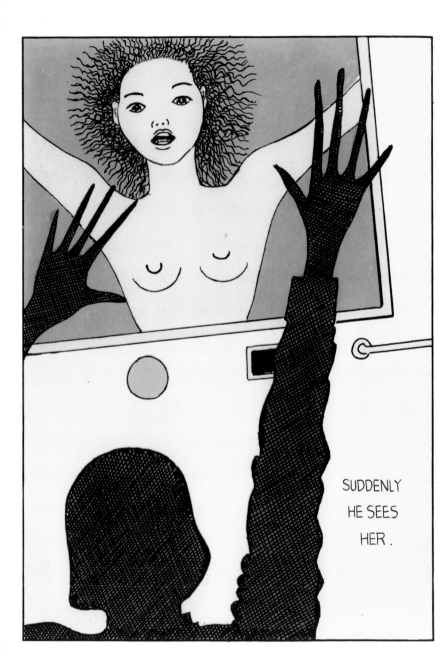

SUDDENLY
HE SEES
HER.

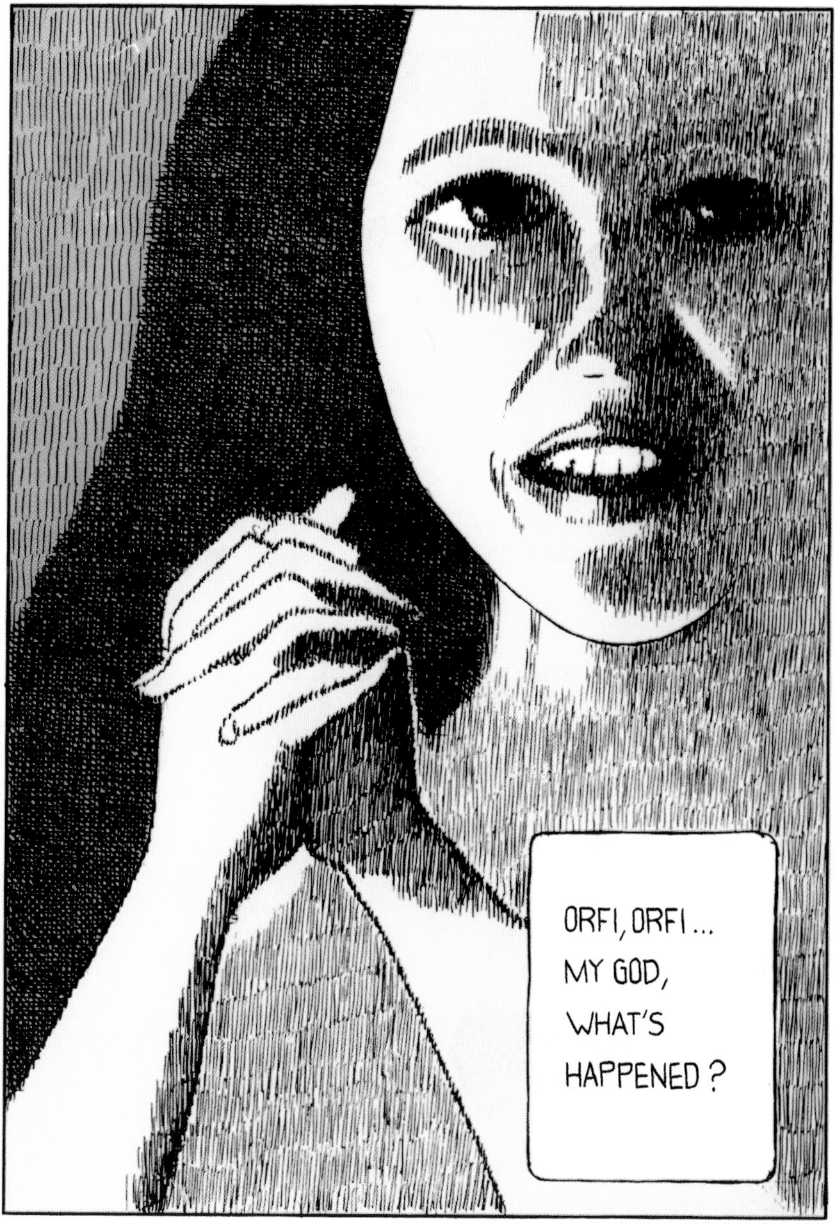
ORFI, ORFI...
MY GOD,
WHAT'S
HAPPENED?

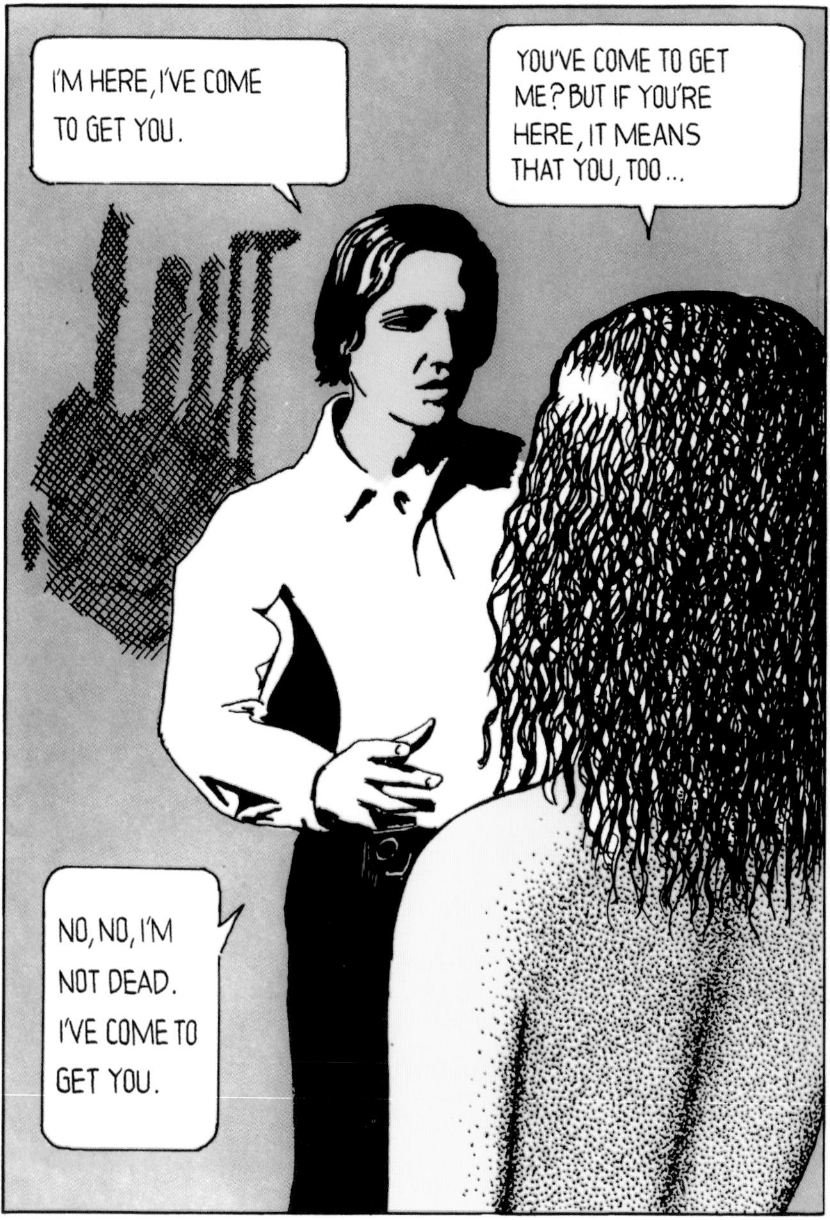
I'M HERE, I'VE COME TO GET YOU.
YOU'VE COME TO GET ME? BUT IF YOU'RE HERE, IT MEANS THAT YOU, TOO...
NO, NO, I'M NOT DEAD. I'VE COME TO GET YOU.

-OH, YOU'RE SO WARM, ORFI. YOU'RE ALIVE!
YOU SCARED ME.

   - EURA, WE MUST LEAVE. I ONLY HAVE A FEW
   HOURS LEFT. WE MUST REACH THE DOOR.

-LET'S STAY LIKE THIS FOR A MOMENT, MY DARLING, HOLD
ME CLOSE. HOW TERRIBLY HOT YOU ARE. YOU'RE BURNING UP.

   - LET'S GO, MY LOVE. THERE ARE STILL TWO
   HOURS LEFT. WE'LL HAVE TO RUN.

–LET'S STAY LIKE THIS. AFTER ALL, YOU KNOW IT'S POINTLESS.

–I'LL TAKE YOU WITH ME. WE'LL GO BACK TO THE POLYPUS CLUB. TONIGHT I'LL TAKE YOU DANCING. COME, MY LOVE, COME, WE MUST REACH THE DOOR.

–THERE IS NO DOOR, NOT ON OUR SIDE.

–WE'LL FIND IT, I'LL FIND IT. BUT HURRY, FOR HEAVEN'S SAKE. WE ONLY HAVE AN HOUR AND THREE-QUARTERS LEFT.

-LET ME SEE. YOUR WATCH! A REAL CLOCK WITH
TIME THAT PASSES, THE CLOCK OF THE LIVING.
LET ME HEAR IT. YES, THERE IT GOES: TIC

TOC. YOU KNOW THAT HERE, THERE IS NO TIME.
AND NO ONE ARRIVES HERE WITH A WATCH. GIVE
IT TO ME, ORFI, WILL YOU PLEASE?
I WOULD BE SO HAPPY. IN RETURN
I'LL GIVE YOU THIS RING.

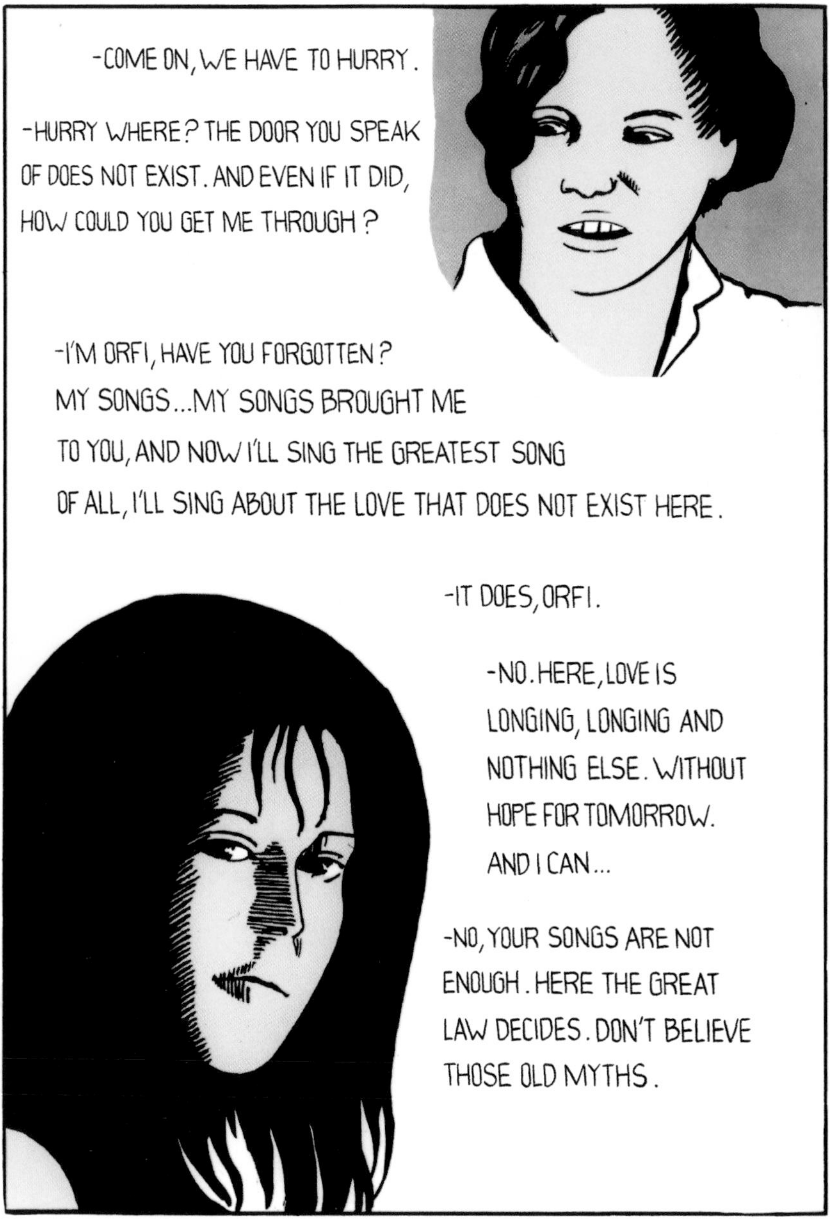
-COME ON, WE HAVE TO HURRY.
-HURRY WHERE? THE DOOR YOU SPEAK OF DOES NOT EXIST. AND EVEN IF IT DID, HOW COULD YOU GET ME THROUGH?
-I'M ORFI, HAVE YOU FORGOTTEN? MY SONGS...MY SONGS BROUGHT ME TO YOU, AND NOW I'LL SING THE GREATEST SONG OF ALL, I'LL SING ABOUT THE LOVE THAT DOES NOT EXIST HERE.
-IT DOES, ORFI.
-NO. HERE, LOVE IS LONGING, LONGING AND NOTHING ELSE. WITHOUT HOPE FOR TOMORROW. AND I CAN...
-NO, YOUR SONGS ARE NOT ENOUGH. HERE THE GREAT LAW DECIDES. DON'T BELIEVE THOSE OLD MYTHS.

–ONLY SEVENTY MINUTES LEFT. COME, EURA.
WE MUST FIND THE DOOR.

–DEAREST ORFI, MY DARLING, THERE ARE POWERS COMPARED TO
WHICH EVEN MEN LIKE YOU ARE DUST, TINY SCATTERED ANTS. BUT
ONE DAY WE'LL MEET AGAIN, PERHAPS.

–COME ON, EURA, ONLY FIFTY MINUTES LEFT.

–DARLING, I TOLD YOU. IT'S POINTLESS. I CAN'T FOLLOW YOU UP
THERE. IT'S JUST A SAD OLD MYTH, THE MYTH OF ORPHEUS.
EVEN IF YOU DON'T TURN AROUND, IT WILL STILL BE POINTLESS.
SLOW DOWN, ORFI, PLEASE, I'M TIRED. WE'RE ALL TIRED HERE.

—I BEG YOU, DON'T STOP, WE ONLY HAVE HALF AN HOUR.

> —LET'S SAY GOODBYE INSTEAD, MY LOVE. A REAL GOODBYE. THE DOOR YOU SPEAK OF DOES NOT EXIST.

—THOSE PEOPLE, THE GUARDIANS, THEY'LL OPEN THE DOOR FOR ME. WHEN I SING, NO ONE CAN RESIST.

> —LET'S SAY GOODBYE, ORFI. KISS ME, THOUGH I'M SO TERRIBLY COLD.

—I'LL COVER YOU WITH KISSES, BUT REAL ONES. NOW WE MUST GO.

> —I CAN'T GO ANY FARTHER. LET'S REST HERE A MOMENT, LET ME CATCH MY BREATH.

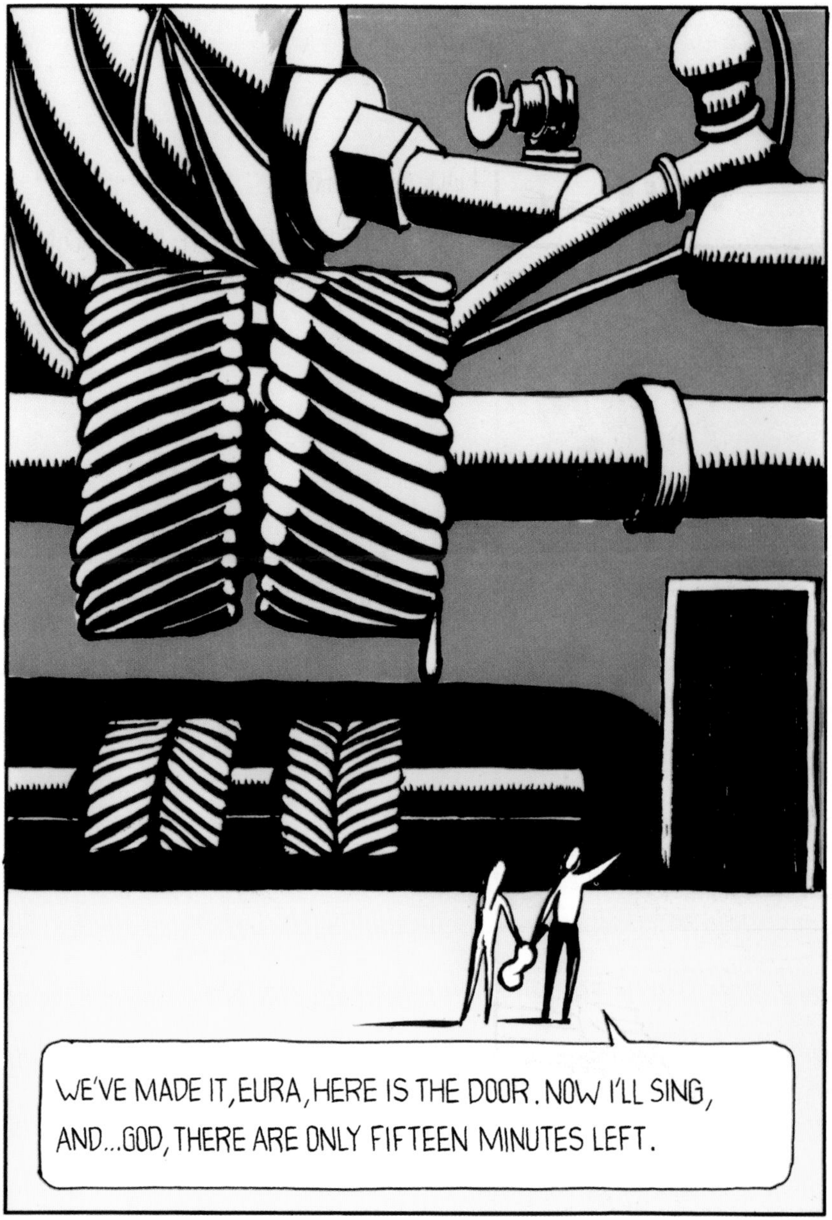
WE'VE MADE IT, EURA, HERE IS THE DOOR. NOW I'LL SING, AND...GOD, THERE ARE ONLY FIFTEEN MINUTES LEFT.

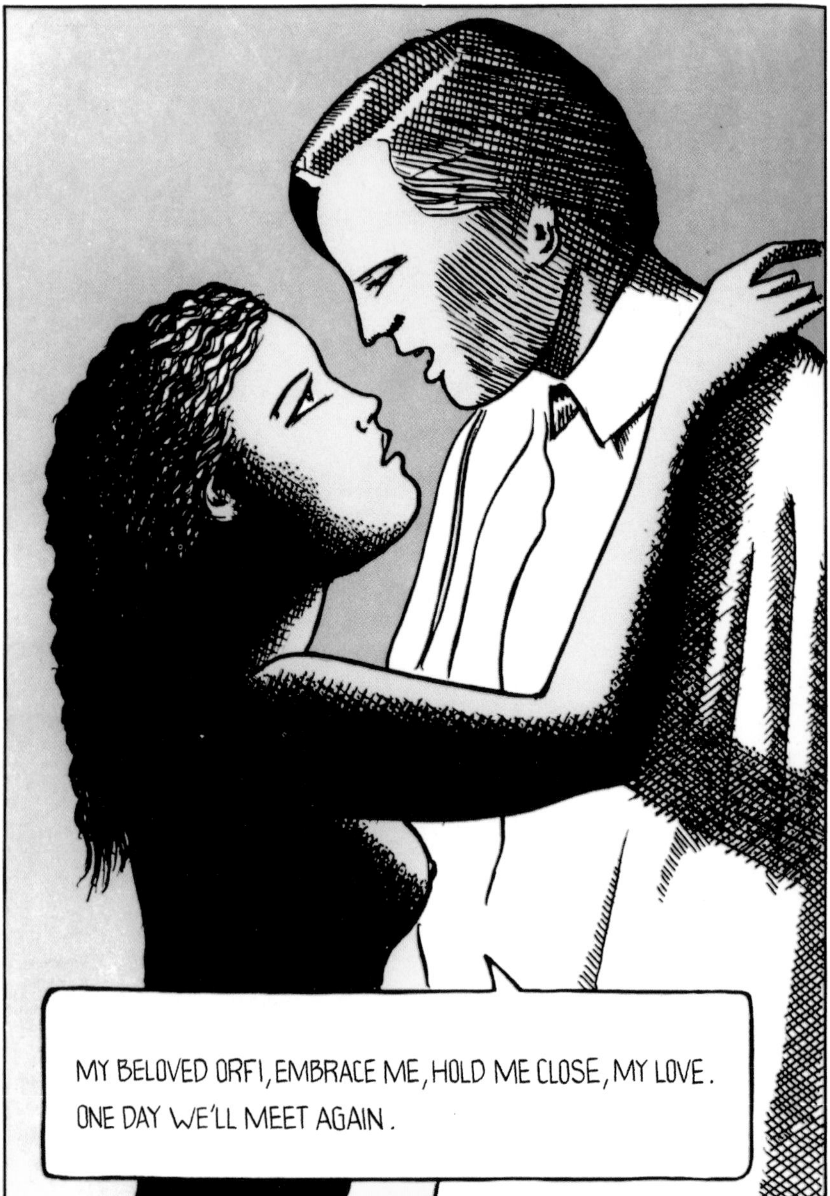
MY BELOVED ORFI, EMBRACE ME, HOLD ME CLOSE, MY LOVE. ONE DAY WE'LL MEET AGAIN.

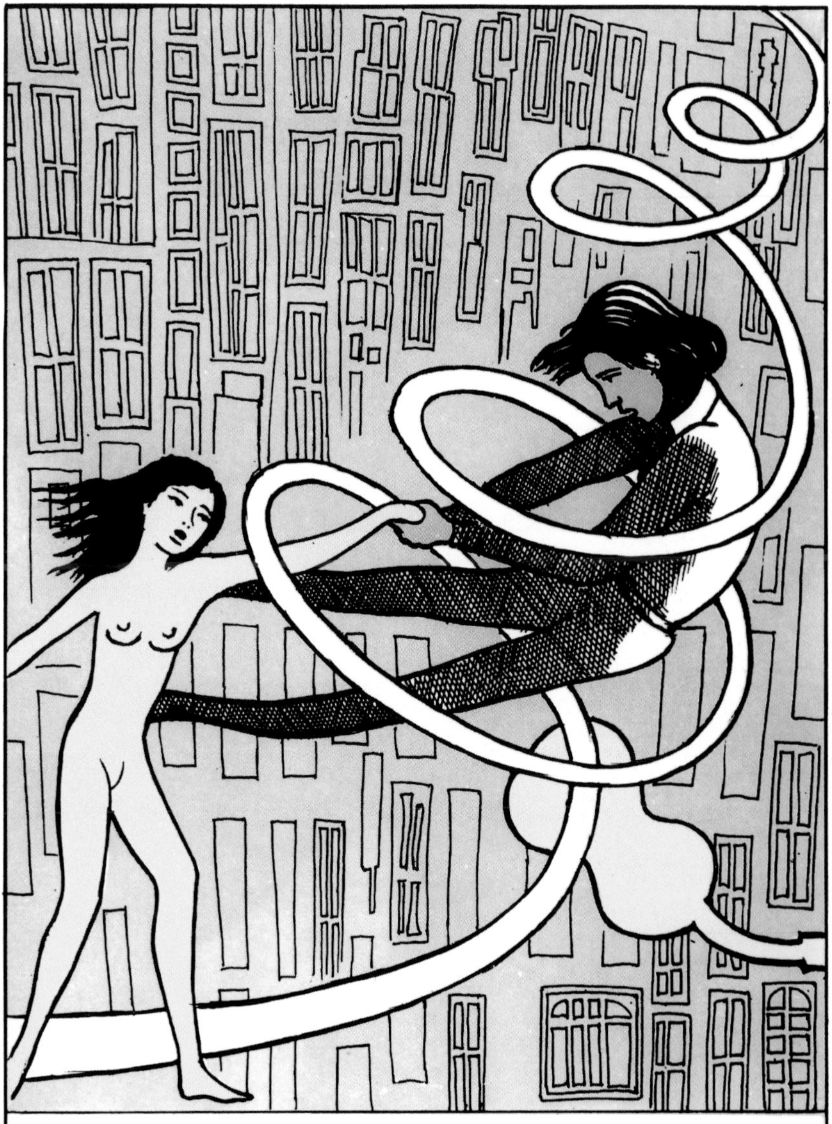

BUT AN IRRESISTIBLE FORCE SEIZED HIM, PULLED HIM AWAY.

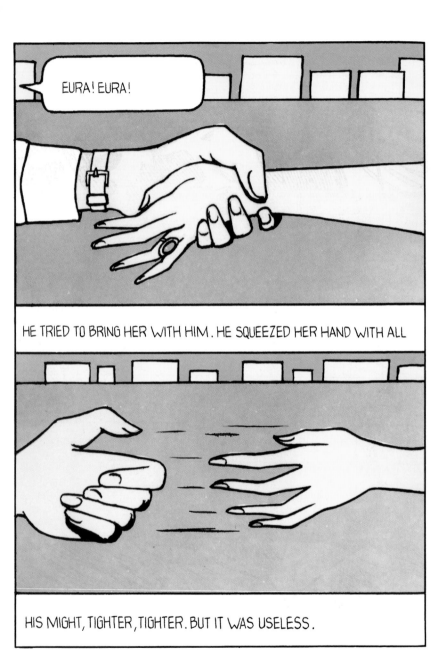

EURA! EURA!

HE TRIED TO BRING HER WITH HIM. HE SQUEEZED HER HAND WITH ALL

HIS MIGHT, TIGHTER, TIGHTER. BUT IT WAS USELESS.

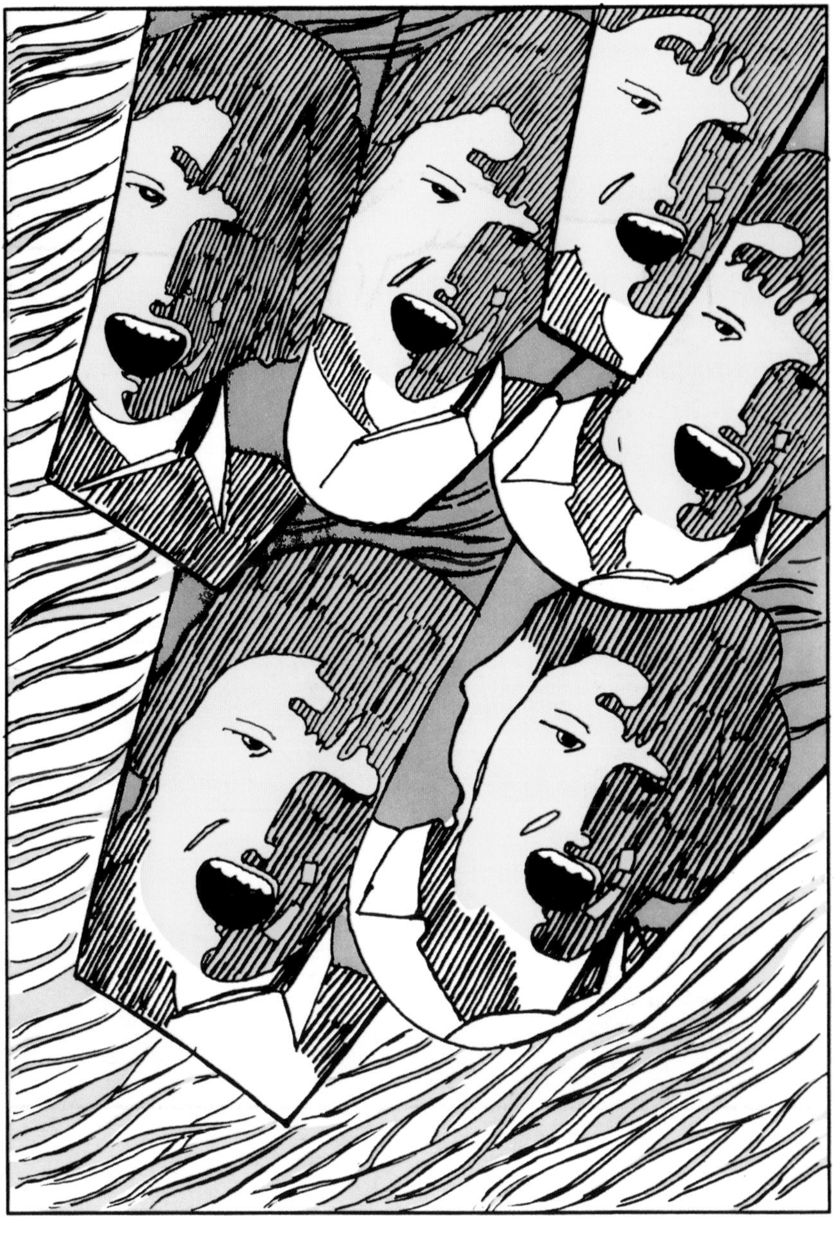

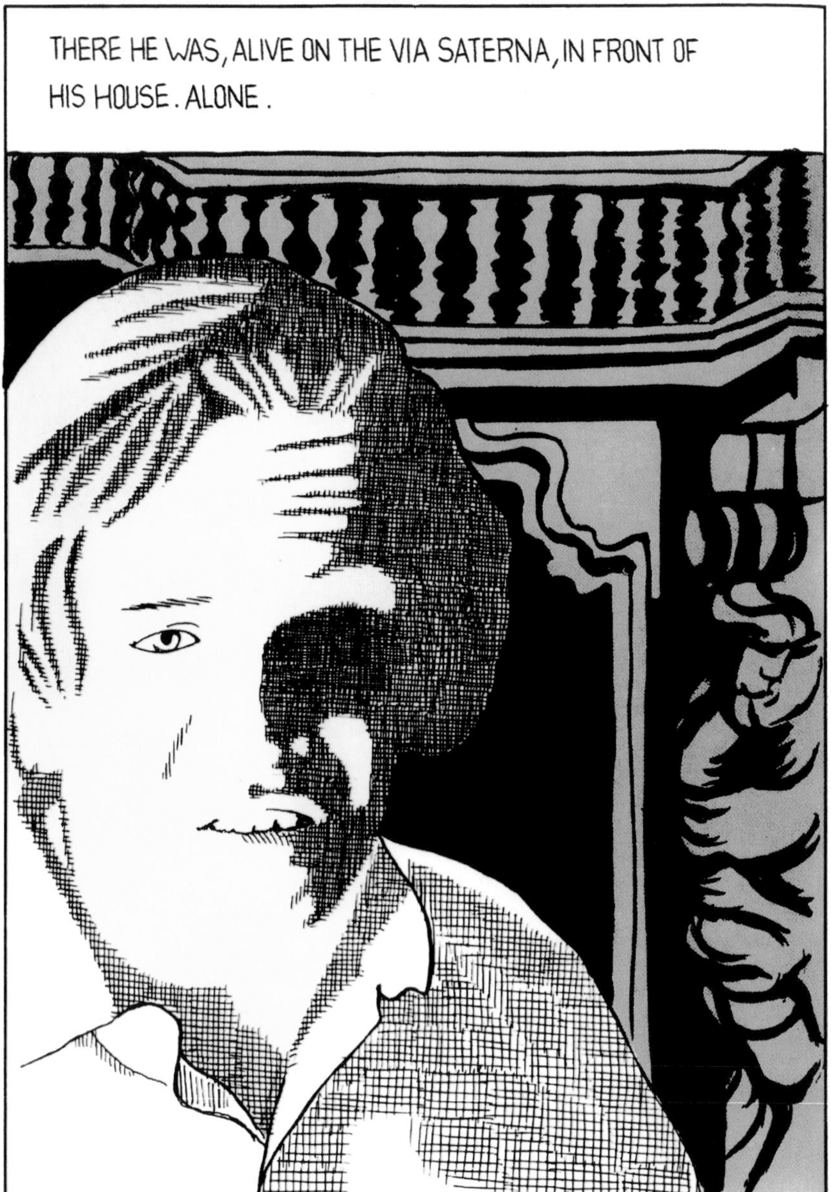
THERE HE WAS, ALIVE ON THE VIA SATERNA, IN FRONT OF HIS HOUSE. ALONE.

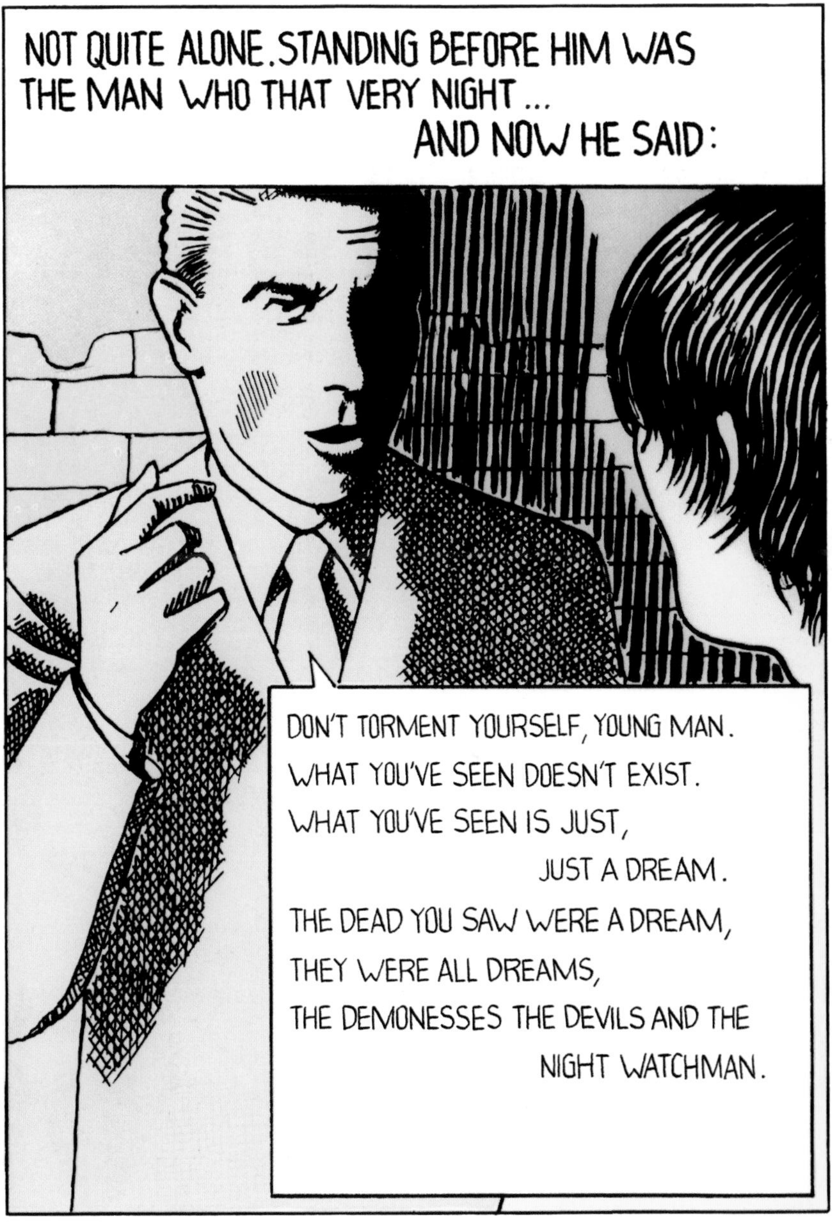
NOT QUITE ALONE. STANDING BEFORE HIM WAS THE MAN WHO THAT VERY NIGHT... AND NOW HE SAID:
DON'T TORMENT YOURSELF, YOUNG MAN. WHAT YOU'VE SEEN DOESN'T EXIST. WHAT YOU'VE SEEN IS JUST, JUST A DREAM. THE DEAD YOU SAW WERE A DREAM, THEY WERE ALL DREAMS, THE DEMONESSES THE DEVILS AND THE NIGHT WATCHMAN.

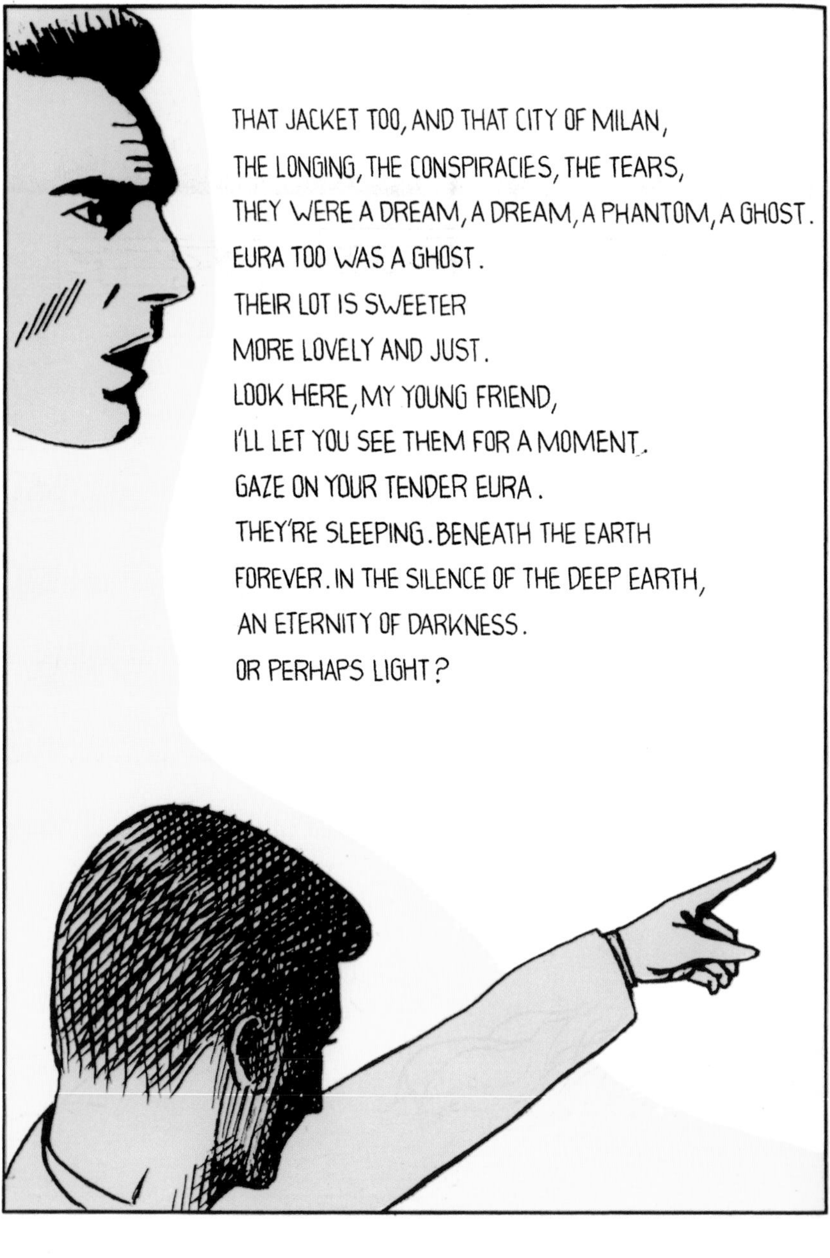
THAT JACKET TOO, AND THAT CITY OF MILAN,
THE LONGING, THE CONSPIRACIES, THE TEARS,
THEY WERE A DREAM, A DREAM, A PHANTOM, A GHOST.
EURA TOO WAS A GHOST.
THEIR LOT IS SWEETER
MORE LOVELY AND JUST.
LOOK HERE, MY YOUNG FRIEND,
I'LL LET YOU SEE THEM FOR A MOMENT.
GAZE ON YOUR TENDER EURA.
THEY'RE SLEEPING. BENEATH THE EARTH
FOREVER. IN THE SILENCE OF THE DEEP EARTH,
AN ETERNITY OF DARKNESS.
OR PERHAPS LIGHT?

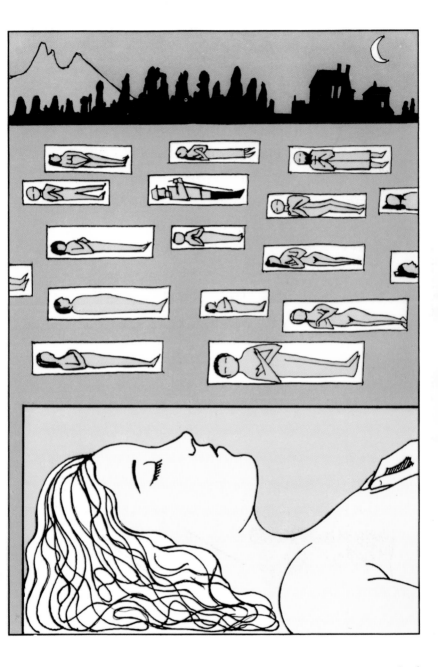

211

PERHAPS LIGHT, RECKLESS YOUNG MAN?
THEY'RE SLEEPING, SEE HOW THEY SLEEP,
SMALL, WELL-BEHAVED, SHRINKING SLOWLY,
MORE EARTH, MORE DUST, MORE NOTHINGNESS,
MUSIC AND SONGS ARE NOTHING
COMPARED TO THIS SLEEP.
SHE TOO LIES THERE. AND THE DAY WILL COME
WHEN YOU WILL GO THROUGH THAT DOOR
WITH YOUR OWN PERSONAL PASS,
AND YOU'LL SLEEP, YOU'LL SLEEP BESIDE HER,
IN NOTHINGNESS, IF WE CAN CALL IT THAT ?
ADIEU.

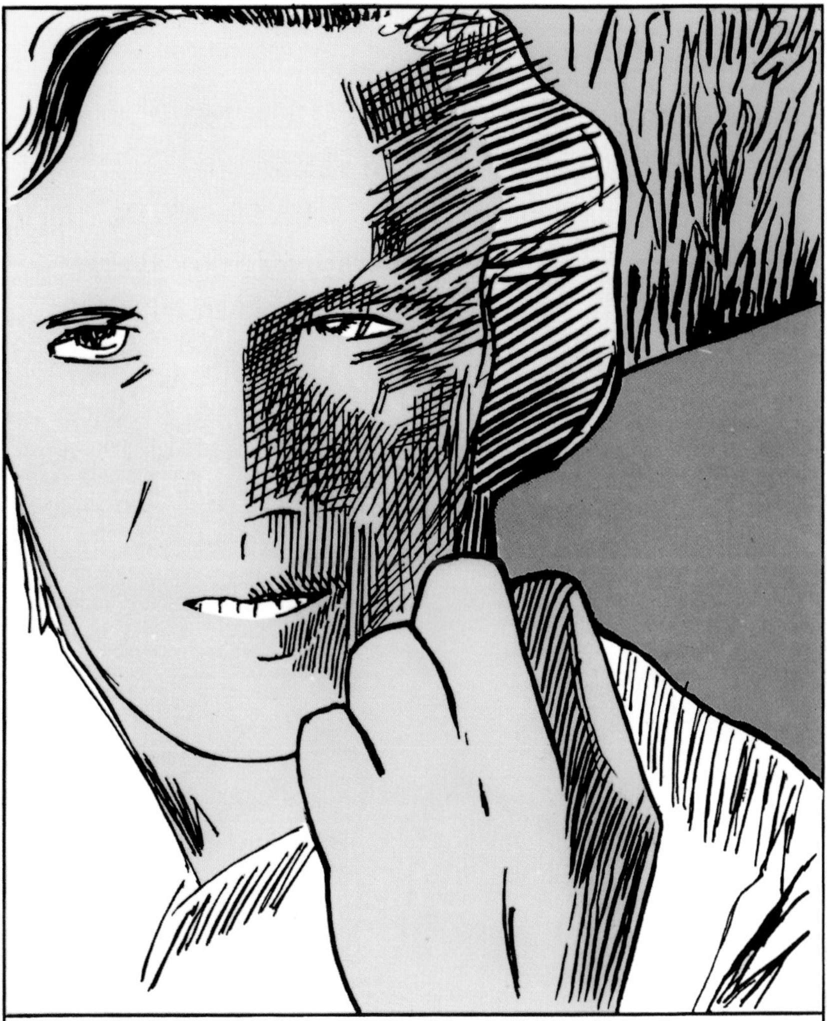

AS HE LISTENED, ORFI REALIZED HE WAS HOLDING SOMETHING IN HIS LEFT HAND.

HE OPENS HIS HAND. THERE'S A RING.
A SPECIAL RING. EURA'S RING. WITHOUT REALIZING
IT, HE HAD TAKEN IT FROM HER AS HE FLED.

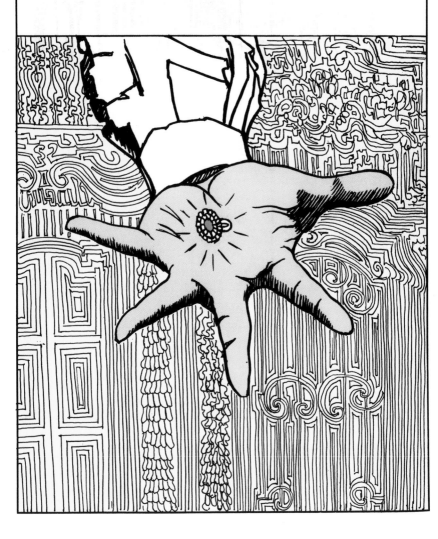

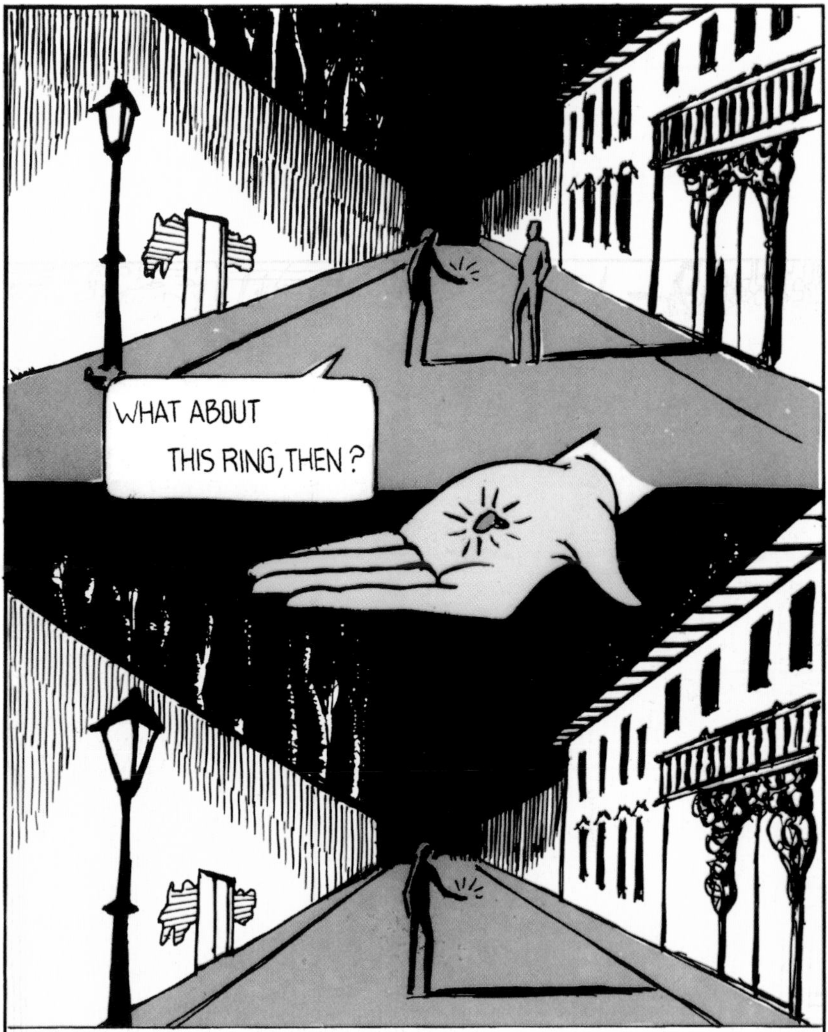
WHAT ABOUT THIS RING, THEN?
BUT THE STRANGER WAS GONE. THE STREET WAS EMPTY.

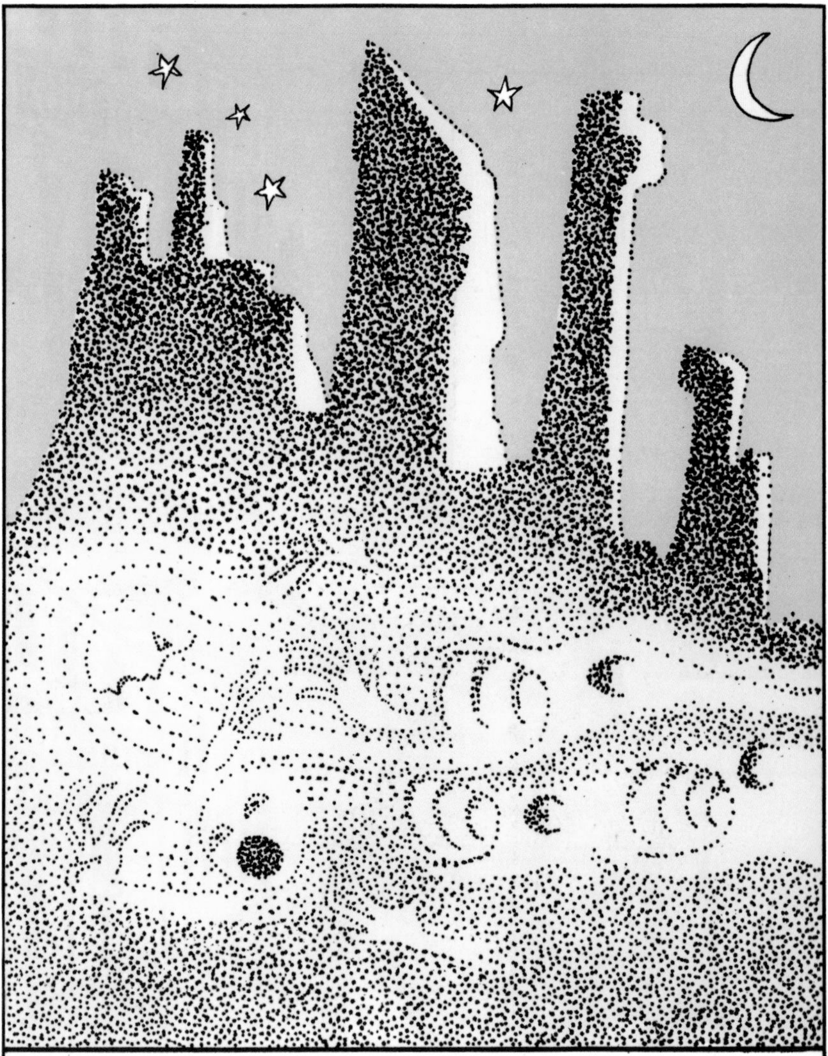

AT THAT VERY MOMENT ABOVE THE PEAKS OF THE GRAN FERMEDA THE STORM WAS SWIRLING WITH THE USUAL SOULS IN TORMENT.

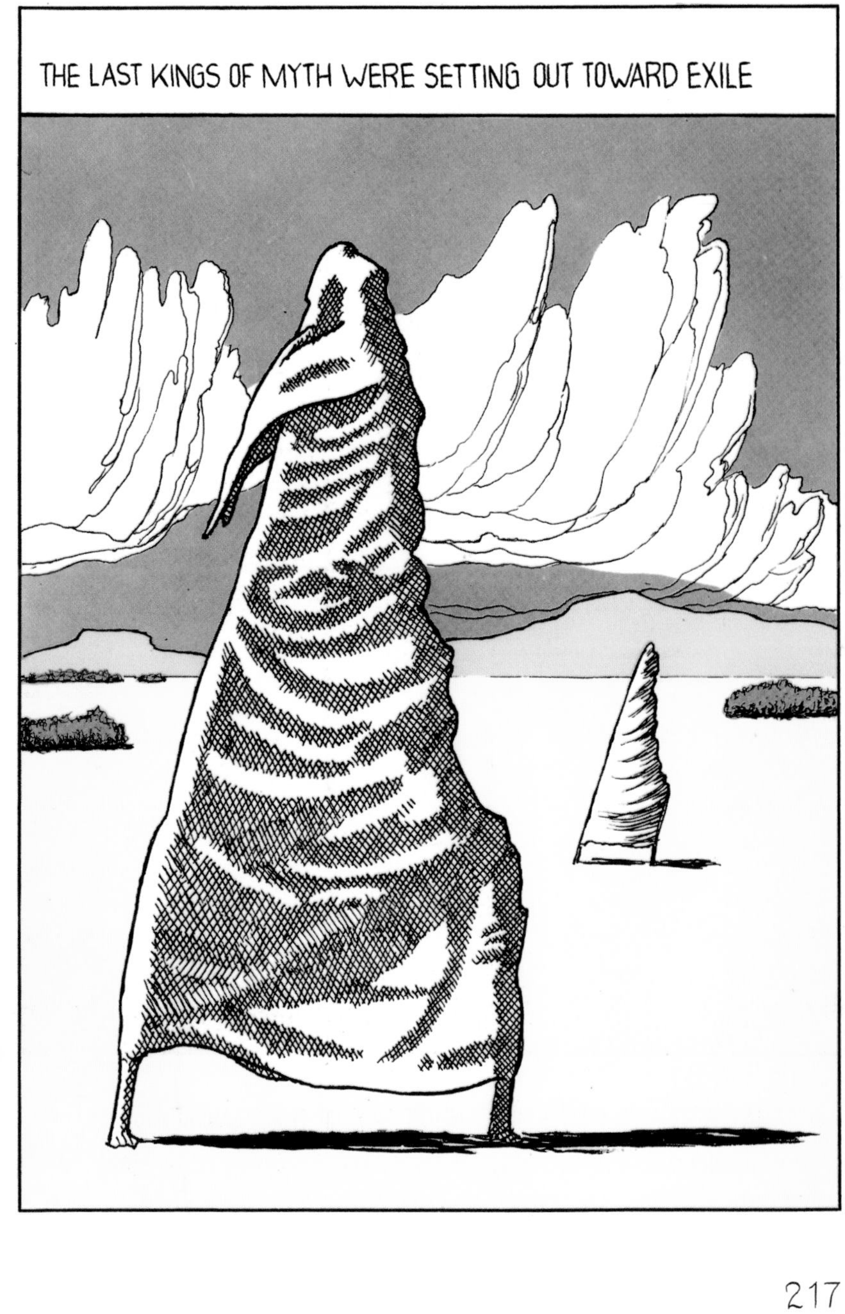
THE LAST KINGS OF MYTH WERE SETTING OUT TOWARD EXILE

AND OVER THE KALAHARI DESERT THE TURRETED
CLOUDS OF ETERNITY FLOATED SLOWLY BY.